D1758169

Citizenship in Hard Times

What do citizens do in response to threats to democracy? This book examines the mass politics of civic obligation in the US, UK, and Germany. Exploring threats like foreign interference in elections and polarization, Sara Wallace Goodman shows that citizens respond to threats to democracy as partisans, interpreting civic obligation through partisan incentives that are shaped by a country's political institutions. This divided, partisan citizenship makes democratic problems worse by eroding the national unity required for democratic stability. Employing novel survey experiments in a cross-national research design, *Citizenship in Hard Times* presents the first comprehensive and comparative analysis of citizenship norms in the face of democratic threat. In showing partisan citizens are not a reliable bulwark against democratic backsliding, Goodman identifies a key vulnerability in the mass politics of democratic order. In times of democratic crisis, defenders of democracy must work to fortify the shared foundations of democratic citizenship.

SARA WALLACE GOODMAN is Associate Professor of Political Science at the University of California, Irvine. She is the author of *Immigration and Membership Politics in Western Europe* (Cambridge, 2014).

Citizenship in Hard Times

How Ordinary People Respond to Democratic Threat

SARA WALLACE GOODMAN

University of California, Irvine

CAMBRIDGE
UNIVERSITY PRESS

CAMBRIDGE
UNIVERSITY PRESS

University Printing House, Cambridge CB2 8BS, United Kingdom

One Liberty Plaza, 20th Floor, New York, NY 10006, USA

477 Williamstown Road, Port Melbourne, VIC 3207, Australia

314–321, 3rd Floor, Plot 3, Splendor Forum, Jasola District Centre, New Delhi – 110025, India

103 Penang Road, #05-06/07, Visioncrest Commercial, Singapore 238467

Cambridge University Press is part of the University of Cambridge.

It furthers the University's mission by disseminating knowledge in the pursuit of
education, learning, and research at the highest international levels of excellence.

www.cambridge.org
Information on this title: www.cambridge.org/9781316512333
DOI: 10.1017/9781009058292

© Sara Wallace Goodman 2022

First published 2022

A catalogue record for this publication is available from the British Library.

Library of Congress Cataloging-in-Publication Data
NAMES: Goodman, Sara Wallace, 1979– author.
TITLE: Citizenship in hard times : how ordinary people respond to democratic threat /
Sara Wallace Goodman, University of California, Irvine.
DESCRIPTION: Cambridge, United Kingdom ; New York, NY : Cambridge University Press, 2022. |
Includes bibliographical references and index. | Contents: Introduction – Citizenship and democratic
instability – Measuring citizenship norms: behavior, belief, and belonging – Patterns of partisan
citizenship – Polarization – Foreign interference in elections – Conclusion.
IDENTIFIERS: LCCN 2021029697 (print) | LCCN 2021029698 (ebook) |
ISBN 9781316512333 (hardback) | ISBN 9781009061049 (paperback) | ISBN 9781009058292 (epub)
SUBJECTS: LCSH: Citizenship–United States–History. | Democracy–United States–History. | Elections–
Corrupt practices–United States. | Minorities–United States–Social conditions. | United States–Politics and
government–21st century. | BISAC: POLITICAL SCIENCE / General
CLASSIFICATION: LCC JK1759 .G587 2022 (print) | LCC JK1759 (ebook) | DDC 323.60973–dc23
LC record available at https://lccn.loc.gov/2021029697
LC ebook record available at https://lccn.loc.gov/2021029698

ISBN 978-1-316-51233-3 Hardback
ISBN 978-1-009-06104-9 Paperback

Dedicated to Micah and Silvia

Contents

Figures

Tables

Acknowledgments

This book's origins drew from an observation that percolated for a decade while I was researching immigrant integration. In studying citizenship requirements for immigrants in Western Europe and the United States, I was tracing this new policy trend (civic integration) that made sure immigrants knew liberal democratic values and behaved in ways that demonstrated a genuine commitment to them. I kept thinking to myself: "Wow – policymakers seem to have a very clear understanding of what it takes for immigrants to become 'good' citizens. I wonder how much people who are already citizens believe these things."

This observation was on the forefront of my mind as I saw citizens in the United States, the United Kingdom, and Germany vote for parties and political leaders that rejected some of the core tenets of liberal democracy. With the rise of intolerance, illiberalism, and extremism, I felt compelled to ask what citizens think their obligations to protect democracy should be. How did they perceive threats to democracy? Did they even see them as threats? What did it mean to be a good citizen in the context of democratic hard times?

I started to sketch the bones of this project on coloring book pages, the first of which is still pinned to my bulletin board. It reminds me that academic moms do the very best we can. There are infinite barriers to success, but there are also generous wellsprings of support if you're brave and humble enough to ask for help. This book would not have been possible without the many people in my life who were kind enough to read a vignette or a draft, answer questions, or just lend an ear of compassion.

For feedback, comments, and support, thank you to Ariel Ahram, Hannah Alarian, Simone Chambers, Alexandra Filindra, Robert Ford,

Shana Kushner Gadarian, Justin Gest, Seth Jolly, Samara Klar, Jeff Kopstein, Adam Seth Levine, Davin Phoenix, Cristian Rodriguez, Jae-Jae Spoon, Daniel Stid, Michael Tesler, Danielle Thomsen, Catherine de Vries, Christopher Williams, and Conrad Ziller. I feel so lucky to call these brilliant people my friends.

A special thank you to Tom Pepinsky for your exceptional patience, superhuman efficiency, and honest and supportive words. And, while you're here, I have an idea for another paper...

I am also grateful for the research assistance from outstanding scholars on various parts of the project: Maneesh Arora, Nathan Chan, Sargis Karavardanyan, Julius Lagodny, and Nina Obermeier.

Thank you to the University of California, Irvine Office for Inclusive Excellence's Combatting Extremism project and to the Jack W. Peltason Center for the Study of Democracy for funding portions of this research.

Parts of this book were presented at Aarhus University (Denmark), the Center for the Study of International Migration at UCLA, the University of California, San Diego, the University of British Columbia, and the London School of Economics. Thank you to these audiences, as well as anonymous reviewers, for the constructive feedback along the way. The joke's on you: no one is a harsher critic of my work than myself.

For my nonacademic friends – Missy, Deb, Tiger, Claudia, Brie, and Rachel – thank you for being supportive and understanding, for dragging me to the beach when I needed it, and for being there no matter what. Sorry I returned your texts three days late. I did my best.

To my family, Mom and Dad, Howard and Nicky, thank you for your encouragement, milestone incentives, and the occasional hot meal. To my husband, Adam, I am eternally grateful for your unwavering love, steadfast care, delicious cappuccinos, and tech assistance.

This book is dedicated to my children, Micah and Silvia. I can't believe I finished this book during the COVID-19 pandemic. It would never have been possible without the commitment of your elementary school, your amazing teachers, and the loving support staff. I am forever grateful our community pulled together to make it work. COVID turned out to be a special time in our lives, when – for over a year – I never missed a goodnight kiss or a morning cuddle. You are my light, my Huckleberry friends. I love you with all my heart. I know it seemed my work took me away from you, but I wrote this book for you. I believe in democracy, and I want it to be better for you. This is Mama's small attempt to figure out what's wrong so we can start doing what's right.

I

Introduction

We live in difficult times for democracy. If this book found its way to your hands, this is probably not new information. In the United States (US), democratic insecurity may seem rather sudden, with the presidential election of Donald Trump in 2016, an outsider candidate with weak commitments to liberal democratic norms, uncomfortable admiration for authoritarian strongmen, a toxic mix of xenophobic and racial politics, and little deference to the Constitution. This view culminates in the violent January 6, 2021, insurrection, where Trump supporters broke into the US Capitol building to disrupt the certification of Electoral College votes confirming Joe Biden the successful and legitimate winner of the 2020 Presidential Election. For others, 2016 and everything that followed only laid bare the fragility of American democratic institutions, preserving counter-majoritarian institutions and exposed by gerrymandering practices and decades of voting suppression and, with it, a persistent second-class citizenship for America's ethnic and racial minorities. From either perspective, ordinary Americans are confronting an unprecedented crisis of democracy. This crisis is both sudden and systemic, and not easily resolved by changing presidents.

Democratic hard times are hardly unique to the US. Across the Atlantic, European democracies have far more practice with antidemocratic and illiberal politics. Yet this familiarity does not make it quotidian, and has not inured Europe to illiberalism and democratic instability. Exclusionary, national populist parties have gained alarming levels of support. In Germany, the extreme right-wing Alternative for Germany (*AfD; Alternative für Deutschland*) emerged as the third largest party in the 2017 federal elections. Successful far-right parties in France, Austria,

Denmark, Switzerland, and the Netherlands also exhibit traditional authoritarian attributes and issue positions that align with a broader populist transformation. In the United Kingdom (UK), British citizens narrowly voted to exit the European Union (EU) – a political and economic organization whose core purpose is shared peace, prosperity, and democratic commitment – supported by a campaign fueled on nationalism and xenophobia. Meanwhile, leaders like Turkey's Recep Tayyip Erdogan and Hungary's Viktor Orban have done serious, ongoing damage to their countries' democratic governments, with the latter successfully accumulating unchecked executive power through emergency law during the 2020 COVID-19 pandemic. From Brazil to Poland to Israel and India, illiberal, exclusionary populism has surged, eroding democratic norms and institutions in the undertow.

Given the rise of antidemocratic movements and the frequent violation of democratic principles by leaders and political elites, even the casual observer would note democratic "backsliding" in some of the world's most advanced democratic states. Together, the past few years comprise what Larry Diamond labels a "democratic recession" and what others have variously characterized as democratic deconsolidation, erosion, decay, or instability. It is a process of democratic undoing or, as Adam Przeworski puts it, "manifest signals that democratic institutions are under threat."[1] This, of course, makes it challenging to identify a threat *a priori*, that is, before it happens and wreaks consequences. A threat could also be temporary or long-term, swift or slow-moving, as can the consequences. Furthermore, democratic backsliding may not present as a "one-time *coup de grâce*" but a "discontinuous series of incremental actions."[2]

Democratic threats take many different shapes, but a shared definition that I use here is that they present an event or period of difficulty, with the intent to inflict damage upon and undermine the integrity and legitimacy of democratic institutions. A democratic threat – which can produce a democratic crisis – damages core features of democracy itself, such as free, fair, and regular elections, or participation. Under a maximal definition of democracy, democratic threat also includes harm to liberal democratic values that enable the functioning of democratic institutions, including

---

[1] Adam Przeworski, *Crises of Democracy* (New York: Cambridge University Press, 2019), 15.
[2] David Waldner and Ellen Lust, "Unwelcome Change: Coming to Terms with Democratic Backsliding," *Annual Review of Political Science* 21 (2018): 95.

checks and balances, rule of law, government neutrality, as well as the norms and values of individual rights and civil liberties.

The contemporary democratic crisis is at once new but not unique; with every wave of democratization there is always a backlash in its wake. And each generation has experienced self-declared democratic crises. In Europe's interwar period, the democratic crisis was an existential one.[3] In the 1970s, Michel Crozier, Samuel Huntington, and Joji Watanuki describe a different "crisis of democracy," as the "increasing delegitimation of authority" through the "decline in the confidence and trust which the people have in government, in their leaders."[4] Written at the intersection of the Cold War and the Oil Crisis, the central concern was pessimism about democracy in the context of a dismal economic downturn. By the 1990s, the phrase "crisis of democracy" had taken on an altogether new meaning. The threat was not institutional replacement or erosion but participation. Declining levels of engagement in community life, political trust, and faith in government – as well as low voter turnout and union and party membership – were all treated as symptoms of a serious democratic crisis. Succinctly put by Macedo et al. in the US context, "Americans have turned away from politics and the public sphere in large numbers, leaving our civic life impoverished."[5] In Britain, the specter of indifferent citizens also loomed large in a scenario described as post-democratic, noting that while "elections certainly exist and can change governments, public electoral debate is a tightly controlled spectacle."[6]

And today's crisis of democracy is different still. While internal tensions and even dysfunction are inherent to complex systems, it manifests today as a type of gridlock in a uniquely hyper-partisan political arena – what Jennifer McCoy and Murat Somer term "pernicious polarization."[7] From political parties to mass attitudes, "team" identity is stronger than ever, where average citizens are willing to suffer democratic – even

---

[3] Giovanni Capoccia, *Defending Democracy: Reactions to Extremism in Interwar Europe* (Baltimore: Johns Hopkins University Press, 2005).

[4] Michel Crozier, Samuel P. Huntington, and Joji Watanuki, *The Crisis of Democracy*, vol. 70 (New York: University Press New York, 1975), 162.

[5] Yvette M. Alex-Assensoh, *Democracy at Risk: How Political Choices Undermine Citizen Participation and What We Can Do about It* (Washington, DC: Brookings Institution Press, 2005).

[6] Colin Crouch, *Coping with Post-Democracy*, vol. 598 (London: Fabian Society, 2000).

[7] Jennifer McCoy and Murat Somer, "Toward a Theory of Pernicious Polarization and How It Harms Democracies: Comparative Evidence and Possible Remedies," *The ANNALS of the American Academy of Political and Social Science* 681, no. 1 (2019).

economic – losses for ideological or partisan-motivated gains.[8] This may lead political elites to disregard threat, deny the seriousness of threat, or even perpetuate threat outright. In this context, we increasingly see evidence of a solidifying and deepening regime cleavage, or conflict, over the foundations of the democratic government itself, between those who support democracy and those who do not, with elected officials sometimes siding against democracy. As Tom Pepinsky observes, writing about the US, "Regime cleavages emerge only in governing systems in crisis, and our democracy is indeed in crisis."[9]

Moreover, the current moment is so disturbing not just because of its substantive features – the values it is attacking and how – but its breadth. There is a global dimension to today's illiberal turn.[10] Economically aggrieved and racially resentful voters have found voice in populist parties around the world, as a network of illiberal leaders prop up one another from the US to Brazil to Russia. Today's wide-reaching democratic backsliding is occurring among recent democratizers and advanced democracies alike.

But unlike late democratizers, which are described as weakly institutionalized and fragile to begin with,[11] explanations for backsliding in advanced democracies present a different set of constraints. We not only expect to see different mechanisms at work, where elite-driven coups or

---

[8] Christopher H. Achen and Larry M. Bartels, *Democracy for Realists: Why Elections Do Not Produce Responsive Government*, vol. 4 (Princeton, NJ: Princeton University Press, 2017); Diana C. Mutz, "Status Threat, Not Economic Hardship, Explains the 2016 Presidential Vote," *Proceedings of the National Academy of Sciences* 115, no. 19 (2018); Tyler T. Reny, Loren Collingwood, and Ali A. Valenzuela, "Vote Switching in the 2016 Election: How Racial and Immigration Attitudes, Not Economics, Explain Shifts in White Voting," *Public Opinion Quarterly* 83, no. 1 (2019).

[9] Thomas Pepinsky, "Why the Impeachment Fight Is Even Scarier Than You Think," *Politico*, October 31, 2019.

[10] Valeriya Mechkova, Anna Lührmann, and Staffan I. Lindberg, "How Much Democratic Backsliding?," *Journal of Democracy* 28, no. 4 (2017).

[11] For instance, democratizers of Eastern and Central Europe face unique institutional and economic circumstances from incomplete democratic transitions as well as frustrations of EU accession. See Milada Vachudova, *Europe Undivided: Democracy, Leverage, and Integration after Communism* (New York: Oxford University Press, 2005); Ulrich Sedelmeier, "Anchoring Democracy from Above? The European Union and Democratic Backsliding in Hungary and Romania after Accession," *JCMS: Journal of Common Market Studies* 52, no. 1 (2014); Mitchell Alexander Orenstein, *Out of the Red: Building Capitalism and Democracy in Postcommunist Europe* (University of Michigan Press, 2001). Also see Robert R. Kaufman and Stephan Haggard, "Democratic Decline in the United States: What Can We Learn from Middle-Income Backsliding?," *Perspectives on Politics* 17, no. 2 (2019).

declarations of emergency powers[12] are thought of as challenges for new democracies or things of the past, there is also a different time horizon for crisis. In democracies that have been consolidated for a century or more, it may be unthinkable to imagine a coup-driven regime change overnight but much more likely to envision small, gradual, and layered changes that add up to erosion. Also, unlike coups or a violent insurrection, these piecemeal changes are much more likely to go unnoticed (or, even more worrying, unchecked). Thus, in advanced democracies, the nature of erosion may be slow-moving and experienced in increments but noticed only in hindsight and in the aggregate. Finally, they may also be more consequential. Long seen as constitutive of the global liberal order and immune to most sources of erosion, as democracy is widely considered to be "the only game in town,"[13] backsliding in advanced democracies upends regime stability.

Most of what we know about democratic crises in advanced democracies focuses on the role of elites. For instance, many contemporary studies as well as a large current of historical comparative work drawing insight from Europe's interwar years place elites at the front and center.[14] These accounts detail how elites employ a series of institutional and rhetorical strategies to undermine liberal democracy. The successes of these "bad actor" strategies are reflected in the failure of elections to constrain illiberal and antidemocratic interests, lack of checks on executive and legislative power,[15] as well as elite polarization.[16]

Examples of elite-centered definitions abound. In *How Democracies Die*, Steven Levitsky and Daniel Ziblatt focus on the diminished role of party gatekeeping. They flag specifically whether "political leaders, and especially political parties, work to prevent [extremist demagogues] from gaining power in the first place" as an "essential test for democracies."[17]

---

[12] For coups, see Nancy Bermeo, "On Democratic Backsliding," *Journal of Democracy* 27, no. 1 (2016). For institutional careening, see Dan Slater, "Democratic Careening," *World Politics* 65, no. 4 (2013). These produced immediate and rapid regime change.

[13] Juan J. Linz and Alfred C. Stepan, "Toward Consolidated Democracies," *Journal of Democracy* 7, no. 2 (1996): 15.

[14] Juan J. Linz, *Crisis, Breakdown and Reequilibration* (Baltimore: Johns Hopkins University Press, 1978); Capoccia, *Defending Democracy: Reactions to Extremism in Interwar Europe*; Sheri Berman, *Democracy and Dictatorship in Europe: From the Ancien Régime to the Present Day* (Oxford: Oxford University Press, 2019).

[15] Bermeo, "On Democratic Backsliding."

[16] Berman, *Democracy and Dictatorship in Europe: From the Ancien Régime to the Present Day*; Daniel Ziblatt, *Conservative Political Parties and the Birth of Modern Democracy in Europe* (New York: Cambridge University Press, 2017).

[17] Steven Levitsky and Daniel Ziblatt, *How Democracies Die* (New York: Crown, 2018), 7.

Elites are responsible for who gets on the ticket, as well as preserving norms of mutual tolerance and forbearance. Stephen Haggard and Robert Kaufman describe democratic backsliding outright as "a process in which democratically elected leaders weaken democratic institutions."[18] Nancy Bermeo defines backsliding as a "*state-led* debilitation or elimination of any of the political institutions that sustain an existing democracy" (emphasis added).[19] And Milada Vachudova's definition also focuses on "the work of incumbents," which dismantles counter-majoritarian institutions, state and media independence, and advances illiberal, ethnopopulist appeals "to control the cultural, academic, artistic, and economic life of the country."[20] Other accounts of the contemporary crisis drill into institutional aspects of electoral integrity,[21] the weakening of horizontal checks,[22] and the skillful interests of outsider, far right populist parties.[23] But, by and large, these are all top-down stories about political elites – about their naked, authoritarian aspirations, their tenuous allegiance to rule of law or civil liberties, or their failure to enforce institutional and political checks to prevent erosion.

We know much less about the role of everyday citizens in times of democratic crises. What we do know focuses mostly on how eroding support for democracy among citizens allows for these power grabs to take place,[24] or when citizens choose undemocratic leaders through

---

[18] Stephan Haggard and Robert Kaufman, *Backsliding: Democratic Regress in the Contemporary World* (New York: Cambridge University Press, 2021).

[19] Bermeo, "On Democratic Backsliding," 5.

[20] Milada Vachudova, "Ethnopopulism and Democratic Backsliding in Central Europe," *East European Politics* 36, no. 3 (2020): 328.

[21] Pippa Norris, Sarah Cameron, and Thomas Wynter, *Electoral Integrity in America: Securing Democracy* (Oxford: Oxford University Press, 2018).

[22] Tom Ginsburg and Aziz Z. Huq, *How to Save a Constitutional Democracy* (Chicago: University of Chicago Press, 2018).

[23] William A. Galston, *Anti-Pluralism: The Populist Threat to Liberal Democracy* (New Haven, CT: Yale University Press, 2017); Ronald Inglehart and Pippa Norris, "Trump and the Populist Authoritarian Parties: The Silent Revolution in Reverse," *Perspectives on Politics* 15, no. 2 (2017); Cas Mudde, *Populist Radical Right Parties in Europe* (New York: Cambridge University Press Cambridge, 2007); Milada Vachudova, "From Competition to Polarization in Central Europe: How Populists Change Party Systems and the European Union," *Polity* 51, no. 4 (2019).

[24] Yascha Mounk, *The People Vs. Democracy: Why Our Freedom Is in Danger and How to Save It* (Cambridge, MA: Harvard University Press, 2018); Matthew H. Graham and Milan W. Svolik, "Democracy in America? Partisanship, Polarization, and the Robustness of Support for Democracy in the United States," *American Political Science Review* 114, no. 2 (2020).

popular elections.[25] To be sure, public support for democratic survival is essential,[26] and mass support by ordinary people plays a crucial role in sustaining democracy when elites try to subvert it.[27] But the role played by citizens extends beyond voting. Citizens may have a weak understanding of democratic norms, or support democracy in the abstract while endorsing illiberal, undemocratic actions.[28] We can study illiberal cultural contexts[29], or ask about political leanings and attitudes toward authoritarianism,[30] but we want to know the role democratic citizens play during these moments of crisis. Political elites play a central role in times of democratic uncertainty, but so do citizens.

Mass politics is not merely the field in which elite politics play out, nor are the masses passive recipients of antidemocratic or illiberal messages by political leaders. A democracy, by definition, draws legitimacy from its citizens. Through participation and liberal value commitments, citizens not only shape elite preferences and decisions, they also ensure democratic quality and good governance. Indeed, what distinguishes advanced liberal democracies from weakly institutionalized alternatives is not just the quality and endurance of democratic institutions but citizens' commitment to – and participation in – them. Citizens do not just support abstract democratic principles but practice them; they may hold intensely opposing views while also accepting the legitimacy of elections and commitment to rules that structure transfers of power. Given their capacity for mobilization, citizens can be either the bulwark against or handmaid of erosion. And, unlike most theories about democratic backsliding that

---

[25] Bermeo, "On Democratic Backsliding."

[26] Seymour Martin Lipset, "Political Man: The Social Bases of Politics," (1959); David Easton, *A Framework for Political Analysis*, vol. 25 (Hoboken, NJ: Prentice-Hall Englewood Cliffs, 1965).

[27] Nancy Gina Bermeo, *Ordinary People in Extraordinary Times: The Citizenry and the Breakdown of Democracy* (Princeton, NJ: Princeton University Press, 2003); Larry Diamond, *Developing Democracy: Toward Consolidation* (Baltimore: JHU Press, 1999); also see Christopher Claassen, "Does Public Support Help Democracy Survive?," *American Journal of Political Science* 64, no. 1 (2020).

[28] John L. Sullivan, James Piereson, and George E. Marcus, *Political Tolerance and American Democracy* (Chicago: University of Chicago Press, 1982).

[29] Marc Morjé Howard, *The Weakness of Civil Society in Post-Communist Europe* (New York: Cambridge University Press, 2003); James Dawson and Seán Hanley, "What's Wrong with East-Central Europe?: The Fading Mirage of The Liberal Consensus," *Journal of Democracy* 27, no. 1 (2016).

[30] Graham and Svolik, "Democracy in America? Partisanship, Polarization, and the Robustness of Support for Democracy in the United States."; Pippa Norris and Ronald Inglehart, *Cultural Backlash: Trump, Brexit, and Authoritarian Populism* (New York: Cambridge University Press, 2019).

"treat citizens as a relatively homogenous group,"[31] differences exist *between* citizens – in the form of socioeconomic and political cleavages – which may exacerbate erosion where commitment to institutions that traditionally structure and balance those differences are weak. Thus, democratic breakdown may be as much about the decisions that citizens make – to engage in politics, to guard against elites' authoritarian impulses – as it is about the violation of norms by those in charge. Especially in advanced democracies, this means that looking at citizens is essential for understanding the contemporary crisis.

The insight that "mass politics matters" is hardly novel. On top of being core to the definition of democracy, one of the most prominent areas of research in comparative politics examines democratic quality through the lens of citizen attitudes and behavior. Its analytical starting point is that citizens and mass politics are the origin of democratic legitimacy and performance. These works – from Ron Inglehart and Pippa Norris to Russ Dalton, Christian Welzel, and others[32] – take citizens seriously, looking at the cross-national character of citizenship and quality of democracy and using surveys to get at comparative mass politics of support for democracy. But there is a significant gap in this literature, too, as it has not engaged with backsliding more directly, in which citizens don't just change alongside a crisis but in response to it. Here, I endeavor to bring the backsliding and citizenship literatures together. Centering citizens in an analysis of democratic crisis requires looking beyond who citizens vote for and why,[33] and to a wider array of citizen attitudes and norms that, when confronted with democratic crisis, may make undermining democracy feasible or frictional.

So, what are citizens doing in the face of democratic crisis? What does democratic crisis do to public norms? Are citizens upholding liberal democratic values or abandoning them? There are at least two different ways to think about citizens in these hard times. We can look at protests

---

[31] Waldner and Lust, "Unwelcome Change: Coming to Terms with Democratic Backsliding," 103.

[32] Ronald Inglehart, *The Silent Revolution: Changing Values and Political Styles among Western Publics* (Princeton, NJ: Princeton University Press, 2015); Russell J. Dalton, *The Good Citizen: How a Younger Generation Is Reshaping American Politics* (Washington, DC: CQ Press, 2021); Russell J. Dalton, *Citizen Politics: Public Opinion and Political Parties in Advanced Industrial Democracies* (Washington, DC: CQ Press, 2013); Christian Welzel, *Freedom Rising* (New York: Cambridge University Press, 2013); Pippa Norris, *Critical Citizens: Global Support for Democratic Government* (New York: Oxford University Press, 1999).

[33] Norris and Inglehart, *Cultural Backlash: Trump, Brexit, and Authoritarian Populism*.

as an example of these different views. From one perspective, civil society and civic activism have never been stronger. The Women's March of January 21, 2017, the day after the inauguration of President Donald Trump, was the largest single day of protest in modern US history, with an estimated 4 million marchers turning out. Voter turnout in the 2018 US midterm election reached record numbers. The Black Lives Matter movement protests against police brutality in the wake of the death of George Floyd were widespread and well-attended, even during social distancing and stay-at-home orders of the COVID-19 pandemic. Enthusiasm spread across the world. In Europe, where marches are more typical and frequent features of expression since 1968, there have regularly been large protests in support for the science of climate change, and against nationalist politics, like the UK leaving the EU, and anti-Islamophobic and far right politics in Germany. In this vision of the contemporary crisis, the citizenry has never been more active, vocal, and critical in speaking out against government abuse and ethnopopulism. And, in some cases, protests not only give voice but produce real change, such as removing long-standing monuments to the Confederacy.

The second view of contemporary citizenship today, however, is quite different. Despite the overwhelming turnout at the Women's March – where Facebook feeds filled up with pictures, knitting circles showed off their bespoke pink pussy hats, and social media circulated the cleverest and wittiest signage – in reality, the March drew only 1% of the US population. Furthermore, unlike traditional social movements, it did not capitalize on its moment of support and transform into an organized political structure but petered out, a result of in-fighting, divisive leadership, and supporter fatigue. Subsequent political moments that generated strong outrage were not met with similarly sized protests – not on the eve of Impeachment, nor to protest family separation of asylum seekers at the border. Black Lives Matter in May–June 2020 is a notable exception, but that too ebbed with many cosmetic changes, like changing the Mississippi state flag, but not widespread or substantive police reform and accountability.

Perhaps more significant we also see the rise of illiberal citizen mobilization, like that witnessed in Washington, D.C. on January 6th. PEGIDA, a German nationalist, anti-immigrant movement, and the Unite the Right rally in Charlottesville, VA are two further examples. These protests do not match their liberal counterparts in size but, by their presence and through their web of supporters, present a very real and often violent threat to liberal democracy. Extremist groups often mobilize to expressly oppose and physically intimidate progressive marches, such as those of the Black Lives Matter movement. And, in France, a country accustomed to regular protesting, the Yellow Vest movement (*Mouvement des gilets jaunes*) seems to combine both liberal and illiberal elements. Motivated by rising fuel prices, high costs of living, and tax burdens on the working class, the movement spans the political spectrum to include both left and right and has often resulted in violent clashes between and amongst protestors, bystanders, and police. Or, in a further example of blended purpose, antiracism protests in Paris to protest the death of Adama Traoré (a Malian French man who died in police custody in 2016) interlaced antiracism with anti-Semitic slogans, shouting "*Sale juif*" (dirty Jew) at counter-protestors.

But, to look beyond protesting, most citizens are not marching. They are passive, or – arguably worse – living online in social circles defined by polarization and insularity, sharing information and opinions largely among other like-minded citizens within their ideological silos. And evidence suggests that exposure to opposing views on social media only leads to further polarization.[34] These divisions are deepening over time. In a 2014 Pew Research Center poll, 27% of Democrats and 36% of Republicans saw members of the opposite party not only as unfavorable but as a "threat to the nation's well-being."[35] By 2016, those percentages increased to 41% and 45%, respectively.[36] And polarization, while certainly pronounced in the US system, is not exceptional to the US system; cross-national evidence shows a number of advanced democracies characterized by problematic and deepening rifts.[37]

The most vital dimension of a strong democracy is uncoerced political participation,[38] but civic participation itself does not guarantee democratic strength. Like protesting, voting offers a second example of the

---

[34] Christopher A. Bail et al., "Exposure to Opposing Views on Social Media Can Increase Political Polarization," *Proceedings of the National Academy of Sciences* 115, no. 37 (2018).

[35] Pew Research Center. "Political Polarization in the American Public." June 12, 2014, available at https://www.pewresearch.org/politics/2014/06/12/political-polarization-in-the-american-public/ (accessed January 2, 2021).

[36] Pew Research Center. "Politics and Foreign Policy Survey. April 12–19, 2016, available at https://www.pewresearch.org/politics/dataset/april-2016-politics-and-foreign-policy-survey/ (accessed January 2, 2021).

[37] Noam Gidron, James Adams, and Will Horne, "American Affective Polarization in Comparative Perspective," *Elements in American Politics* (2020).

[38] Robert D. Putnam, *Making Democracy Work: Civic Traditions in Modern Italy* (Princeton, NJ: Princeton University Press, 1993); Gabriel Almond and Sidney Verba, *The Civic Culture : Political Attitudes and Democracy in Five Nations* (Princeton, NJ: Princeton University Press, 1963).

Janus-face of participation. Voter turnout may be high, but voters can choose extreme and even antidemocratic parties. In other words, sometimes democrats vote for authoritarians.[39] In a study of US voters, Matthew Graham and Milan Svolik find "only a small fraction of Americans prioritize democratic principles in their electoral choices."[40] Or, in proportional representation systems, as voters move away from mainstream parties they can lean toward fringe, even extremist alternatives.[41] This "center-fleeing polarization"[42] is potentially unstable on its own, a fact made worse when citizens are increasingly willing to choose undemocratic options. In this new era of emboldened illiberalism, we also see unprecedented spikes in hate crimes against immigrants, refugees, Jews, Muslims, and other minorities, making this era of extreme polarization dangerous for democracy in general and for citizens directly.

Both views are accurate. We are – at the same time – engaged and demobilized; composed of democratic and illiberal impulses. An active and engaged citizenry can simultaneously buttress and undermine the foundations of democracy. These views paint a difficult road ahead for advanced democracies, especially for those who wish to safeguard liberal democratic institutions and values against threats both foreign and domestic. These views also add up to a larger point: Our explanations of democratic instability need to look beyond elites and put citizens into the picture. We need to understand what citizens do in hard times. And it has never been more important than right now. Given the breadth of polarization (and no signs of centripetal forces), regularity – even normalization – of democratic threat, and the stakes for ordinary individuals, we can employ advanced social science tools in order to see (1) how citizens are affected by threat; (2) whether and in what ways democratic norms have eroded; and, (3) how ubiquitous this problem is across advanced democracies.

[39] Sheri Berman, *The Social Democratic Moment* (Cambridge, MA: Harvard University Press, 1998); Samuel P. Huntington, *Political Order in Changing Societies* (New Haven, CT: Yale University Press, 2006).

[40] Graham and Svolik, "Democracy in America? Partisanship, Polarization, and the Robustness of Support for Democracy in the United States."

[41] With those on the left experiencing historical decline, see Sheri Berman and Maria Snegovaya, "Populism and the Decline of Social Democracy," *Journal of Democracy* 30, no. 3 (2019).

[42] Giovanni Sartori, *Parties and Party Systems: A Framework for Analysis* (Cambridge: Cambridge University Press, 1976), 163.

I.I THE PUZZLE

This book investigates citizenship norms during democratic crises. What makes a good citizen in hard times? Do good citizens value activation and mobilization to protect democracy? Or do they remain silent and deferential? Do good citizens uphold commitments to liberal democratic principles, like vigilance and mutual tolerance? Or do they seek greater authoritarian control, asking their compatriots for obedience and system loyalty? Do good citizens embrace diversity, or do they "hunker down" and rally around the flag of national identity? What factors determine how individuals respond to challenges? And do citizens respond similarly across advanced democracies?

These questions – and the objects of analysis (the dependent variables) in this study – are all about citizenship norms. Why norms? Citizenship norms comprise "a shared set of expectations about the citizen's role in politics" telling "citizens what is expected of them, and what they expect of themselves."[43] These include expectations about what to do (behavior), believe (liberal democratic commitments, ideas about solidarity), and how to imagine the national political community. A skeptic might ask, "If we want to know what citizens do in hard times, why not look at what they *do?*" – that is, their behavior. However, norms support, guide, and – therefore – precede behavior. There is an accumulation of evidence pointing to norms – referred to interchangeably as citizen/civic duty, good citizenship, and obligation – as a motivation to vote[44] and participate more generally.[45] But looking at behavior only captures observable consequences of norms and provides a very narrow understanding of what citizens value. As Russ Dalton succinctly puts it, norms of citizenship "are the key to understanding what is really going on."[46]

---

[43] Russell J. Dalton, "Citizenship Norms and the Expansion of Political Participation," *Political studies* 56, no. 1 (2008): 78.

[44] André Blais and Christopher H. Achen, "Civic Duty and Voter Turnout," *Political Behavior* 41, no. 2 (2019); André Blais, *To Vote or Not to Vote?: The Merits and Limits of Rational Choice Theory* (Pittsburgh, PA: University of Pittsburgh Press, 2000); William H. Riker and Peter C. Ordeshook, "A Theory of the Calculus of Voting," *The American Political Science Review* 62, no. 1 (1968).

[45] For example, Catherine Bolzendahl and Hilde Coffé, "Are 'Good' Citizens 'Good' Participants? Testing Citizenship Norms and Political Participation across 25 Nations," *Political Studies* 61 (2013).

[46] Russell J. Dalton, *The Good Citizen: How a Younger Generation Is Reshaping American Politics* (Washington, DC: CQ Press, 2008), 11.

The central research question – what happens to norms of citizenship in democratic hard times? – is first and foremost empirical. How are norms about behaviors, beliefs, and sense of national belonging affected by democratic threat? The short answer is: we don't know. Existing work readily acknowledges that norms shift in response to changing social conditions, but we do not have rigorous, systematic answers to the acute effects of democratic threat on these norms. This question also raises a normative concern. If we believe democracy is the best form of government and want to preserve it, then we should want to identify what citizens think they *should* do to offset the threat to the democratic order; that is, how they interpret their role in democratic safeguarding. The answer to this question can help us to understand what kind of citizen serves as a bulwark against democratic erosion, and what kind of citizen accelerates its decline. It also helps us to chart out a route forward to determine what kind of civic work needs to take place.

Characterizing the contemporary political moment as one of democratic crisis may not be a statement everyone agrees with. While cross-national measures of regime quality – like V-Dem, Freedom House, and The Economist Intelligence Unit's Democracy – all show a global decline in liberal democracy and its features, some observers of contemporary politics consider institutions to be robust, threat to be cyclical, and talk of a democratic crisis to be overblown.[47] Indeed, there are many historical cases of democratic breakdown, but none among advanced liberal democracies. To wit, the January 6 insurrection was put down and a peaceful transfer of power occurred two weeks later. Advanced democracies are consolidated and, by definition, have proven themselves to be durable, able to weather passing fads of populism, economic downturns, and even institutional erosion. Skeptics may further argue that it is easier to rebuild and repair institutions then it is to construct new rules from scratch and optimistically hold out for an election that brings democrats back into leadership. But these views presume that the current threats to democracy are temporary and reversible. To hold this belief, one also must have confidence that democracies and their citizens are resilient when core institutions are attacked, and that these attacks are no worse than they were in previous decades.

---

[47] "Cycles of optimism and pessimism are not new: they have accompanied previous democratic waves and the backsliding that followed them" (377). Berman, *Democracy and Dictatorship in Europe: From the Ancien Régime to the Present Day.*

But can citizens trust the results of future elections if recent ones were not free and fair? Can citizens have faith in democracy if abuses of power go unchecked or unpunished? What are the consequences for democracy when institutions endure but values – liberal democratic practices, rule of law, but also participatory and trust norms – decline? The central point is this: Even a skeptic should want to know how democratic threat affects citizens in some of the world's oldest and strongest democracies.

1.2 THE ARGUMENTS

This book makes two interconnected arguments about citizenship in hard times. First, citizenship – as a status and source of national identity – is a foundational institution for democratic stability. It secures minimal national unity required for defining group goals and, as a coordinating device, establishes and conveys legitimacy to governing elites. Second, when this unity is weakened, citizens become a source of instability. Specifically, this happens when individuals define their role in democratic hard times not as citizens but as partisans, interpreting obligation in response to positional incentives of the party they support. In other words, citizens decide whether to recognize and respond to crisis or not by what benefits or hurts their "side." By centering the citizen, I present a theory of democratic instability that defines when individuals respond to crisis and how. I discuss each in turn.

1. *Citizenship is a foundational institution for democratic governance and stability.* Individuals obtain rights, privileges, and protections *from* a state and, in exchange, they owe certain duties or obligations *to* the state.[48] These obligations can be actions or behaviors, commitments to liberal democratic beliefs, or aligning with norms of belonging. Through status and identity, citizens are meaningfully connected to other citizens, or "nationals," to comprise a national political community of "insiders." This understanding of citizenship is elemental to making democracy work. It creates legitimacy for a regime by defining a community to express shared group goals – from representation to human flourishing, and builds habits of participation and patience that enable representation and democratic turnover. It also resolves coordination dilemmas.

---

[48] Charles Tilly characterized this formal tie as a transactional relationship connecting individuals directly to the administrative state. Charles Tilly, "Citizenship, Identity and Social History," *International Review of Social History* 40, no. S3 (1995).

Not only is citizenship not an inherently partisan identity, it also establishes a connection between an individual and national polity that *deliberately supersedes* other identities *to create its own*. It encompasses differences by constructing a framework of national unity, coordinating common, unifying values and attributes. This category – in which a plurality of views and interests, even ethnocultural and religious differences, can be encapsulated in a single status – makes citizenship a source of democratic stability.

Within this system, individuals *as citizens* are not passive receivers of elite actions and decisions, but agenda-setters, legitimacy-conferrers, and custodians of the soft guardrails preventing backsliding. And not just in attitude or support for elites,[49] but *as a citizen's raison d'être*. It is what citizens do and who they are. This fundamental observation pushes citizenship to the center of the puzzle of democratic erosion. If we want to know how and why democracies erode, and what elites can get away with, we need to understand individuals as citizens.

2. *Citizenship becomes divided in hard times, where individuals respond to democratic threat as partisans.* Having centered citizens in our understanding not just democratic legitimacy but stability, the second argument describes how citizenship becomes a source of *instability*: when citizenship becomes political. This occurs when individuals interpret their obligation as preserving and defending partisan or political goals, which may conflict with democratic, regime-level goals. The most accessible form of political identity for citizens is found in partisanship, as it links individuals to political processes of representation and decision-making. It also provides heuristic cues and informational shortcuts for responding to events. Partisanship is a type of social identity that guides individuals to pay attention to elites that share their views and oppose those that do not.[50] While, principally, citizenship is an identity committed to democratic norms that supersede partisan factionalism, partisan citizenship can be "activated" in hard times, especially when the threat itself is politicized. As a result, individuals respond to democratic threat as partisans, not citizens – as Democrats, not democrats.

Partisan citizenship is not inevitable (nor inevitably pernicious). To account for this outcome, I present a theory of democratic instability that

---

[49] Cf. Roberto Stefan Foa and Yascha Mounk, "The Signs of Deconsolidation," *Journal of Democracy* 28, no. 1 (2017).

[50] Lilliana Mason, *Uncivil Agreement: How Politics Became Our Identity* (Chicago: University of Chicago Press, 2018).

places citizens at the center of analysis to argue divided citizenship, that is, national disunity, is a product of *positional incentives*. Two factors shape an understanding of political incentives and the decision to respond or not. First is *incumbent versus challenger status,* which considers incentives to react based on whether a party is in power and incumbent (thus benefitting from preserving the status quo) or a challenger party out of power (and benefits from upending it). This position may determine what is threatening and whether or not to react. Second is the *institutional system in which parties compete*. Institutional design matters in terms of whether it is a two or multiparty system and, related, whether competition is structured through zero-sum majoritarian systems or consensus-based systems,[51] the latter of which are better at reducing winner/loser dynamics than their majoritarian counterpart. Where consensus-based systems create positive-sum games for the greatest number of participants, zero-sum, majoritarian systems create fewer opportunities for consensus, and polarizing tendencies of a two-party system magnify differences.[52] As such, consensus systems are more conducive to collaborative responses to democratic threat, while majoritarian systems see threat – and potential gains and losses – through a sharper set of partisan trade-offs.

But how do these system-level features affect citizens? In centering the citizen, I argue that citizens perceive incentives to redefine good citizenship in response to crisis according to potential gains or losses of their "side," defined by partisanship. Partisanship as a social identity connects the idea of *who* Democrats or Republicans are to *what Democrats or Republicans do* and *who they listen to.* One way that people navigate the political world – especially in the face of crisis when they have little information – is to rely on partisanship as a cue to guide political choices such as who to vote for, what policy positions to adopt, and how to process information.[53] As parties navigate incentives to challenge or preserve the status quo, informational cue-takers (i.e., citizens) interpret

---

[51] These two types of democratic political systems derive from Arend Lijphart's influential *Patterns of Democracy*. Other examples comparing these *types* of institutional arrangements include G. Bingham Powell and G. Bingham Powell Jr., *Elections as Instruments of Democracy: Majoritarian and Proportional Visions* (New Haven, CT: Yale University Press, 2000); George Tsebelis, *Veto Players: How Political Institutions Work* (Princeton, NJ: Princeton University Press, 2002); Donald L. Horowitz, *Ethnic Groups in Conflict, Updated Edition with a New Preface* (Berkeley: University of California Press, 2000).

[52] Steven W. Webster and Alan I. Abramowitz, "The Ideological Foundations of Affective Polarization in the Us Electorate," *American Politics Research* 45, no. 4 (2017).

[53] John Zaller, *The Nature and Origins of Mass Opinion* (New York: Cambridge University Press, 1992).

a threat in kind. This is especially the case when it comes to uncertain or new political events. In these instances, citizens view politicians like experts, and trust their information.[54] This, I argue, includes how to interpret what is threatening and whether a response benefits their "side."

Thus, not all threats are equally "threatening" to citizens. Unlike some threats, democratic threats are squarely political, undermine democratic institutions, and are oftentimes perpetrated by the very people elected to run those institutions. This makes recognizing and responding to threat confusing and potentially conflicting for individuals who want to be good partisans *and* good citizens. Confusion is amplified when threat is perpetrated by office holders, which may paint a patina of legitimacy over destructive behavior. Finally, threats to democratic institutions are often distant from the lived experiences of ordinary people. Acting on norms of good citizenship is not a part of an average citizen's day-to-day life (even voting as a basic civic duty is not something many citizens participate in), so we do not expect every threat to alter democratic norms, but where they do it is because it benefits challengers and threatens status quo holders. Examining citizenship norms in hard times, through the unique use of survey experiments, lets us get closer to answering questions like "*which* types of threat do citizen find threatening?"

Elites remain a vital part of the story. They frame and filter a threat, identify incentives of cooperation or zero-sum gamesmanship, provide cues for citizens, and set party priorities. But citizens adjust norms (or not) that may legitimize power grabs and facilitate further backsliding. Or, equally concerning, if only opposition supporters rally around liberal values, a ruling party has less incentive or constraints to stay in line.

Building on these two arguments – citizens are critical to democratic stability and citizenship norms become political in hard times – I introduce a third and final argument in the conclusion of the book: Divided citizenship makes democratic problems worse. It exacerbates "sideism," attenuating cross-cutting ties and eroding the minimal national unity necessary to maintain shared national goals and convey legitimacy to a democratic regime. Before presenting the book outline, I next discuss case selection and methodology.

---

[54] Bethany Albertson and Shana Kushner Gadarian, *Anxious Politics: Democratic Citizenship in a Threatening World* (New York: Cambridge University Press, 2015).

1.3 THREE COUNTRIES, TWO THREATS

To explore the effects of democratic threat on citizenship, namely, under what conditions do citizens update norms of obligation as an extension of their partisan identity, this book employs original surveys and experimental data in three countries: the US, the UK, and Germany.[55] I show that partisan citizenship as a response to threat is sharper in majoritarian political systems, which enhances partisan differences through polarizing, zero-sum institutions. This institutional context not only contributes to democratic instability, where citizens are meant to serve as an institutional guardrail; it also intensifies it by limiting potential paths for consensus and compromise.

These cases share many features that make their comparison useful for reaching broader generalization about citizenship in hard times. They are all advanced democracies with industrial economies and, relatedly, similar political cultures.[56] Each has also faced real threats to democratic institutions in recent years, where scenario realism and cross-case control are both highly valued in experimental research. Finally, the partisan right is the majority power holder in each of the cases during the time period of survey fielding (May–August 2019[57]), which enables us to control for partisan interests across a range of incumbency-challenger models. That is, while Republicans (US), Conservatives (UK), and the Christian Democratic Union (Germany) are all right-wing majority power holders (or coalition leaders), they experience different incumbency benefits and pressures as a result of institutional design. Holding constant incumbent party orientation limits the

---

[55] In a sense, one might say these are traditional cases for studying democratic citizenship, as they were featured in Gabriel Almond and Sidney Verba's canonical text, *The Civic Culture* wherein, they identified the US ("participant civic culture") and UK ("deferential civic culture") as exhibiting citizens most compatible to democratic stability, while (West) Germany's culture was not civic but portrayed subject competence alongside political detachment." Almond and Verba explain this as a consequence of German political history: "as if the intense commitment to political movements that characteristic Germany under Weimar and the Nazi era is now being balanced by a detached, practical, and almost cynical attitude toward politics" Almond and Verba, *The Civic Culture: Political Attitudes and Democracy in Five Nations*, 429.

[56] Specifically, they have similar self-expression value correlates that relate to a similar sense of political empowerment and agency. Christian Welzel and Ronald Inglehart, "The Role of Ordinary People in Democratization," *Journal of Democracy* 19, no. 1 (2008).

[57] This is a representative snapshot for studying democratic threat in all three cases. The timing was chosen to reduce political salience of previous and scheduled forthcoming elections (as well as to avoid overlap with what ended up being an ever-changing Brexit deadline).

study's ability to generalize to the full scope of party reactions both inside and outside of government. However, including Germany – where a left party (Social Democrats; SPD) was in a long-standing power-sharing coalition with the CDU at the time of writing – gives leverage on that question. This cross-case research design allows for analysis of the effects of institutions on shaping incentives to retain or challenge status quo arrangements in response to threat.

As such, this case selection leverages important variation in institutional design to gain analytical insight on how systems shape citizen incentives to respond to democratic threat or not. The US is a majoritarian system par excellence. And, because it is also a presidential system, with separate and scheduled elections for the executive and legislative branches, its first-past-the-post (FPTP) elections produce effective two-party systems and, therefore, distinct zero-sum incentives. Unsurprising, it is also the most polarized of the three cases. The UK is also a majoritarian system that uses FPTP, but combines these features with a multiparty, parliamentary system. This alters incentives for citizens; a vote for a third party does not "throw away" their choice at the constituency level. This has led to durable third parties, like the Liberal Democrats, as well as regional parties, including Scotland's Scottish National Party and Northern Ireland's Democratic Unionist Party, who supported the Conservatives in coalition during the fielding of the survey (ending their support in November 2019). Finally, Germany is a multiparty system that uses a type of proportional representation and other power-sharing arrangements consistent with a consensus-based political system. Citizens can choose between several national parties on the left and right, with a strong likelihood that their party will represent their interests in the Bundestag (the federal parliament), where any party that gains above 5% of the vote gets seats. And, in a case like Germany, we observe parties on the left that are both in (SPD) and out (Green, Die Linke) of power. This lets us examine more closely what elements of citizen norms are affected by being on the losing side versus being on the left. In sum, across these three systems, different institutional designs produce different incentives for citizens to maintain or challenge the status quo.

Across these three cases, I use a series of vignette experiments to examine two types of democratic threat: polarization and electoral interference. Advanced democracies have experienced any number of threats in recent years, from the erosion of rule of law to the rise of nativist, populist parties. And some of these have been more threatening than the threats presented here. But there is a trade-off of cross-national survey experimentation that requires reducing within-country specificity while maintaining realism and fidelity, in order to maximize cross-national comparability for increased generalizability. As such, I select two phenomena that have been framed as a democratic threat in each case. So, for example, the far right AfD in Germany represents a clear democratic threat in embracing an illiberal policy agenda, and comparison to the UKIP/Brexit party in the UK and the Republican Party in the US would be possible. But it is an inherently partisan premise – it is about political parties – and invites a partisan response, whereas the puzzle here is how democratic threats that are not inherently partisan can *become* partisan because of positional incentives. Unlike populist threats, foreign interference and polarization do not point the finger at any specific national group or side, thus allowing the survey respondent to infer positional incentives on their own or in response to party cues, consistent with my theory of democratic instability.

The first democratic threat is polarization. Political science uses two related but distinct definitions of this term. One is structural, defined as the sharp ideological differentiation between parties. Polarization in this sense occurs in both two-party and multiparty systems. In fact, multiparty systems tend to produce strong polarization, especially where convergence between and dissatisfaction with mainstream parties lead to the creation and support for extreme parties on the fringe.[58] A second meaning, which I use here, refers not to parties but people, existing at both the elite and mass levels, and is defined as the "simultaneous presence of opposing or conflicting principles, tendencies, or points of view."[59] Polarization is not just a condition of hard times; it may produce further democratic instability when it erodes the liberal democratic norms and cross-cutting ties that bind differing views together and makes unity possible. Because it is a type of horizontal threat – that is, it exists between ostensibly equal citizens – positional incentives of winners and losers are more ambiguous. Therefore, I consider polarization a type of crucial case for whether citizens intuit positional incentives in either preserving or challenging the status quo. It is, at the same time, also a typical case for testing the strength of citizen responses. This type of threat is closest to

---

[58] For example, Sheri Berman and Hans Kundnani point out that democratic dysfunction in Germany stems from *convergence*. Sheri Berman and Hans Kundnani, "The Cost of Convergence," *Journal of Democracy* 32, no. 1 (2021). But also see Ernesto Calvo and Timothy Hellwig, "Centripetal and Centrifugal Incentives under Different Electoral Systems," *American Journal of Political Science* 55, no. 1 (2011).

[59] Morris P. Fiorina and Samuel J. Abrams, "Political Polarization in the American Public," *Annual Review of Political Science* 11 (2008): 566.

citizens – it exists *between* citizens. Citizens are therefore complicit in the problem but may also perceive greater individual agency to affect outcomes. In other words, citizen work can be consequential.

The study of affective polarization – which focuses on outgroup derogation of others based on partisan identity – has, with a few exceptions, been confined to the US context. However, in the growing field of comparative affective polarization – that is, how individuals feel about people in other parties – consensus finds the US and UK to be broadly, similarly polarized, and Germany less so.[60] One study depicting change over time finds a sharp increase in polarization in the US, a more gradual slope for the UK, and Germany depolarizing considerably.[61] This type of intensity variation allows for an additional layer of analysis into civic responses across advanced democracies.

All three countries exhibit polarization, though the substance or source of division differs. In the US, consistent with a traditional definition of polarization as the distance between two parties, polarization has solidified around partisanship.[62] In the UK, the Leave vs. Remain cleavage is the most salient political issue in 2019, an issue that runs perpendicular to partisanship, as Brexit negotiations remained ongoing, even consolidating as its own social identity.[63] And in Germany, as we see rising support not only for the extreme right but also extreme left, social fracturing and the disintegration of cross-cutting ties present clear challenges to social cohesion ("sozialen Zusammenhalt").

The second democratic threat is foreign interference in elections. Foreign electoral interference occurs when an external force, country, or power "uses rhetoric and/or resources to give specific parties or candidates an electoral advantage."[64] This is a violation of an election's freeness and supposed fairness. Because elections produce clear winners and

[60] Andres Reiljan, "'Fear and Loathing across Party Lines' (Also) in Europe: Affective Polarisation in European Party Systems," *European Journal of Political Research* 59, no. 2 (2020): 386; Noam Gidron, James Adams, and Will Horne, *American Affective Polarization in Comparative Perspective* (New York: Cambridge University Press, 2020).

[61] Slopes of affective polarization increase/decrease over time are 0.48 (US), −0.11 (UK), and −0.40 (Germany). Levi Boxell, Matthew Gentzkow, and Jesse M. Shapiro, "Cross-Country Trends in Affective Polarization," in *NBER Working Paper No. 26669* (2020).

[62] Matthew Levendusky, *The Partisan Sort: How Liberals Became Democrats and Conservatives Became Republicans* (Chicago, IL: University of Chicago Press, 2009).

[63] Julian Hoerner and Sara Hobolt, "Unity in Diversity? Polarization, Issue Diversity and Satisfaction with Democracy," *Journal of European Public Policy* (2019).

[64] Michael Tomz and Jessica L. P. Weeks, "Public Opinion and Foreign Electoral Intervention," *American Political Science Review* (2020).

losers, this is a "most likely" case for where we should see motivated reasoning and positional incentives predict how citizens interpret obligation, in which acknowledging or responding to interference may threaten the status quo. It is also a hard test for citizen response. I expect a muted citizen response overall. While positional incentives to respond or not are clear, a citizen is actually quite far removed from being able to affect change. As agency is inherently lower in this type of vertical threat (between citizen and institution/state), the benefits to "doing something" – even something as minimal as updating civic norms – is unclear.

All three cases experienced degrees of Russian meddling in national elections – specifically the US Presidential election of 2016, the British referendum on European Union Membership, or "Brexit" of 2016, and the German Federal election of 2017, through hacked information, campaigns of disinformation and propaganda as well as illegal campaign funding. There exists variation in both the impact and awareness of interference among citizens, but the external nature and similar strategies enable a comparison across the three cases that can support generalizations about citizens in democracy (as opposed to nationally specific conclusions).

To preview the book's findings, I show across both threat types that modal attitudinal responses among citizens are determined by *positional incentives*. That is, citizenship norms align with the incentives of the party an individual supports. In both polarization and interference, incumbents either recoil from democratic citizenship norms or ignore threat altogether. To illustrate, we see Republicans in the US rejecting forbearance in the face of electoral interference. This is an important point. Daniel Ziblatt rightly points to the role of conservative elites in safeguarding democracy[65], but here I present evidence that shows that when they don't, the citizens let them get away with it. These negative responses are reduced in a consensus-based system like Germany, which relies on cross-cutting coalitions. But in the case of Germany, we also see how the SPD – a left party in the grand coalition – exhibits incumbent attitudes, suggesting that positional incentives transcend party orientation.

By contrast, supporters of status quo challenger parties take up the mantle of action. In the face of threat, challenger parties come to value a variety of attributes of good citizenship, including patriotism, vigilance, and many liberal democratic attributes, like tolerance. In short, status quo challengers recognize and respond to threat in a way entirely distinct from those who

---

[65] Ziblatt, *Conservative Political Parties and the Birth of Modern Democracy in Europe*.

benefit from the status quo. Again, the asymmetry of threat response is reduced in Germany, where "ideological polarisation does not lead itself to strong interparty hostility."[66] But, in zero-sum systems with clear status quo beneficiaries and losses, citizens interpret obligation according to the interests and incentives of their political party.

As we see democratic threats alter our traditional institutions – like elections, political parties, rule of law – so, too, do they change the institution of democratic citizenship by elevating political identities. This has deep implications for any possible response to crises of democracy, as solutions prove to be as partisan as the problem itself is perceived. Therefore, when ideological positions coalesce around political parties and, in turn, shape how individuals interpret their role as citizens, we should be very worried about our capacity to resolve democratic problems and, thus, prevent democratic erosion.

1.4 BOOK OUTLINE

The remainder of this book is structured as follows. Chapter 2 presents the concept of citizenship, its unifying function in a national polity, and the way it contributes to – or undermines – democratic stability. I begin by laying out a capacious definition of citizenship norms along three dimensions or types: *behavior*, liberal democratic *beliefs*, and ideals about national *belonging* (the "three B's"). I then present a citizen-centered theory of democratic instability that first locates citizenship as a source of stability, focusing tightly on national unity and cross-cutting ties, followed by a discussion of positional incentives, with a citizen's party's interest in either preserving or challenging status quo, competing in a system that encourages consensus or not. Positional incentives in majoritarian systems increase polarization and division in civic obligation. This undermines national unity as a principal foundation for democratic stability, making the resolution of democratic problems more difficult.

Chapter 3 moves on to how we identify and measure citizenship norms cross-nationally and over time. I introduce my original, three-country survey (approximately N = 3000 per country), and present descriptive evidence of how individuals define a "good citizen" across fourteen different items that span behaviors, beliefs, and belonging. Items range

---

[66] Reiljan, "'Fear and Loathing across Party Lines' (Also) in Europe: Affective Polarisation in European Party Systems."

from voting and obeying the law to tolerating those with different political views to speaking the national language. To capture changes in
democratic norms over time, I compare my original survey evidence from
2019 with International Social Survey Programme (ISSP) data from
2004 and 2014 (pre-democratic crisis snapshots).

Following a discussion of longitudinal and cross-national patterns,
I use factor analysis to explore the interrelationship between these fourteen items. As a measure of construct validity, I confirm the 3-Bs as
durable dimensions of citizenship: *behavior* (defined by voting, watching
government, association, protest, and understanding politics), liberal
beliefs (defined by tolerance, patience in losing, civility, cross-cutting
networks, and valuing diversity), and democratic *belonging* (defined by
obedience, government support, patriotism, and homogeneity preferences). This descriptive overview of good citizenship norms in 2019 sets
up the analysis in the rest of the book.

Chapter 4 presents the partisan structure of democratic citizenship.
First, we see consensus in all three cases, where there are significant
overlaps in civic norms to substantiate a core of common goals and
values. Specifically, behavioral items and liberal beliefs are highly valued
by both the partisan left and right. In fact, in everyday citizenship, there
are more similarities than differences. These are the cross-cutting, minimally necessary values of national unity upon which democratic stability rests. Where we see differences are primarily along items of belonging
and inclusion, that is, community values. In the US and the UK, the
partisan left maintains positive outgroup responsibility, like helping
others and accepting diversity. By contrast, the partisan right strongly
embraces inward-oriented definitions of citizenship, whereby a "good
citizen" obeys the law, supports government, speaks English and feels
American/British. This pattern is less visible in Germany. There is no
division when it comes to liberal democratic beliefs or behavior, though
the partisan right exhibits stronger norms of belonging. I conclude by
comparing 2019 patterns of partisan citizenship with 2004 data, in
which we see no underlying partisan structure in earlier citizenship
norms (and with different parties in government in both the UK and
Germany). This tells us there is something unique about everyday citizenship today – even before taking threat into account – and that
partisanship plays a key role in that story. This lays the groundwork
for how a democratic crisis can magnify and activate partisan differences
to serious consequence.

Chapters 5 and 6 move to the central question: How do individuals interpret civic obligation in the face of democratic threat? Chapter 5 presents the results of vignette experiments on polarization and Chapter 6 on foreign interference in elections. The vignette experiments prime a random sample of survey respondents to consider foreign interference in their country's elections, and others to think about polarization in their country (both compared to a control group receiving nonpolitical information). The goal of this experiment was to increase the salience of a realistic democratic threat to a group of respondents, allowing me to explore how information about the threat shapes respondents' norms, compared to a control group that does not receive information on a democratic threat. In both threat types, I find strong partisan effects, where individuals interpret citizenship norms as a function of party identification.

Asking individuals about the consequences of polarization presents an opportunity to self-reflect on one of the very sources of democratic precarity. It is also a good test for positional incentives, as there are no obvious winners and losers by status. I find polarization as a democratic threat produces an unambiguously strong effect on citizenship norms by partisanship in all three countries. Citizens respond to the problem of polarization with appropriately corresponding solutions, for example, tolerance and understanding others. Likewise, behavioral norms, such as voting or protesting, are seldom activated in the US and not activated at all in the UK, which adequately reflects the ongoing intractable nature of deep polarization. In this, polarization becomes self-perpetuating. By contrast, in the context of German polarization, where we observe low levels of political polarization (not unrelated to its consensus political system), partisans of all stripes are mobilized, taking "shared ownership" of the problem by valuing engaged citizenship (behavioral components) as well as liberal democratic norms. Here, the barriers are low enough to disrupt the status quo allowing for a strong "active citizen" response to polarization, from the far left (Die Linke) to the far right (AfD), and even across distinctions of in- versus out-of-government.

In response to foreign interference in elections, as a threat that designates clear winners and losers, we see strong differences emerge between "sides." Specifically, we see significant changes to challenger norms and little from incumbent supporters. In the US, we see little to no effect on Republicans as status quo recipients, with the notable exception of devaluing forbearance – a guardrail of democratic stability. Some even reject the frame altogether. By contrast, partisan challengers (Democrats and others) express "watching government" (vigilance) and protest as more important attributes of good citizenship, as well as patriotism. A sharper pattern of partisan citizenship emerges in the UK, with the left responding to threat by embracing a strongly engaged citizenship (i.e., behavioral norms) and patriotism, while the right recoils, devaluing attributes like "being informed." In Germany, by contrast, partisanship does not uniquely provoke one group of citizens to respond versus another, though, on the whole, those out of power are substantially motivated to respond to threat.

Chapter 7 asks, "What comes next?" Citizens have the power to defend democracy or deliver autocracy. And yet my findings show that democratic threats generally do not provoke the type of liberal responses essential to safeguarding democracy; that is, obligations that overcome the political divide and reestablish national unity. How do you protect democracy when not all sides accept its fundamental principles? How do you reduce the corrosive effects of polarization when it breeds further polarization? What are the practical consequences when a party in power is not only ambivalent to threat but responsible for it I may be accused of asking more questions than I provide in answers, but I flag some of the central dilemmas for advanced democracies today. While certain countries (and certain citizens) are more vulnerable to authoritarian and illiberal capture, my findings highlight how ordinary citizens can be complicit in democratic erosion. In the end, the most pernicious – and potentially long-lasting – crisis of democracy is the disappearance of an "our," replaced instead with an "us" versus "them."

1.5 CONTRIBUTIONS

The book makes three central contributions. First, by inserting citizenship into the story of democratic hard times, the book shows that everyday citizens recognize and respond to democratic threat but do so in accordance with their partisan identity. Individuals do not see themselves as uniformly affected by threat and depending on whether their "side" benefits or not determines who responds to crisis and who "stays home."[67] These benefits may be incompatible with democracy. It also makes it hard for societies to define democratic threat as a shared problem and unifying threat. And where you have uneven responses, where only

---

[67] This is consistent to what Frances Lee describes as "teamsmanship." Frances E. Lee, *Beyond Ideology: Politics, Principles, and Partisanship in the U. S. Senate* (Chicago: University of Chicago Press, 2009).

certain partisans mobilize, the threat itself becomes politicized. Thus, citizenship foments further division, undermining national unity and thus the foundation or core of democratic stability.

To test these arguments, and in contrast to existing work that has focused on citizenship in democratic "good times" and at a narrow set of civic behaviors, I employ experimental techniques to introduce new public opinion data collected specifically to probe the foundations of citizenship in times of democratic crisis. I find that while different kinds of democratic threats have different effects on citizenship (both within and across countries), they do not affect citizens on all sides, and they generally do not produce renewed commitments to traditional liberal values on the partisan right, like tolerance, forbearance, and valuing diversity. In general, we do not see the public as a whole respond to democratic problems by emphasizing shared liberal values and securing institutional guard rails. Instead, we see strong partisan effects.

My second contribution in this book is to introduce a novel approach to identifying democratic citizenship norms. I use a deliberately broad definition of what it means to be a "good citizen," which includes traditional civic duties like voting and being informed, but also overlooked dimensions of liberal values (patience, tolerance) and belonging. These facets of citizenship are typically taken for granted, particularly when the subject of analysis is native-born citizens. Native-born citizens grow up and are socialized in liberal democratic settings, so their commitments to liberal values and understanding of national identity go unscrutinized. This might explain, for example, why elected officials seem continually surprised when violent acts are perpetuated by (white) citizens, actors that are labeled "vigilante" or "troubled" but would otherwise be called "terrorist" when perpetuated by group outsiders.

But from the perspective of immigration scholarship, commitments to liberal value and patriotic values are the most explicit – if opaque – requirements for acquiring citizenship, and feature prominently in naturalization ceremonies. Immigrants literally sign oaths or stand in front of judges, magistrates, and immigration officers and swear "true faith and allegiance" to national values in all the cases studied here.[68] Given the prominent role that these expectations play in the lives of newcomers, the broader conceptualization of citizenship that I introduce

---

[68] See Sara Wallace Goodman, *Immigration and Membership Politics in Western European* (New York: Cambridge University Press, 2014).

turns the lens around to consider the balance of these norms in everyday citizens, and what happens to them in democratic hard times.

My third broad contribution is to our understanding of the institutional roots of democratic crisis. In majoritarian systems, my analysis shows how institutions reinforce antagonistic conditions between winners and losers and, thus, exacerbates partisan identity. This limits the space to interpret civic obligation as contributing toward a public good, that is, a democratic regime and rule of law, irrespective of winners and losers. By contrast, we expect – and I find – lower partisanship differences in consensus-based systems. Thus, in addition to demographic and attitudinal features, institutional contexts play an integral, mediating role in shaping citizens' attitudes about what makes a good citizen. That studies of partisan and affective polarization typically take place in the US only limits the extent we can examine institutional sources for this rift, or whether it is a feature of democracy more generally. Thus, the imperative to place citizenship at the center of analysis is also a call to look comparatively at the structure of advanced democracies, marrying behavioral tools for studying citizen attitudes with institutional understandings of processes and context.

Taken together, *Citizenship in Hard Times* shows that the contemporary crisis of democracy is changing ordinary people's views of citizenship and therefore what citizens can do to prevent or exacerbate democratic erosion. Worryingly, I find citizenship values align to divisive partisan identities rather than a set of unifying forms of the overall democratic political system in the face of threat. Further, the analysis in this book breaks down simplistic models of citizenship, providing greater empirical nuance to our understanding of citizenship and the conceptual structure needed to make sense of where they come from and how they are changing. It shows that while US, UK, and Germany all face comparable challenges to democracy, the effects of these challenges on citizens differ substantially.

This book is the first to systematically tackle citizenship attitudes and ideals in advanced democracies facing democratic hard times. Politicians and pundits who look to an active citizenry to prevent further democratic backsliding do so without an understanding of what citizens think they should be doing. In fact, the common wisdom that "an active citizenry will redeem democracy" is dangerous when taken to be automatic or unconditional. As this book shows, citizens only respond to certain crises, and only when it is in their interest. And those interests are shaped by partisanship and institutional incentives. These factors determine whether citizens are the custodians of democracy or the midwives of its alternatives.

2

Citizenship and Democratic Instability

This chapter develops the core arguments of the book. First, *citizenship is a foundation for democratic stability*. It binds together deep differences inherent to plural societies to establish a baseline of shared liberal democratic goals and, with those goals in mind, conveys legitimacy to a regime to govern. Second, the division of this national unity is a source of instability as *citizens respond to democratic threat not as citizens but as partisans*, interpreting good citizenship norms by what benefits their "side." A citizen-centered approach focuses on how individuals use partisanship as an informational heuristic in hard times, relying on party cues to determine whether responding to a threat is "in their interest." These interests are determined by *positional incentives* of their side, that is, whether their party is in or out of power and institutional design features, which encourage either costly zero-sum (majoritarian) or positive-sum (consensus) responses.

Citizenship has always been political; it is itself the identity that inserts the individual into the realm of politics. Moreover, the factors that determine who gets citizenship and what constitutes civic duty are often related to political zeitgeists of the day. But "political" is not partisan; the former connotes engagement with and participation in politics, while the latter defines that participation by "teams" or "sideism." Citizenship is a formal institution that weaves distant corners of society into a common patchwork, encompassing but balancing differences under a canopy of shared goals. However, existing but dormant differences can be activated under stressful and threatening conditions, and citizenship can – like other social identities – become defined by divisive, partisan interests. When citizenship is aligned with political identity, and when political institutions encourage contestation along those divisions, citizenship is not a source of democratic stability or resilience but rather an additional factor in backsliding (see Chapter 7).

This chapter proceeds in three parts. First, to locate citizenship as foundational to democratic stability, I lay out a definition of democratic citizenship by the transactional ties between individual and state, and the balance of rights and obligations contained within it. I particularly focus on the understudied side of obligation, including norms of (1) *behavior*, (2) commitments to liberal democratic *beliefs*, and (3) considerations of national *belonging* that comprise notions of "good citizenship." Put another way, good citizenship is a type of moral claim about what citizens are supposed to be, believe, and do. This requires clear delineation of who is and is not a citizen, but also consensus over what the goals of society are that citizens pursue and preserve. Where liberal philosophies of citizenship predominate, this may be as minimal as seeing a citizen as an autonomous bearer of rights, or it may be more maximal, such as extending basic liberal democratic rights to others.

Having defined citizenship norms and why they matter, the second part situates citizenship as a feature of not only democratic legitimacy but also *stability*. Citizens are an integral political institution who practice and preserve system goals, and their attitudes and behaviors both determine and are affected by democratic governance. Citizenship is, thus, a coordinating device that brings together disparate factions and groups under common group goals and status. This is vital; a government cannot be democratically responsive to the will of the people if "the people" are amorphous and "the will" is undefined.[1] This national unity is not only a prerequisite for democratic governance but also a key part of regime stability.

Third, I argue that citizenship becomes a source of instability in democratic hard times by becoming divisive and partisan. Individuals may hold fast to liberal democratic norms like tolerance or being informed as part of everyday citizenship, as a set of latent, costless, and untested beliefs, but in the face of uncertainty, citizens rely on partisan leaders for cues and accordingly respond to threat by whether it challenges or preserves the status quo. These positional incentives are particularly pronounced in majoritarian political systems, which structure politics through a series

---

[1] This characteristic of democracy comes from Robert Dahl, *Polyarchy: Participation and Opposition* (New Haven, CT: Yale University Press, 1973).

of zero-sum competitions, encouraging individuals to respond to democratic problems as status quo winners versus system losers. By contrast, mutual ties of citizenship are more likely to be sustained through consensus-based political institutional arrangements.

By placing citizens at the center of analysis, I show how this vital democratic institution is the foundation of legitimacy and stability in good times, but a source of instability when times get tough. By looking at crisis from the perspective of citizens, I illustrate how their perception of threat is conditioned by an understanding of macro-positional incentives that either help or hurt their "side," and therefore how baseline norms get activated or not in a citizen's decision to react. Thus, a citizen's sense of obligation is shaped by the costs and benefits of reaction. Taking a citizen-centered view of exogenous events and structural features of politics aligns the ontology of the argument with the individual-level survey data collected and analyzed in the remainder of the book.

2.1 WHAT IS CITIZENSHIP?

2.1.1 Defining Citizenship

Citizenship is one of the most widely used concepts in political studies, but scholars often use it to refer to different things. The issue is not that citizenship is an "essentially contested concept" but rather that it is a multidimensional one. First, citizenship is a legal status. It is the passport you hold and the political, civil, and social rights you bear as a function of that status.[2] Second, citizenship is a type of behavior, what individuals do in a civic capacity.[3] Third, citizenship is an identity, a set of values that foster a sense of belonging, creating categories of insiders and outsiders.[4] In other words, citizenship is what you have, what you do, and who you are. In its most generic use, "citizen" is simply a replacement term for individual. In the words of Peter Spiro, it appears as an "anodyne synonym for virtuousness in society and in individuals ... a way of describing

---

[2] T.H. Marshall, *Citizenship and Social Class and Other Essays* (Cambridge, UK: Cambridge University Press, 1950), 41–3.
[3] Dalton, *The Good Citizen.*
[4] Rogers Brubaker, *Citizenship and Nationhood in France and Germany* (Cambridge, MA: Harvard University Press, 1992).

any public audience."[5] And, as Linda Bosniak notes, these concepts "are overlapping but not always coextensive."[6]

Yet, one thread runs through these many definitions: citizenship is a *transactional* relationship between an individual and a polity, wherein a citizen receives rights *in exchange* for certain obligations.[7] An individual requires the state for status, protection, rights, mobility, and even identity. But the state has needs too; as an administrative apparatus, it must identify whom they are obligated to protect, whom to distribute goods to, from whom they can extract resources, and so on – all of which are processes that make individuals "legible" to the state.[8]

As a result of this arrangement, citizenship emerges as a core feature of all regime types but particularly critical for constituting and sustaining democratic systems.[9] Democracy derives sovereignty from its citizens, and citizens exercise authority through consent (conferring legitimacy on the state[10]) and participation in democratic politics. As Benjamin Barber succinctly states, a strong democracy "requires unmediated self-government by an engaged citizenry."[11] Citizens are so elemental to the core definition and functioning of a democracy that, in Robert Dahl's ubiquitous construction, the *only necessary conditions* to create a polyarchy are institutions of contestation – that is, elections – and partici-pation – that is, the involvement of citizens.[12]

---

[5] Peter J. Spiro, *Citizenship: What Everyone Needs to Know®* (Oxford: Oxford University Press, 2019).

[6] Linda Bosniak, *The Citizen and the Alien: Dilemmas of Contemporary Membership* (Princeton, NJ: Princeton University Press, 2006), 3.

[7] Tilly, "Citizenship, Identity and Social History," 8.

[8] James C. Scott, *Seeing Like a State: How Certain Schemes to Improve the Human Condition Have Failed* (New Haven, CT: Yale University Press, 1998).

[9] Authoritarian citizenship is different. In authoritarian regimes, citizenship serves as an instrumental marker of ingroup identity, and its relationship to an authoritarian leader is defined by compliance and obedience. This is consistent with models of rulership like the authoritarian bargain model, an implicit agreement between political elites and citizens in which consolidation of power comprises extending welfare, goods, and protection to citizens in exchange for regime support and quiescence.

[10] Legitimacy is a "requisite of democracy, defined as 'the belief that existing political institutions are the most appropriate or proper ones for the society'." Lipset, "Political Man," 83.

[11] Benjamin Barber, *Strong Democracy: Participatory Politics for a New Age* (Berkeley: University of California Press, 2003), 261.

[12] Dahl, *Polyarchy*. Dahl would later write that there are several other conditions that differentiate robust democracies from diminished subtypes, including inclusive citizenship (full franchise). Robert A. Dahl, "What Political Institutions Does Large-Scale Democracy Require?," *Political Science Quarterly* 120, no. 2 (2005): 187–97.

Within democratic polities, governments may be subject to citizen decisions, but they are responsible for citizen-making. States craft citizenship rules to decide who partakes in democratic activities, by associating participatory rights with a national group – in other words, who is (and who is not) a member of the national political community. They do so through a variety of procedures, conferring citizenship by place of birth (*jus soli*), parentage (*jus sanguinis*), as well as pathways for naturalization. The vast majority of a state's citizenry are born into citizenship and thus rarely think about either the unique benefits or vulnerability of their citizenship. This may lead them to undervalue, or not consider at all, the power of rights and obligations associated with it. Of course, noncitizens play important roles in democratic systems, too. They often use political activity, like protesting and organization, to increase their rights and representation. But only citizens have obligations to participate, to confer legitimacy and consent.

The "correct" balance between rights and obligations in an advanced democracy is a source of debate, but conventional wisdom holds that individual rights have come to predominate, diminishing the counterbalancing role of obligation.[13] Part of the reason is historical. In the postwar, rights-based era – and with the very glaring exception of mandatory military service – the few obligations that citizens owe to a state are banal, like following the law and paying taxes. And even those duties are not reserved for citizens. But the decline in duty-based citizenship models in favor of liberal, rights-based ones does not mean that individual obligation has disappeared; rather, it has moved from being explicit (and formal) to being implicit – a voluntary expression of "good citizenship."[14]

Yet, obligation is an integral and unavoidable component of political life. An obligation becomes political when it refers to an individual's duties to the state, government, or communities therein. Obligation can be externalized behavior, duties like voting and military service, wearing a

---

[13] Thomas Janoski, *Citizenship and Civil Society: A Framework of Rights and Obligations in Liberal, Traditional, and Social Democratic Regimes* (New York: Cambridge University Press, 1998).

[14] As Blais and Aachen pointedly write in their study of voter turnout, "'civic duty' has often functioned as a kind of residual category not worth further investigation, rather like putting down 'old age' as a cause of death." Blais and Achen, "Civic Duty and Voter Turnout."

mask in a pandemic, or even "oppos[ing] injustice perpetrated by one's own government."[15] Obligation can also be internalized, like holding beliefs and commitments to a set of values. These are not mutually exclusive, and internalized norms are often strong predictors of public behavior.[16] Thus, where duty has become implicit, norms are the very site for understanding obligation.

2.1.2 What Are Citizenship Norms? Behavior, Beliefs, and Belonging

Norms comprise "a shared set of expectations about the citizen's role in politics."[17] What are those shared expectations? How do citizens fulfill their obligations and commitments to the state?[18] There is no clear definition of the ideal constellation of norms of democratic citizenship. Citizens agree there are rights and responsibilities to citizenship,[19] but disagree over what they are. If we used a "minimal" or procedural definition of democracy – a system that elects leaders based on free and fair elections[20] – a citizen's *only* obligation is behavioral: to participate in voting. Of course, even in this minimalist conception, participation is not for everyone.[21] One of the enduring legacies of Gabriel Almond and Sidney Verba's *The Civic Culture* is the observation that democracies *require* a "blend of activity and passivity," where "there is political activity, but not so much as to destroy governmental authority; there is

[15] John Horton, *Political Obligation* (London: Macmillan International Higher Education, 2010), 14.
[16] Dalton, *The Good Citizen*; Bolzendahl and Coffé, "Are 'Good' Citizens 'Good' Participants?"
[17] Dalton, "Citizenship Norms and the Expansion of Political Participation," 78.
[18] Individuals "communicate to others that we are persons of a certain sort, who hold certain opinions, and will conduct ourselves in a certain manner. We entitle them to expect things of us, to rely on us, to plan their lives with us in mind as friends, colleagues, allies, or whatever. We give them rights against us and their rights henceforth define our obligations." Michael Walzer, *Obligations: Essays on Disobedience, War, and Citizenship* (Cambridge, MA: Harvard University Press, 1970), xi–xii.
[19] Pamela Johnston Conover, Ivor M. Crewe, and Donald D. Searing, "The Nature of Citizenship in the United States and Great Britain: Empirical Comments on Theoretical Themes," *The Journal of Politics* 53, no. 3 (1991): 800–32.
[20] Joseph A. Schumpeter, *Capitalism, Socialism and Democracy* (New York: Harper & Brothers, 1942); Adam Przeworski, *Capitalism and Social Democracy* (Cambridge: Cambridge University Press, 1986).
[21] In fact, a key argument against mandatory voting laws is that uninformed participation creates information effects that negatively influence an election. Larry M. Bartels, "Uninformed Votes: Information Effects in Presidential Elections," *American Journal of Political Science* 40 (1996): 194–230.

involvement and commitment, but they are moderated; there is political cleavage, but it is held in check."[22] Citizenship is necessarily a big tent, broad enough to include the active and inactive, informed and uninformed, and so on.[23] For Dahl, the ideal citizen is minimally knowledgeable and interested in politics.

But in contemporary democracies, a good citizen is not just an informed participant. Moving from an institutionally minimal to a maximal definition of democracy, a citizen's obligation includes commitments to liberal democratic values. Some of these values consist of respect for the rule of law, equality, and dispositions of mutual tolerance. Liberal democracy further requires values and norms for sustaining cross-cutting ties and social interactions in plural societies. These values are defined in accordance with the tenets of political liberalism and include political liberties like freedom of expression and freedom to form and join organizations. In this philosophical framework, a government is obligated to protect the rule of law as a practice of limited sovereignty and a means to enable individual liberty, thus ensuring equality before the law, the protection of minority rights, and individual civil liberties. It also does so through the principle of neutrality. In fact, a *nonpartisan* state plays a critical role in economic and democratic development,[24] and evidence of blurred lines between party and state is a traditional signpost of authoritarianism.

Within this liberal democratic framework, then, a citizen's obligation is to comply with and uphold liberal democratic norms like following the law, practicing tolerance as equal respect and in recognition of each individual's "right to rights," and committing to a set of shared values. Thus, a good citizen understands their rights and duties[25] and participates to varying degrees in duty and engagement beyond voting.[26] These

---

[22] Furthermore, the model citizen is "not the active citizen; he is the potentially active citizen"; Almond and Verba, *The Civic Culture*, 347.

[23] Schattschneider famously mused that "it is not necessary to know how to *make* a television set in order to buy one intelligently" in Elmer Eric Schattschneider, *The Semisovereign People: A Realist's View of Democracy in America* (New York: Holt, Rinehart and Winston, 1960).

[24] Francis Fukuyama, *Political Order and Political Decay: From the Industrial Revolution to the Globalization of Democracy* (New York: Macmillan, 2014). This is why, for example, so many civil servants and career bureaucrats continue to work in government despite a change in political party.

[25] Conover, Crewe, and Searing, "The Nature of Citizenship in the United States and Great Britain."

[26] Dalton, *The Good Citizen*.

behaviors may include characteristics of what Russell Dalton and Christian Welzel describe as the "assertive citizen": exhibiting low trust in institutions and more willing to confront elites with demands, giving high value to voice and participation.[27] Such an understanding of citizenship embodies the political liberal ideal, where government distance and inherent distrust inform individual participation. And, just as democracies do not require all citizens to participate, so too does liberalism tolerate degrees of illiberalism. It is tolerant of the intolerant, though this is bounded within reasonable limits,[28] and illiberal individuals and groups must still comply with those values that are enshrined in law.

Finally, civic obligation may be conceived as expressing or adhering to norms of national belonging. It is easier to think about whether an individual complies with belonging norms from the perspective of an immigrant, who often has to complete a set of language and country knowledge requirements to gain citizenship through naturalization.[29] It is more challenging to think about how native-born citizens learn and habituate into a set of norms about belonging. "Belonging" is probably the element of citizenship that is most taken for granted among the native-born, included as part of grade school education or through socializing experiences. It is also often the case that there is no single answer for "who belongs" but that national citizenship is composed of a mix of civic and ethnic attributes.[30] For immigrants and native-born citizens alike, however, the central idea here is that "good citizens" carry certain loyalties. These might be ascriptive (like being born into a certain religion), achievable (like learning a national language), or dispositional (expressing patriotism or loyalty). These are not integral to good democratic governance, but they may be for national unity and identifying shared goals in hard times.

Scholars typically do not study good citizenship norms and definitions of national belonging together. For instance, the omnibus International

---

[27] Russell J. Dalton and Christian Welzel, *The Civic Culture Transformed: From Allegiant to Assertive Citizens* (New York, NY: Cambridge University Press, 2014).

[28] This is not an unqualified toleration. Karl Popper, *The Open Society and Its Enemies* (London: Routledge, 1945). Also see John Rawls, *Political Liberalism* (New York, NY: Columbia University Press, 2005).

[29] Goodman, *Immigration and Membership Politics.*

[30] Bart Bonikowski and Paul DiMaggio, "Varieties of American Popular Nationalism," *American Sociological Review* 81, no. 5 (2016): 949–80; Sara Wallace Goodman and Hannah M. Alarian, "National Belonging and Public Support for Multiculturalism," *Journal of Race, Ethnicity and Politics* 6, no. 2 (2021): 305–33.

Social Survey Programme runs two separate survey batteries reflecting this disjuncture: one titled "Citizenship" and the other "National identity." In a second example, Dalton's extensive work on citizenship norms compares engaged and duty-based norms but excludes attributes of belonging.[31] Both approaches exhibit a type of taken-for-grantedness, in which it is assumed the ingroup already adheres to norms, not just "feeling American" or "speaking English" but also commitments to liberal democratic values. If the end of the 2010s has revealed anything, it is that citizens – from presidents to patrons of the proverbial diner – do not inherently hold democratic values.

Thus, I propose here a capacious *definition of citizenship norms* to include expectations about democratic *behaviors*, commitments to liberal democratic *beliefs*, and standards for *national belonging* held by individuals who are subject to a state's rule of law and derive rights from it. This inductive approach stretches beyond behaviorally-oriented trade-offs between engagement and duty to include items of liberal democratic values, and bridges disparate literatures to consider norms of national belonging, which may or may not be a feature of democratic citizenship but are expectations that we typically interrogate of outsiders to join democratic communities. In short, norms of citizenship cover how good citizens should behave, what they should believe, and how they should belong.

In theory, these citizenship norms should not vary across advanced liberal democracies. There may be slight differences based on historical traditions (e.g., the practice of joining associations, or protesting) and in subtleties of content; belonging in Germany means something different than in the US, but the principle is that both *have* expectations of belonging attached to good citizenship. Through different permutations of behavioral attributes, normative beliefs, or expectations of belonging, citizenship constitutes a distinct social identity.[32] It is a quotidian, typically latent identity – rarely experienced in an individual's everyday life – but gets "activated" at certain times, like voting but also travel or opportunities for patriotism (e.g., the Olympics), and – as we shall see – democratic hard times.

---

[31] Dalton, "Citizenship Norms and the Expansion of Political Participation"; Dalton and Welzel, *The Civic Culture Transformed*; Dalton, *The Good Citizen*.

[32] Elizabeth Theiss-Morse, *Who Counts as an American?: The Boundaries of National Identity* (Cambridge UK and New York NY: Cambridge University Press, 2009).

2.2 CITIZENSHIP AS A SOURCE OF DEMOCRATIC STABILITY

To understand how citizenship contributes to democratic *in*stability in hard times, we need to first understand how citizenship is a foundation for democratic stability. How does citizenship make democracy stable, not just legitimate? I argue here citizenship establishes national unity, balancing and subduing otherwise divisive group differences through a consensus of ideas, establishing cross-cutting ties and predictable inter-actions (e.g., the rule of law). It coordinates most different citizens to establish shared goals and convey legitimacy. Citizenship does not reduce differences but defangs them to allow for democratic governance.

Many scholars discuss the critical role of mass support for democratic stability. Again, Almond and Verba were early observers of this phenom-enon, noting civic culture plays a stabilizing role in democracy because it establishes consensus over values, and noting, "If there is no consensus within society, there can be little potentiality for the peaceful resolution of political differences that is associated with the democratic process."[33] Dahl also observed that demarcating a national political community through inclusive citizenship conveys democratic legitimacy.[34] But *why* and *how* does mass support convey stability? This section highlights the role of citizenship in democratic stability, including the role of liberal democratic principles in plural societies and the value of national unity.

There is a critical, unstated assumption in behavioral studies of demo-cratic citizenship: citizenship is unitary. "Citizens believe X" or "Citizens do Y" are not uncommon constructions. This assumption and these constructs are true, but they are superficial. Citizenship is a national political community, broadly conceptualized by the distinction it draws between insiders and outsiders. This national political community is surrounded by a hard shell of membership criteria (e.g., naturalization requirements, immigration rules), while the inside is composed of a soft core of intersubjective meanings about who "we" are and what "we" value. "We" all have the same rights in a democracy, but in practice, not everyone experiences them equally. Or "we" might not be as tolerant toward the expression of rights by some as we are of others. "We" all have obligations and duties, though they may vary from person to person.

---

[33] Almond and Verba, *The Civic Culture*, 358.
[34] Robert Alan Dahl, *Democracy and Its Critics* (New Haven, CT: Yale University Press, 1989).

And "we" belong to the national group, though we may strongly disagree on the attributes that comprise it.

That citizenship appears internally coherent is no small accomplishment; for many states, it takes centuries to achieve a sufficiently common understanding of the "we" group. And because citizenship is also a political category, the standards for joining this membership group and what it means to belong are frequently changing, subject to political concerns and priorities of the day.[35] But citizens are a baseline category from which we can observe mass beliefs and participation. And here we also see broad generalizations about a country having a specific identity or set of norms, referring to different national philosophies (e.g., liberal or republican) or models of citizenship (e.g., ethnic or civic, ascriptive or achievable)[36] or political attitudes.[37]

Yet disagreement and variation remain within that soft core. These differences not only *shape* the liberal democratic nature of citizenship, where competition of ideas is just as vital as competition of parties and candidates, they also *reflect* it, through values like mutual toleration. At a minimum, the liberal beliefs that support democratic citizenship include equality – that individuals merit equal concern, rights and respect – and limited state power, an idea dating back to Locke and Mill, out of fear it may favor one group over another or infringe on individual autonomy. And while it is easy to miss these basic principles among a citizenry that is socialized into citizenship from birth, these standards are quite visible in requirements for immigrants striving to become insiders. In naturalization ceremonies – in all three countries studied here but also beyond – we see explicit oaths and statements to liberal values and the rule of law, specifically to "support and defend the Constitution and laws of the United States of America," "give my loyalty to the United Kingdom and respect its rights and freedoms. I will uphold its democratic values," and "respect and observe the Basic Law and the laws of the Federal Republic of Germany."

---

[35] In the US, for example, there is enormous variation over time in what it means to be a "good American citizen." Sara Wallace Goodman, "'Good American Citizens': A Text-as-Data Analysis of Citizenship Manuals for Immigrants, 1921–1996," *Journal of Ethnic and Migration Studies* 47, no. 7 (2020): 1474–97.

[36] Matthew Wright, "Policy Regimes and Normative Conceptions of Nationalism in Mass Public Opinion," *Comparative Political Studies* 44, no. 5 (2011): 598–624. Or, states can be a hybrid of models, for example, Rogers M. Smith, *Civic Ideals: Conflicting Visions of Citizenship in US History* (New Haven, CT: Yale University Press, 1999).

[37] Norris and Inglehart, *Cultural Backlash*.

These basic liberal commitments allow for the inherent differences of opinions, and other characteristics of a diverse society, to flourish while being bound together in common national purpose, or national unity. These differences may reflect any number of salient cleavages that shape political identity, including partisanship, age, occupation, gender, ideology, religion, to name only a few. In fact, national unity among diverse citizens does not demand the homogenization or flattening of these differences, nor does it imply nationalism. Instead, national unity establishes a "fellow feeling," composed of shared system goals and common purpose. J. S. Mill described it as a "strong and active principle of cohesion among the members of the same community or state" by which he clarifies, a "principle of sympathy, not of hostility; of union, not of separation. We mean a feeling of common interest among those who live under the same government."[38] Further, as David Miller observes: "liberal states do not require their citizens to believe liberal principles, since they tolerate communists, anarchists, fascists, and so forth. What they require is that citizens should conform to liberal principles in practice and accept as legitimate policies that are pursued in the name of such principles, while they are left free to advocate alternative arrangements."[39] Layered on top of this foundational set of values, states may add norms about linguistic proficiency ("A good American speaks English") or belief in a common heritage ("America is a nation of immigrants") or related ethics ("A good American works hard"), which may be contested by other citizens, but citizenship unites across differences by commitments to liberal democratic values.

This liberal democratic core is critical. Not only does it establish national unity, it makes democracy *possible* in plural democracies. Many have puzzled over why it is difficult to achieve democratic stability in divided societies.[40] Dankwart Rustow expounds on this point in great detail. In fact, he argues that national unity (in which "people agree that they are a political entity") is the "single background condition" for a thriving democracy.[41] Describing the case study of Sweden, Rustow writes: "This implies nothing mysterious about Blut und Boden or daily

---

[38] John Stuart Mill, "Collected Works," (1963).CW VIII, p. 923.

[39] David Miller, "Immigrants, Nations, and Citizenship," *Journal of Political Philosophy* 16, no. 4 (2008): 14.

[40] For example, Donald L. Horowitz, "Democracy in Divided Societies," *Journal of Democracy* 4, no. 4 (1993).

[41] This point is also made more recently in Berman, *Democracy and Dictatorship in Europe: From the Ancien Régime to the Present Day.*

pledges of allegiance. .... It simply means that the vast majority of citizens in a democracy-to-be must have no doubt or mental reservations as to which political community they belong to."[42] National unity is not "shared attitudes and opinions," it is not nationalism or national identity, but a background against which political struggle can take place with the understanding that losing to one's opponents in an election is an acceptable outcome.

Rustow is unequivocal that national unity must precede the processes of accommodation, conflict, consensus, and decision-making inherent to democratic governance. We do not have a perfect sense of what national unity means, or what it looks like "in the wild," but at a minimum it includes the basic values that unite democratic citizens behind common national goals. Absent national goals, plural or deeply divided societies "lack consensus," which allow for subnational (or other groupings) to serve as the "primary basis of citizen loyalty."[43]

This is where *liberal* norms are so important for stability.[44] Liberal values make democracy possible not only in sectarian contexts but in demographically diverse societies, keeping ethnocultural impulses at bay or, at least, in check. A strong, well-functioning democracy requires citizens to respectfully engage with one another, even on controversial subjects.[45] Conflict may be a feature of democracy, but ties that enable compromise are necessary for effective governance.[46] It also confers on a democratic government legitimacy to represent and make rules that reflect common group goals. So, partisans – as an example – may hold different ideas about what makes a good citizen, where parties on the left value engagement and parties on the right value loyalty, but there are minimum overlaps that reflect shared values and enable cross-group consensus and coordination to establish common group goals and, therefore, democratic legitimacy.

---

[42] Dankwart A. Rustow, "Transitions to Democracy: Toward a Dynamic Model," *Comparative Politics* 2, no. 3 (1970): 350.

[43] Alvin Rabushka and Kenneth A. Shepsle, Politics in Plural Societies: A Theory of Democratic Instability. Columbus, OH: Charles E. Merrill 232 (1972): 12.

[44] Arend Lijphart, *The Politics of Accommodation; Pluralism and Democracy in the Netherlands* (Berkeley CA: University of California Press, 1968); *Democracies: Patterns of Majoritarian and Consensus Government in Twenty-One Countries* (New Haven, CT: Yale University Press, 1984).

[45] Lipset, "Political Man: The Social Bases of Politics."

[46] Schattschneider, *The Semi-Sovereign People: A Realist's View of Democracy in America.*

Differences are real and significant, but in ordinary times they are innocuous. By that I mean, they may define an individual's sense of civic duty and participation, but citizens rarely think about civic duty in their day-to-day lives. But threat can disrupt an equilibrium to activate deep divisions, though not in predictably similar ways. It may activate some groups but not others. It may activate differences or heighten similarities. For example, external threats, like terrorism or invasion from another country, are shown to produce a converging effect, where attitudinal differences decrease between groups, often producing a type of rallying-around-the-flag or follow-the-leader effect. Conversely, when the threat is internal, existing theories suggests this produces the opposite effect, wherein individuals take sides against one another.[47] The next section looks directly at the reasons why threat elicits divided responses, what sort of obligation might emerge in democratic hard times, and how this transforms citizenship from a source of democratic strength to one of instability.

2.3 A CITIZEN-CENTERED THEORY OF DEMOCRATIC INSTABILITY

This section turns to the book's core theoretical argument: how citizenship becomes fractured in crisis, as changes in norms reflect and align with what is best for one's "side." I develop a citizen-centered theory of democratic instability in hard times that focuses on the conditions under which citizenship devolves from national unity to disunity – or, how the answer to what makes a good citizen differs based on what side you're on.

I argue that divided citizenship, that is, national disunity, is a product of perceiving threat through positional incentives. Two factors shape a citizen's understanding of political incentives and the decision to respond or not: (1) whether they support an incumbent party (which benefits from keeping the status quo) or a challenger party (which benefits from upending it), and (2) the institutional system in which parties compete. Institutional design matters in terms of whether party competition occurs in zero-sum (majoritarian) or positive-sum (consensus) systems, the latter of which reduces the costs of collaborative responses.

First, a word about crises themselves. Democratic crises, perhaps more so than other types of crises, are ripe for politicization because they are

---

[47] For more on these differences, see Albertson and Gadarian, *Anxious Politics: Democratic Citizenship in a Threatening World*.

about politics. A democratic threat is centrally a threat against regime practices, from the rule of law and norms of tolerance to brick-and-mortar institutions like Congress and the Capitol building. The threat is about how politics works, and thus potentially divides people according to how they see politics. Absent unifying messaging, citizen's default to political sideism.

This isn't a trivial point; it is what makes democratic threats unique. We can think of other types of threat – terrorism, pandemics, and economic meltdowns – and how they create other types of "sidedness." For example, terrorism may pit civil libertarians against protectionists and economic crises may divide people on distributional grounds.[48] They may even be partisan; in the case of COVID-19, apolitical health behaviors, like wearing a face mask and social distancing, became defined by partisanship in the US.[49] Yet, the inherent "partisanness" of democratic threat itself makes it a crisis because it punctuates the status quo, potentially affecting some (those in power) more than others (those out of power). Parties and citizens can choose to recognize a violation or problem as a threat or ignore it; that choice alone makes democratic threats unique. If party elites decide that responding is too costly, so will partisans. Citizens are, then, potentially not serving as a check on power grabs or other democratic threats – often perpetrated by their own political party – and instead of a bulwark against democratic backsliding, citizens become an additional source (even a catalyst) for instability.

And because a democratic threat may feel distant, difficult to understand, or is out of reach for agentic, ordinary citizens, a citizen-centered theory describes *how* citizens respond, not *that* citizens respond. I flag and leave open here the potential for causal equifinality. In other words, there could be many factors that determine nonresponse, not simply the absence of factors that induce response. Citizens may decide that a threat is too distant or large for their response to be meaningful. Citizens may also think of obligations of "good citizenship" as time consuming, or of activities that only work in coordination with others, both of which may be disincentives to respond to threat. A reasonable citizen would not respond to threat by updating norms if they think it is futile or a waste

---

[48] Thomas B. Pepinsky, *Economic Crises and the Breakdown of Authoritarian Regimes: Indonesia and Malaysia in Comparative Perspective* (New York, NY: Cambridge University Press, 2009).

[49] Shana Kushner Gadarian, Sara Wallace Goodman, and Thomas B. Pepinsky, "Partisanship, Health Behavior, and Policy Attitudes in the Early Stages of the Covid-19 Pandemic," *PLOS ONE* (2021).

of time. Thus, underlying this theory is an assumption that citizens are rational. Related to this I also expect correspondence between potential threat type and response. In other words, if citizens are going to participate in the costly work of updating citizenship norms – often as a precursor to acting on them – the response will fit the problem. For example, citizens might respond to the problem of populist parties by increasing the importance of voting (for other parties) or to the deprivation of civil liberties by emphasizing their importance. Citizens are problem-solvers, but not everything is a seen as a problem.

With those caveats and assumptions in mind, we now turn to how individuals perceive and respond to threats in line with positional incentives, that is, pursuing what is best in accordance with their political identity or side, focusing on incumbent versus challenger interests and incentives of competition structured by institutional rules.

2.3.1 Incumbents versus Challengers

In an ideal world, responding to a democratic threat is the obligation of all democrats. That is, those who value and participate in a liberal democracy should want to protect it. But political elites and citizens act on incentives, not ideals, specifically, positional incentives. Some have more to gain by responding than others. The principle here is uncomplicated: Incumbent power holders have less incentive to change the status quo by acknowledging and responding to a democratic threat than do challengers, parties, and individuals outside of positions of power. Power holders want to keep power and power seekers want to get it. For this latter group, disrupting the status quo may or may not yield payoffs, but any gains outweigh the steep costs incumbents may potentially incur.

On its own, incumbency advantage is just about power. And positional gains and losses are calculated by party elites seeking to obtain or retain it. But partisanship defines the groups that are incumbents and those that are not; it is partisans that fight over access to holding power. Individual attitudes on their own are relatively unstructured[50] and do not change much over time,[51] so the linkage between party and partisan is key for structuring mass attitudes under normal circumstances, and exceptionally so during a

---

[50] Philip E. Converse, "The Nature of Belief Systems in Mass Publics," in *Ideology and Discontent*, ed. David E. Apter (New York: The Free Press of Glencoe, 1964).
[51] Morris P. Fiorina, Samuel J. Abrams, and Jeremy Pope, *Culture War?: The Myth of a Polarized America* (London: Longman Publishing Group, 2006).

crisis. This is where a citizen-centered theory of instability dovetails with elite-centered ones. As Elmer Schattschneider stated, "Political leaders and parties have the responsibility for organizing conflict"[52] and "the dimensions of conflict set the strategy of politics."[53] The thing about democratic hard times is that citizens see themselves as partisans, and consequently insert themselves through obligation into this matrix of incentives. And, in line with Barry Weingast's equilibrium perspective, elected officials are constrained by civic culture, writing that "mass behavior is relevant" for democratic stability because "citizen reactions [...] provide a component of the elite incentives."[54] Even in contexts with partisan de-alignment,[55] where party identification may be weaker, democratic politicians are still heavily constrained because they are vulnerable electorally. Not everyone joins the game; but those that do, follow their captain and wear a partisan jersey.

Partisanship is critical to understanding positional incentives from the perspective of ordinary people. It is not just the cleavage that defines competition, but how individuals see themselves as vested in that political competition. Even individuals that identify as party independents are affected by partisanship, in which they take on status quo challenger incentives ipso facto. Partisanship connects ordinary people to the stakes of winning and losing, of power gains and losses. The next section examines more closely how partisanship works for citizens in discerning democratic threat. It grounds an otherwise institutional account of party politics in the perspective and agency of citizens.

2.3.2 How Does Partisanship Work

According to the Campbell et al. study, *The American Voter*,[56] partisanship works as a "perceptual screen" through which individuals form political attitudes and behavior, especially – but not limited to – voting. But partisanship is not just the political party one chooses at election time or the type of policy platforms one supports. Partisanship is a *social*

---

[52] Schattschneider, *The Semi-Sovereign People: A Realist's View of Democracy in America*, xxv.

[53] Ibid., xxiv.

[54] Barry R. Weingast, "The Political Foundations of Democracy and the Rule of Law," *American Political Science Review* (1997): 246.

[55] Russell J. Dalton and Martin P. Wattenberg, *Parties without Partisans: Political Change in Advanced Industrial Democracies* (New York: Oxford University Press, 2002).

[56] Angus Campbell et al., *The American Voter* (Ann Arbor, MI: University of Michigan Press, 1960).

identity – a sense of self that one derives from group membership and attachment that persists over time.[57] Partisanship guides which social groups are allies,[58] who you should socialize with,[59] which groups you should avoid,[60] what leaders you should listen to,[61] and vote for,[62] and also, increasingly, *who you are.*

This argument is constructed upon social identity theory.[63] Group categorization leads to intergroup social differentiation, and ultimately positive social identification. And as a group's salience increases, people begin to identify with it and use it to guide behavior.[64] As a social identity, individuals use partisanship to filter facts and information about the political world,[65] and it accordingly shapes how they, as citizens, develop attitudes and engage with issues across the political landscape.[66]

As politics today is defined by the "perpetual campaign,"[67] individuals are constantly receiving partisan cues from elites. For this reason,

---

[57] Steven Greene, "Understanding Party Identification: A Social Identity Approach," *Political Psychology* 20, no. 2 (1999); Leonie Huddy, "From Social to Political Identity: A Critical Examination of Social Identity Theory," *Political Psychology* 22, no. 1 (2001); Mason, *Uncivil Agreement: How Politics Became Our Identity.*

[58] Leonie Huddy, Lilliana Mason, and Lene Aarøe, "Expressive Partisanship: Campaign Involvement, Political Emotion, and Partisan Identity," *American Political Science Review* 109, no. 1 (2015).

[59] Shanto Iyengar and Sean J Westwood, "Fear and Loathing across Party Lines: New Evidence on Group Polarization," *American Journal of Political Science* 59, no. 3 (2015).

[60] Eli J. Finkel et al., "Political Sectarianism in America," *Science* 370, no. 6516 (2020); Shanto Iyengar, Gaurav Sood, and Yphtach Lelkes, "Affect, Not Ideology: A Social Identity Perspective on Polarization," *Public Opinion Quarterly* 76, no. 3 (2012).

[61] Gabriel S. Lenz, *Follow the Leader?: How Voters Respond to Politicians' Policies and Performance* (Chicago, IL: University of Chicago Press, 2013).

[62] Marc J Hetherington, "Resurgent Mass Partisanship: The Role of Elite Polarization," *American Political Science Review* 95, no. 3 (2001).

[63] Henri Tajfel and John C. Turner, "An Integrative Theory of Intergroup Conflict," *The Social Psychology of Intergroup Relations* 33, no. 47 (1979).

[64] Henri Tajfel et al., "Social Categorization and Intergroup Behaviour," *European Journal of Social Psychology* 1, no. 2 (1971).

[65] Martin Bisgaard, "How Getting the Facts Right Can Fuel Partisan-Motivated Reasoning," *American Journal of Political Science* 63, no. 4 (2019); Milton Lodge and Charles S. Taber, *The Rationalizing Voter* (New York, NY: Cambridge University Press, 2013).

[66] Thomas M. Carsey and Geoffrey C. Layman, "Changing Sides or Changing Minds? Party Identification and Policy Preferences in the American Electorate," *American Journal of Political Science* 50, no. 2 (2006); Richard Johnston, "Party Identification: Unmoved Mover or Sum of Preferences?," *Annual Review of Political Science* 9 (2006).

[67] Frances E. Lee, *Insecure Majorities: Congress and the Perpetual Campaign* (Chicago, IL: University of Chicago Press, 2016).

I concentrate tightly on partisanship rather than core beliefs[68] or the more generic and frequently aligned political orientation (left–right spectrum).[69] I will discuss analysis using these terms of left–right orientation to capture cross-national patterns, where party names are nationally specific but orientation is not. Orientation also coalesces around parties,[70] so a focus on parties can also be considered a conservative test for ideology. But I am centrally interested in the *politics of citizenship,* that is, the theoretical way in which individuals interpret democratic threat and their role in it, based on their connections and loyalties to the major actors in it – the parties and elites. Parties have a distinct role in framing issues, connecting individuals to positional incentives, and, as a result, creating sides that win or lose that is unmatched by an untethered, ideological orientation.

Partisanship is a powerful social identity that can lead individuals to reject liberal democratic norms,[71] even abandon personal safety during a health pandemic.[72] There are several potential ways in which partisanship shapes threat response. First, when a threat is new, citizens may default to partisanship as an information shortcut.[73] It would especially be the case that individuals draw on political identity to navigate political problems. We might expect other types of problems (e.g., health scares, immigration) to activate other types of cleavages. However, when a crisis occurs and is effectively framed with partisan cues, we anticipate strong follow-the-leader effects. Research finds strong follow-the-leader effects on a range of issues, from the budget, to health and welfare, in both

---

[68] Geoffrey Evans and Anja Neundorf, "Core Political Values and the Long-Term Shaping of Partisanship," *British Journal of Political Science* (2018); Cf. Paul Goren, "Party Identification and Core Political Values," *American Journal of Political Science* 49, no. 4 (2005).

[69] John Huber and Ronald Inglehart, "Expert Interpretations of Party Space and Party Locations in 42 Societies," *Party Politics* 1, no. 1 (1995). Partisanship and ideological position have effectively consolidated in the US,

[70] Levendusky, *The Partisan Sort: How Liberals Became Democrats and Conservatives Became Republicans.*

[71] Graham and Svolik, "Democracy in America? Partisanship, Polarization, and the Robustness of Support for Democracy in the United States."

[72] Gadarian, Goodman, and Pepinsky, "Partisanship, Health Behavior, and Policy Attitudes in the Early Stages of the Covid-19 Pandemic."

[73] Albertson and Gadarian, *Anxious Politics: Democratic Citizenship in a Threatening World.*

majoritarian and consensus-based systems.[74] And research shows the public generally takes cues on what issue to be concerned about from the leaders of their own party,[75] and can use – in the case of the US – a president's position to benchmark their own preferences.[76]

Second, partisanship shapes information-gathering. Partisanship is both an informational shortcut and decision-making tool, and individuals systematically select sources of information that confirm their own ideological views.[77] Partisan-motivated reasoning is aided by political leaders who emphasize different interpretations of the same facts,[78] and "directionally motivated reasoning" makes it difficult to correct misperceptions about salient political or social issues,[79] especially if individuals are disinclined to seek out information that contradicts their beliefs.[80] The consequences of partisan-motivated reasoning may lead individuals to follow their party's leader regardless, or reject the opposition's positions out of principle and then accept their own party's position, regardless of actual beliefs or ideological compatibility.[81] Incumbents can exploit partisan-motivated reasoning to subvert the rules of democracy.[82]

A third mechanism is less of an active process than it is inertia. Milan Svolik writes that political polarization undermines the public's ability to serve as a democratic check, arguing, "In polarized electorates, voters are

---

[74] Martin Bisgaard and Rune Slothuus, "Partisan Elites as Culprits? How Party Cues Shape Partisan Perceptual Gaps," *American Journal of Political Science* 62, no. 2 (2018).

[75] Lenz, *Follow the Leader?: How Voters Respond to Politicians' Policies and Performance.*

[76] Adam J. Berinsky, "Assuming the Costs of War: Events, Elites, and American Public Support for Military Conflict," *The Journal of Politics* 69, no. 4 (2007).

[77] Michael Bang Petersen et al., "Motivated Reasoning and Political Parties: Evidence for Increased Processing in the Face of Party Cues," *Political Behavior* 35, no. 4 (2013); R. Kelly Garrett and Natalie Jomini Stroud, "Partisan Paths to Exposure Diversity: Differences in Pro-and Counterattitudinal News Consumption," *Journal of Communication* 64, no. 4 (2014).

[78] Bisgaard and Slothuus, "Partisan Elites as Culprits? How Party Cues Shape Partisan Perceptual Gaps."

[79] D. J. Flynn, Brendan Nyhan, and Jason Reifler, "The Nature and Origins of Misperceptions: Understanding False and Unsupported Beliefs About Politics," *Political Psychology* 38, no. S1 (2017).

[80] David P. Redlawsk, "Hot Cognition or Cool Consideration? Testing the Effects of Motivated Reasoning on Political Decision Making," *The Journal of Politics* 64, no. 4 (2002).

[81] Howard G. Lavine, Christopher D. Johnston, and Marco R. Steenbergen, *The Ambivalent Partisan: How Critical Loyalty Promotes Democracy* (New York, NY: Oxford University Press, 2012).

[82] John S. Ahlquist et al., "How Do Voters Perceive Changes to the Rules of the Game? Evidence from the 2014 Hungarian Elections," *Journal of Comparative Economics* 46, no. 4 (2018).

willing to trade off democratic principles for partisan interests."[83] Related to this is the role of social norms. In more polarized settings, the social identities that shape social networks are increasingly partisan and we know "partisan pressure," generated by ingroup social pressure, determines civic duty and impacts voter turnout.[84] In other words, polarization isolates partisans into a social space where there is simply less competition of ideas and more ingroup pressure.

These mechanisms – follow the leader, informational cueing, community pressures – are all ways in which partisanship works as a social identity. And these accounts are generally agnostic to the *content* of those partisan groups; that is, partisanship works the same on the left as it does on the right. But might partisanship – specifically, the programmatic and philosophical content of the party a citizen supports – impact how they respond to democratic threat?

There is some evidence from the US that partisans think about citizenship norms differently. Coffé and Bolzendahl, for example, observe while "Democrats and Republicans differ little in regard to many key rights and duties ... compared to Republicans, Democrats attach more importance to social duties and rights for political participation and minority groups."[85] Dalton also identifies "widening partisan differences" in the US between 2014 and 2018, where Republicans are more likely than Democrats to emphasize duty-based citizenship, like voting and serving in the military, while Democrats are more likely to value engaged citizenship.[86] These findings are also broadly consistent with a large literature on tolerance, where left parties focus on solidarity and inclusion and right parties focus on personal individualism and social conformity.[87] And indeed, I will show in Chapter 4 that across these

---

[83] Milan W. Svolik, "Polarization Versus Democracy," *Journal of Democracy* 30, no. 3 (2019).

[84] Edward Fieldhouse, David Cutts, and Jack Bailey, "Who Cares If You Vote? Partisan Pressure and Social Norms of Voting," *Political Behavior* (2020).

[85] Hilde Coffé and Catherine Bolzendahl, "Partisan Cleavages in the Importance of Citizenship Rights and Responsibilities," *Social Science Quarterly* 92, no. 3 (2011).

[86] Dalton, *The Good Citizen: How a Younger Generation Is Reshaping American Politics*, 47.

[87] Theodor W. Adorno et al., "The Authoritarian Personality," (1950); Robert A. Altemeyer and Bob Altemeyer, *The Authoritarian Specter* (Cambridge, MA: Harvard University Press, 1996); Norris and Inglehart, *Cultural Backlash: Trump, Brexit, and Authoritarian Populism*; Steven V. Miller, "Economic Threats or Societal Turmoil? Understanding Preferences for Authoritarian Political Systems," *Political Behavior* 39, no. 2 (2017).

three countries, there are now systematic differences across parties in citizenship values.

But how do partisans respond to democratic threat? It could be that these baseline differences in partisan values mean that we can trace out partisan responses to democratic threat by looking to parties' programmatic views: liberal parties respond to threat by expressing even greater commitment to liberal citizenship norms, whereas conservative parties respond with even greater commitment to national belonging. But it could also be – as I argue here – that partisan responses to democratic threat are positional in nature: that is, that they depend less on parties' programmatic ideals and values, and more on institutional incentives. Parties in the opposition may respond to democratic threat with greater support for calls for tolerance regardless of whether they are parties of the left or the right. By contrast, governing parties may respond to democratic threat with even more support for obeying the law and national identity, again regardless of their partisan stance. We would expect these differences between governing and opposition parties to be most noticeable in majoritarian systems with winner-take-all politics.

The argument here is not that left party supporters respond with more engagement because they are programmatically inclined or philosophically predisposed to do so, but that they see positional incentives (potential gains) in doing so. Likewise, parties on the right may be more inclined generally to support exclusive conceptions of national belonging, but that does not mean they are always inclined to respond to democratic problems with the blunt instrument of nationalism. They, too, respond primarily to positional incentives – to mobilize in opposition or avert in power. And this is contingent on institutional context and the factors that create incentives, to which we now turn.

2.3.3 Institutional Design

Power dynamics are moderated by different rules of competition, that is, institutional settings that encourage or encumber consensus. Simply put, rules make responses to democratic threat more costly in some contexts versus in others. For this, we turn to a large comparative politics literature that focuses on institutional design, specifically structural differences between majoritarian and consensus democracies.[88] Drawing from

---

[88] Lijphart, *The Politics of Accommodation; Pluralism and Democracy in the Netherlands; Democracies: Patterns of Majoritarian and Consensus Government in Twenty-One*

Arend Lijphart's influential work, institutional design broadly distinguishes two types of democratic models, derived from differences in electoral systems and power-sharing arrangements. Generally speaking, consensus democracies are multiparty systems, with parliamentarism, inclusive cabinet coalitions, and proportional electoral systems, among other power-dispersing institutions. Lijphart describes these as "kinder and gentler" systems,[89] more likely to produce robust welfare systems and reduce differences between winners and losers. Examples can be found in Germany, the Netherlands, and Denmark, and are especially desirable in deeply divided societies,[90] as consensus-based systems are structured around integrating opponents, and preventing one ethnic or sociolinguistic group from gaining too much power by increasing minority representation. Several studies have also shown that consensus systems engender more political activism.[91]

By contrast, majoritarian (or Westminster) models are defined by majority rule, where power is concentrated in one-party and bare-majority cabinets, effective two-party systems, and plurality electoral systems. The US and the UK are quintessential majoritarian system.[92] The shortcomings of majoritarian systems are an extension of its structure. Two-party systems become defined by fractionalization by virtue of an "environment of intensified party competition for the control of governing institutions,"[93] and, through this, can directly undermine democratic stability.[94] In short, the stark differences between winners and losers can exacerbate social cleavages and undermine faith in the

Countries; Arend Lijphart, *Patterns of Democracy. Government Forms and Performance in Thirty-Six Countries* (New Haven CT [u.a.]: Yale University Press, 1999).

[89] Lijphart, *Patterns of Democracy. Government Forms and Performance in Thirty-Six Countries*, 275.

[90] Renske Doorenspleet, "Electoral Systems and Good Governance in Divided Countries," *Ethnopolitics* 4, no. 4 (2005).

[91] Hanspeter Kriesi et al., *New Social Movements in Western Europe: A Comparative Analysis* (Routledge, 1995); Jeffrey A. Karp and Susan A. Banducci, "Political Efficacy and Participation in Twenty-Seven Democracies: How Electoral Systems Shape Political Behaviour," *British Journal of Political Science* (2008). Cf. Tom W. G. Van der Meer, Jan W. Van Deth, and Peer L. H. Scheepers, "The Politicized Participant: Ideology and Political Action in 20 Democracies," *Comparative Political Studies* 42, no. 11 (2009).

[92] Though the UK is also an exception in that it maintains a multiparty system – an irony not lost to Lijphart.

[93] Frances E. Lee, "How Party Polarization Affects Governance," *Annual Review of Political Science* 18 (2015): 262.

[94] Scott Mainwaring, *Rethinking Party Systems in the Third Wave of Democratization: The Case of Brazil* (Palo Alto, CA: Stanford University Press, 1999).

rules of the game. We look at the US compared to the UK and see even further potential for winner–loser dynamics because it is a presidential system. In studying democratic transitions, Juan Linz describes presidentialism (and its executive-legislative arrangement defined by separation of powers) as inherently flawed, because it creates independence for both the executive and legislature, which creates inevitable conflict.[95] This is unlike a parliamentary system, defined by a fusion of powers in which one national election takes place and the executive emerges *from* the legislature.

For our purposes, the key dimension of each system is whether they incentivize cooperation by design. Consensus systems are positive sum while majoritarian are zero sum. What do these terms mean? They are derived from game theory and refer to situations in terms of total gains and losses. A positive-sum game occurs when gains (e.g., resources) can be achieved by multiple participants or parties. Specifically, total gains and losses are greater than zero (thus, the *positive* sum). Distributive bargains are one way in which more participants can meet their needs. By contrast, a zero-sum game refers to situations when one party benefits at the direct expense of another. Someone has to lose for you to win.

As a series of positive-sum interactions, consensus systems are structurally inclusive; they "satisfy large groups' interests on a great number of issues."[96] That they do so across a large number of parties reduces the likelihood that any single party obtains a majority after an election, necessitating coalition building and cooperation. As a result, costs of cooperation are lower and attitudinal gaps between winners and losers are smaller than majoritarian systems.[97] In fact, Anderson and Guillory find that losing matters less in consensus-based systems and losers express more satisfaction with democracy than those with majoritarian characteristics.[98] Milner finds consensus-based political institutions facilitate civic literacy to produce optimal, welfare-based outcomes.[99] Van der

[95] Juan J. Linz, "The Perils of Presidentialism," *Journal of Democracy* 1, no. 1 (1990).

[96] Josep M. Colomer, *Political Institutions: Democracy and Social Choice* (Oxford: Oxford University Press, 2001), 2.

[97] Christopher J. Anderson et al., *Losers' Consent: Elections and Democratic Legitimacy* (Oxford, UK: Oxford University Press, 2005).

[98] Christopher J. Anderson and Christine A. Guillory, "Political Institutions and Satisfaction with Democracy: A Cross-National Analysis of Consensus and Majoritarian Systems," *American Political Science Review* 91, no. 1 (1997).

[99] Henry Milner, *Civic Literacy: How Informed Citizens Make Democracy Work* (UPNE, 2002).

Meer et al. reach a different conclusion – that citizens are less likely to participate in consensus democracies, from voting to campaigning to contacting officials.[100] But, of course, behavior is only one obligation of citizenship.

By contrast, it is not coincidental that zero-sum, majoritarian systems are highly politically polarized. As political parties become more polarized, they become better at "sorting individuals along ideological lines"[101] and become "tightly clustered around the party mean."[102] As parties polarize, citizens follow suit. Noam Lupu finds consistent cross-national evidence that "if citizens perceive party polarization, they are more likely to become partisan."[103] As individuals strengthen their party attachment, they use partisan cues to shape civic attitudes, behavior, and often rely on parties to serve as an information shortcut.[104] And, in turn, partisanship increases polarization over time.[105]

Polarization is not inherently negative; in systems that use proportional representation, we actually see higher levels of polarization, that is, a higher proportion of noncentrists, and this is correlated with reducing income inequality.[106] A multiparty system, however, creates more poles, reducing costs of compromise because consensus in typically required for coalition-building and governing. In bipolar systems, citizens necessarily exhibit greater distance in their opinions by party.[107] This type of center-fleeing polarization is conducive to negative affective polarization, where individuals not simply *disagree* over matters of policy but *dislike*

---

[100] Van der Meer, Van Deth, and Scheepers, "The Politicized Participant: Ideology and Political Action in 20 Democracies," 1447.

[101] Delia Baldassarri and Andrew Gelman, "Partisans without Constraint: Political Polarization and Trends in American Public Opinion," *American Journal of Sociology* 114, no. 2 (2008).

[102] Keith T. Poole and Howard L. Rosenthal, *Ideology and Congress*, vol. 1 (Transaction Publishers, 2011), 105.

[103] Noam Lupu, "Party Polarization and Mass Partisanship: A Comparative Perspective," *Political Behavior* 37, no. 2 (2015).

[104] Jeffery J. Mondak, "Public Opinion and Heuristic Processing of Source Cues," *Political behavior* 15, no. 2 (1993); Wendy M. Rahn, "The Role of Partisan Stereotypes in Information Processing About Political Candidates," *American Journal of Political Science* (1993).

[105] Nicole Satherley et al., "If They Say "Yes," We Say "No": Partisan Cues Increase Polarization over National Symbols," *Psychological Science* 29, no. 12 (2018).

[106] Torben Iversen and David Soskice, "Information, Inequality, and Mass Polarization: Ideology in Advanced Democracies," *Comparative Political Studies* 48, no. 13 (2015).

[107] See, for example, James N. Druckman, Erik Peterson, and Rune Slothuus, "How Elite Partisan Polarization Affects Public Opinion Formation," *American Political Science Review* (2013).

individuals who identify with the opposing political party.[108] This condition strengthens internal echo chambers of information and social relations,[109] and externally damages the ability of groups to compromise and trust,[110] which may erode democratic legitimacy.[111] It certainly reduces the likelihood of consensus.

To wit, while the US predominates as a case study in this literature,[112] recent work has also identified polarization and affective partisanship as factors in multiparty systems, particularly – for our purposes – in Europe.[113] Stephan Haggard and Robert Kaufman also focus tightly on democratic regression as an incremental product of polarization.[114] Pippa Norris shows democratic backsliding is correlated specifically with party polarization over cultural, moral and liberal democratic values.[115] Westwood et al. show in countries as diverse as the US, Belgium, the UK, and Spain, that affective polarization has a stronger influence than social cleavages on levels of trust, observing a rising trend of "partyism" in modern democracies.[116] In Reiljan's study, he finds significant hostility toward out-partisans in Europe[117] and, thus, consistent with social identity theory, strength in ingroup identity. Huddy et al. also see strong partisanship in Europe through several expressive attributes.[118] De-alignment may have eroded the religious and class bases of

[108] Alan I Abramowitz and Steven Webster, "The Rise of Negative Partisanship and the Nationalization of US Elections in the 21st Century," *Electoral Studies* 41 (2016); Iyengar, Sood, and Lelkes, "Affect, Not Ideology: A Social Identity Perspective on Polarization.")

[109] Matthew Levendusky, *How Partisan Media Polarize America* (Chicago, IL: University of Chicago Press, 2013); Bail et al., "Exposure to Opposing Views on Social Media Can Increase Political Polarization."

[110] Michael MacKuen et al., "Civic Engagements: Resolute Partisanship or Reflective Deliberation," *American Journal of Political Science* 54, no. 2 (2010).

[111] Anderson et al., *Losers' Consent: Elections and Democratic Legitimacy.*

[112] Nolan McCarty, Keith T. Poole, and Howard Rosenthal, *Polarized America: The Dance of Ideology and Unequal Riches* (Cambridge, MA: MIT Press, 2016).

[113] Gidron, Adams, and Horne, "American Affective Polarization in Comparative Perspective."; Boxell, Gentzkow, and Shapiro, "Cross-Country Trends in Affective Polarization."

[114] Haggard and Kaufman, *Backsliding: Democratic Regress in the Contemporary World.*

[115] Pippa Norris, "It Happened in America," *Foreign Affairs* (2021).

[116] Sean J. Westwood et al., "The Tie That Divides: Cross-National Evidence of the Primacy of Partyism," *European Journal of Political Research* 57, no. 2 (2018).

[117] Reiljan, "'Fear and Loathing across Party Lines'(Also) in Europe: Affective Polarisation in European Party Systems."

[118] Leonie Huddy, Alexa Bankert, and Caitlin Davies, "Expressive Versus Instrumental Partisanship in Multiparty European Systems," *Political Psychology* 39 (2018).

partisanship in Europe,[119] but it has been supplanted with realignment, where party preferences become based on different cleavage politics, including education and new cultural values, like immigration and the EU.[120] These observations make the US comparable to Europe when it comes to positional incentives, but also the role of the individual interpreting those stakes through partisanship.

Let me summarize the argument of positional incentives as a driver of divided citizenship. First, as a baseline assumption, I recognize citizens are rational. Civic duty can be time-consuming (or perceived as such), so if a citizen is going to recognize and respond to a threat, it will have correspondence; that is, the response will be meaningful and appropriate to the perceived threat. For example, citizens would respond to the problem of polarization with more patience or tolerance and not, for instance, protesting.

Second, I expect citizens supporting incumbent parties (status quo beneficiaries) to either ignore or respond defensively to democratic threat. If they respond at all, it would be in norms that value demobilization and illiberalism, and perhaps a defensive circling of the nationalist wagons. By contrast, citizens that support status quo challenger parties are more likely to see and pursue gains in acknowledging and responding to threat. This may be increasing the importance of political behavior norms and rallying around national values – from liberal democracy to patriotism.

Third, these positional incentives are conditioned and contextualized by the institutional context in which parties compete and govern. Zero-sum, two-party majoritarian systems make everything about winning and losing. Thus, political threats also become about winning or losing, and citizens update conceptions of good citizenship in kind. In positive-sum, multiparty consensus systems, where parties regularly compromise and build coalitions, winning and losing is more diffuse, so it is not as costly for even incumbent power holders to respond. As more citizens are likely to perceive shared effects of threat, we accordingly expect a greater share in the response.

---

[119] Seymour Martin Lipset and Stein Rokkan, eds., *Party Systems and Voter Alignments: Cross-National Perspectives*, vol. 7 (New York, NY: Free Press, 1967); Hanspeter Kriesi et al., *West European Politics in the Age of Globalization* (2008).

[120] Hanspeter Kriesi, "Restructuration of Partisan Politics and the Emergence of a New Cleavage Based on Values," *West European Politics* 33, no. 3 (2010); Robert Ford and Will Jennings, "The Changing Cleavage Politics of Western Europe," *Annual Review of Political Science* 23 (2020).

To conclude, we can predict that democratic threat will divide citizens, wherein individuals adjust citizenship norms that forward their side's positional interest and are moderated by institutions. When these institutions exacerbate "sideism," we see an uneven response to a democratic problem and, ultimately, a weakening of cross-cutting ties and erosion of national unity. This is how "good citizens" may end up undermining citizenship – the keystone to democratic stability.

3

Measuring Citizenship Norms

Behavior, Belief, and Belonging

In this chapter, I operationalize and measure citizenship norms. What does it mean to be a good citizen? Do norms change over time? Do they vary cross-nationally? In Chapter 2, I laid out a new conceptualization of citizenship norms composed of behavior, liberal democratic beliefs, and conceptions of national belonging, as well as set up an argument for how citizens interpret norms differently in the face of democratic threat. This chapter pivots to strategies for identifying and comparing individual responses.

After a brief examination of existing research practices for measuring citizenship norms in advanced democracies, I operationalize my conception of citizenship norms by examining items that make for a "good citizen" across these three dimensions. Specifically, I measure norms along fourteen different attributes of democratic citizenship, and present each in turn. Six items replicate previously asked questions on democratic citizenship by the International Social Survey Programme (ISSP), which mostly cover civic behavior. Eight items are novel, either new questions never before asked for survey research (items on liberal values, categorized here as "beliefs") or reframed questions from ISSP's National Identity survey (questions on attributes of belonging). These fourteen items capture the variety of good citizenship attributes and contextualize them by looking at patterns of similarity and difference both cross-nationally and over time. This descriptive exercise establishes the range of support across a variety of items on our outcome of interest, setting up the rest of the book to explore individual determinants and national differences.

The third section employs two techniques to organize and think about these items. First, I use factor analysis to explore the interrelationships among these fourteen attributes. This theory-driven exercise confirms that fourteen items group into three factors or dimensions of democratic citizenship norms: *behavior* (citizens who value active attributes of citizenship, like voting), liberal *beliefs* (citizens who value commitment to norms of individualism, equality, and tolerance), and national *belonging* (citizens who value attributes of membership, like speaking the national language). As these fourteen items load similarly across the three factors in all three countries, we can conclude that they represent stable, unique, and generalizable dimensions of democratic citizenship.

Finally, I test whether these norms predict political behavior, to see if there is congruity or not between ideas about what makes a good citizen and action, that is, what citizens do. The data show that individuals who hold behavioral citizenship norms also practice those values by engaging in active citizenship. Moreover, citizens who hold strong belief and belonging norms are not necessarily active; in fact, they may exhibit more passive behavior. Specifically, obedient and loyal ("belonging") citizens do not exercise voice and make demands but stay at home, while liberal ("belief") citizens are the most behaviorally inconsistent and vary cross-nationally. This analysis helps to bolster the approach that I take in the book, focusing on norms that capture a wider set of obligations rather than simply focusing on participation, which may miss the more important shifts that are happening out of sight.

3.1 DISCIPLINARY FOUNDATIONS TO MEASURING GOOD CITIZENSHIP

We begin with *The Civic Culture,* which established early a strong conceptualization of good citizenship, what they term the "allegiant citizen." Found especially in the US and Britain, allegiant citizens show deference to authority (institutional affect), trust in institutions, and support for the principles and practice of democracy (like voting and other forms of participation). These citizens coexist with subjects and parochials – other citizen types with less activity or trusting dispositions toward government – and are the key to unlocking a democracy's civic potential. While their conceptualization of political culture is clear and enduring, their measurement is nonstandard and complex, including features of both the individual and the system, as well as orientations of the former to the latter in terms of cognition, affect, and evaluation. Representative of early functional, systems theory, they conceive of civic culture to be as much about individual attitudes and behavior as it is about attitudes toward and support for the political system in which they operate.

In response to large structural changes and political realignment in the 1970s, this allegiant citizen became more assertive and self-expressive,[1] and with it so too did conceptualization and measurement become more parsimonious and precise. By the third "visitation" to civic culture, *The Civic Culture Transformed*, the transition from allegiant to assertive citizens and its operationalization became visible across many works.[2] In particular, Dalton focuses on four elements of citizenship: participation (vote, active in politics and associations), autonomy (independently forming opinions), acceptance of state authority (obeying laws, serving on a jury or in the military if called), and solidarity (looking out for the welfare of others). These roughly group into two dimensions of democratic citizenship norms: engagement and duty.[3]

This provides a useful baseline for studying citizenship norms. But a more expansive conceptualization is necessary. First, missing from this literature is any way to capture the importance of belonging. Recall from Chapter 2, citizenship is not only a status but also an identity. Fundamentally, citizenship is belonging to a community of national members. Studies of political behavior that do not consider the fluidity and liminality of membership may miss this dimension, taking for granted that national unity exists. Yet a separate literature centrally questions mass beliefs about belonging and national identity, and finds potentially relevant within-case variation.[4] In other words, citizens within the same state may hold wide-ranging understandings of national definitions of belonging, from achievable attributes (like holding liberal democratic

---

[1] Ronald Inglehart, *The Silent Revolution: Changing Values and Political Styles among Western Publics* (Princeton, NJ: Princeton University Press, 1977).

[2] Dalton, *Citizen Politics: Public Opinion and Political Parties in Advanced Industrial Democracies*; *The Good Citizen: How a Younger Generation Is Reshaping American Politics*.

[3] Dalton, "Citizenship Norms and the Expansion of Political Participation." Also see Bolzendahl and Coffé, "Are 'Good' Citizens 'Good' Participants? Testing Citizenship Norms and Political Participation across 25 Nations."

[4] Matthew Wright, Jack Citrin, and Jonathan Wand, "Alternative Measures of American National Identity: Implications for the Civic-Ethnic Distinction," *Political Psychology* 33, no. 4 (2012): 469–82; Wright, "Policy Regimes and Normative Conceptions of Nationalism in Mass Public Opinion."; Bart Bonikowski, "Nationalism in Settled Times," *Annual Review of Sociology* 42 (2016): 427–49; Theiss-Morse, *Who Counts as an American?: The Boundaries of National Identity*.

values or speaking the national language) to ascriptive attributes (like being white or Christian). We know little about how these measures of belonging correspond to good citizenship for the native born.[5] But, if large-scale immigration and generations of immigrant integration have revealed one thing to liberal democracies, it is that there is more that goes into being a "good citizen" than liberal values and participatory norms. In short, good citizenship may reflect implicit norms of belonging. With the right data, this is a testable proposition.

A second assumption in existing approaches is that citizens of liberal democracies are inherently liberal. The supposition is as follows: Citizens are socialized from an early age to comply with and comport to a set of liberal values, from individual autonomy to tolerance and equality.[6] But this, too, requires testing. A majority of citizens may be liberal, but identifying conditions under which citizens abandon, or only weakly adhere to, liberal values could indicate that mass publics only have a weak foundation for fending off democratic threat. The proliferation of illiberal democracies today – in countries like Turkey, Hungary, and Poland, where illiberal practices render democracy hollow – suggests we cannot assume that liberal values and democratic institutions are inherently or forever linked. We need to ask citizens whether and to what extent they define "good citizenship" as committing to a wide set of liberal democratic values. It also reveals an inherent irony in our understanding of "good citizenship"; over the past two decades, Western European countries have brought immigrants into the national political community by asserting liberal democratic values as a condition of inclusion,[7] all the while – and perhaps dangerously – assuming that native-born citizens already have these values. Put another way, political elites have been preoccupied with protecting national values from immigrant influence, all the while overlooking whether the core itself espouse those values.

Third, but related, similarities and differences can only emerge out of – but are also a product of – the questions we ask. Putting aside the previous points on the consequences of including omitted items (liberal democratic norms, national belonging), the panel of existing items that are typically presented as dimensions of citizenship norms may present an artificial impression of difference as a function of included items. For

---

[5] In the ISSP surveys, for example, "Citizenship" and "National Identity" questionnaires are run independently of each other.
[6] Welzel, *Freedom Rising*.
[7] Goodman, *Immigration and Membership Politics in Western European*.

instance, some items that group as part of "engaged citizenship" include "helping people worse off in the world" and an item of political consumerism while "duty-based citizenship" includes items like serving in the military. We can have reasonable disagreements about whether cosmopolitanism, consumer ethics, and enlisting are core attributes of ordinary citizens, but the central point is that differences can only emerge – and are sometimes created – as a function of the items we ask.

Finally, we simply do not know what individuals think good citizens are or do in democratic hard times. As the post-modernization literature shows, cultures are not inherently stable, and shifts in values can affect an individual's sense of duty or obligation. When the democratic problem is not decline in participation but erosion of institutions, trust, and the rule of law *around* the citizen, what do citizens interpret their civic obligations to be?

3.2 OPERATIONALIZING CITIZENSHIP NORMS

To review, democratic citizenship norms are the shared set of expectations about the citizen's role in politics, and include behavior performed, beliefs held, community standards, or norms complied by individuals who are subject to a state's rule of law and who derive rights therein. This section describes how we can capture these expectations in survey data.

Some indicators of civic obligation can be drawn from previous surveys. This not only provides an external benchmark to assess how these indicators perform, but also gives us another data point in time, enabling us to uncover patterns across country and over time. Missing from previous approaches, however, are a wide set of liberal value measures that may more accurately graft to contemporary democratic challenges, as well as dimensions of belonging, which necessitates adding new and merging old questions.

The ISSP battery provides a useful starting point, as it asks a set of questions that tap into behavior and beliefs about good citizenship. In the ISSP Citizenship panel (run in 2004 and 2014), the question reads: "There are different opinions as to what it takes to be a good citizen. As far as you are concerned personally on a scale of 1 to 7, where 1 is not at all important and 7 is very important, how important is it…" and then includes nine (in 2014) or ten (in 2004) items, from voting to helping people. A factor analysis of the nine, consistent items across thirty-two democracies identifies three dimensions: *participation* (voting, watching government, active in social or political association), *compliance* (obeying laws and not evading taxes), and *communal/solidarity* (and helping people who are worse off, both in your country and around the world, and ethical buying behavior).[8] I begin by selecting representative items from each dimension. Yet, my conceptualization of citizenship holds that we need to look not just at these factors but at a wider set of beliefs about liberal norms and belonging. We need to balance the commitments and activities of good citizens with the beliefs they may hold and the characteristics they may have.

To add national belonging as a dimension of good citizenship, I look again to ISSP questions, this time pulling from the National Identity panel (run in 1995, 2003, and 2013). Respondents in these surveys were asked: "Some people say that the following things are important for being truly [NATIONALITY]. Others say they are not important. How important do you think each of the following is..." and the survey then includes eight different items, including birth in the country, speaking the national language, and respecting political institutions and laws. For national belonging, I select two nonoverlapping achievable attributes: speaking [national language] and feeling [nationality]. It is especially important to add dimensions of belonging for studying democratic crisis, when backsliding so often coincides with ethnopopulism. Because survey-based approaches to citizenship have never put these questions together with the baseline citizenship modules, it remains an open question how attributes of national belonging map on to citizens' views about democratic citizenship norms, despite the theoretical importance of national unity.

Selecting nonoverlapping items from these ISSP modules produced eight items on "what it takes to be a good citizen":

- Obeys laws and regulations
- Votes in elections
- Is active in social or political associations
- Helps people worse off than yourself
- Keeps watch on government
- Understands the reasoning of people with other opinions
- Speaks [national language]
- Feels [nationality]

Of these items, three may be understood as traditional liberal values: "obeys laws and regulations" (i.e., respects rule of law), "keeps watch on

---

[8] This factor analysis included 32 countries, that is all the democracies that had responses to the 2004 and 2014 Citizenship survey waves. On file with author.

government" (i.e., vigilance), and "understands the reasoning of people with other opinions," as a measure of tolerance.

But there is reason to suspect that obeyance, vigilance, and tolerance are insufficient for measuring citizens' commitment to liberal norms in democratic hard times. At the end of *How Democracies Die*, for example, Levitsky and Ziblatt advocate for a civic reawakening, where commitment to liberal values like mutual tolerance and forbearance are "soft guardrails of democracy."[9] Notably, these are suggestions that liberal values need to be renewed or reactivated *among* and *between citizens*. Obeyance (rule of law) and vigilance (watching government) are primarily vertical dispositions, describing the relationship between a citizen and their government. But political liberalism also imposes horizontal obligations, asserting values for how citizens are to treat one another, including but not limited to understanding the reasoning of people with different opinions.

While democracy is inherently conflictual and competitive, liberalism maintains that this disagreement does not have to be rancorous. Tolerance, civility, and forbearance are the type of civic attributes that would preserve cross-cutting social ties and protect civil disagreement. Therefore, to capture a wider range of liberal values, I include four, additional and original questions to the previous eight:

- Maintain friendship or ties with people with different opinions (civility)
- Accept people of diverse backgrounds
- Have patience, recognizing sometimes your side wins and sometimes your side loses (forbearance)
- Understand how government and politics work (politically informed)

Finally, I add two questions about attitudes toward government directly, reflecting the roles that system attitudes and civic activism play in constructing good citizenship. These may contradict each other, which may be a useful tool of internal validity.

- Protest or dissent when you disagree with actions of government
- Support the actions of government

Together, this yields fourteen potential items of good citizenship, capturing norms of behavior, beliefs, and belonging. The next section describes how I measured them in using a new survey-based approach.

---

[9] Levitsky and Ziblatt, *How Democracies Die*.

3.3 MEASURING CITIZENSHIP NORMS: "CITIZENSHIP IN HARD TIMES" SURVEY

The need to ask new questions in a new time period requires a new survey. The survey data employed in this book comes from three, nationally representative surveys conducted over the summer of 2019. An identical survey was fielded in the US, UK, and Germany.[10] In the US, I employed the survey firm YouGov, that fielded the survey June 21–July 9, with an N = 3,111. For Germany and the UK, I used the survey firm Respondi. The German survey was fielded during August 6–14, collecting N = 3,155 respondents; the UK survey was fielded August 6–16, collecting N = 3,225 respondents. Participants were recruited for online participation through a stratified random sampling strategy, with quotas for age, gender, and geographic area.[11] These sample sizes are roughly three times the size of most nationally representative surveys, but they give me the statistical power needed to test a series of hypotheses that examine fourteen items of civic obligation, as well as to conduct the vignette experiments used in Chapters 5 and 6.

Surveying ordinary people is the best way to tap into questions of public opinion. The timing of the survey in summer 2019 coincides with what I might call ambient threat, or creeping power grabs and erosion of norms, but nothing resembling exogenous shock that would make these time points unique or ungeneralizable, like during an election or a terrorist attack. Major democratic crises and liberal norms violations certainly predate this snapshot, including the rise of the AfD, power abuses by the Trump Administration, and further delays in Brexit anticipating a change in government. This prepares citizens to think about democratic threat, but coincides with nothing specific, making summer 2019 a useful time period to gauge general attitudes toward civic obligation in democratic hard times.

Borrowing language from the ISSP Citizenship panels, the question is as follows:

There are different opinions as to what it takes to be a **good citizen** in your country. The following questions will ask you how important each attribute is for being a good citizen. Based on what you think makes a good citizen, rate these

---

[10] This study was approved by the University of California, Irvine IRB (HS# 2019-5181) and the pre-analysis plan registered with EGAP (20190621AA).

[11] In the US, this could be obtained at the metropolitan statistical level; in the UK, it was by the NUTS1 statistical region (11 in total); in Germany, by the 16 Länder.

on a scale of 1 to 5, where 1 is not at all important and 5 is very important. How important is it for a good citizen to...

The fourteen citizenship items were presented in random order.

The next sections present descriptive findings for each of the fourteen items of civic obligation. First, I present items that replicate previous surveys, to illustrate variation both cross-nationally and over time. Second, I present the new survey items, including liberal value items and belonging items. Because they are new, I cannot compare them with previous responses, but this snapshot of 2019 attitudes shows significant variation across our three advanced democracies.

3.4 CHANGE OVER TIME

There are six replicated questions in the survey,[12] which allows us to examine civic norms in 2019 while comparing them to earlier measures, in 2004 and 2014. All figures report respondent means and includes 95 percent confidence intervals. In almost all items, we see statistically significant change between 2004 and 2014 and between 2014 and 2019.[13] This confirms our understanding that political culture and citizenship norms can shift over time. These descriptive findings invite us to consider whether democratic threat is a relevant context for shifts. Further, and despite changes over time, we see broad support overall for most of these items cross-nationally, suggesting that these capture broad characteristics of good citizenship in advanced democracies.

3.4.1 A Good Citizen Obeys Laws and Regulations

"Obeying the law" is the most consistently highly rated norm, both across countries and compared to the other questions. Placing the rule of law at the center of civic obligation also suggests that across each of these cases, the liberal "minimum" is highly valued. Declines in the ratings for

---

[12] ISSP originally uses a seven-point scale for these questions. I reduced the scale to five to emphasize variation, and also rescaled the ISSP measure to allow for direct, longitudinal comparison. While I also borrow two additional questions from the ISSP – speaking X and feeling X – the question wording and framing differs, where immigrants are the explicit referent category. This makes direct comparison inappropriate.

[13] Change is statistically significant, though change may look modest across years. These are small numbers of difference (e.g., moving from a 4.75/5 to a 4.4/5), but these are aggregated through averages, which implies, in this example, more respondents are choosing lower numbers than before.

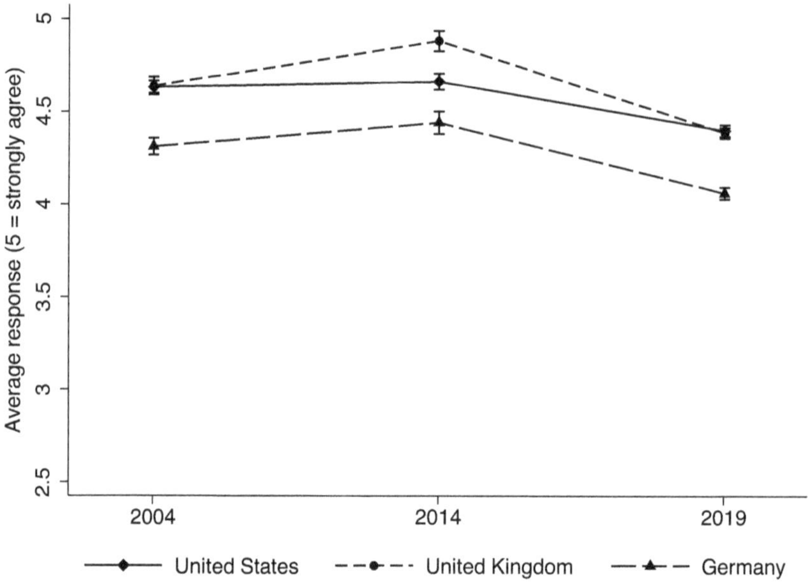

FIGURE 3.1. Obeys laws and regulations

obeyance, therefore, suggest a decline in liberal values. Figure 3.1 shows that citizens in all three countries highly value obeyance before backsliding, but this support drops in 2019. The UK exhibits the sharpest decline, followed by Germany, then the US. One should not overinterpret this finding. There may be a ceiling effect, where support after 2014 – especially for the US and the UK – could not increase much further. Yet, while all countries post a score above 4, statistically significant declines by 2019 suggest there is something happening to citizens and, therefore, citizenship.

3.4.2 A Good Citizen Votes in Elections

Where following the "rule of law" is the most representative liberal value, participating in elections is the most democratic one. In Figure 3.2, we see a divergence in trends when compared to obeyance, and also cross-nationally. Unlike the rule of law, the importance of voting increases or stays statistically similar to 2014 levels in all three countries. By 2019, the importance of voting – consistently high in the US,[14] and already high in

---

[14] This stable attitude is corroborated by Blais and Achen, "Civic Duty and Voter Turnout."

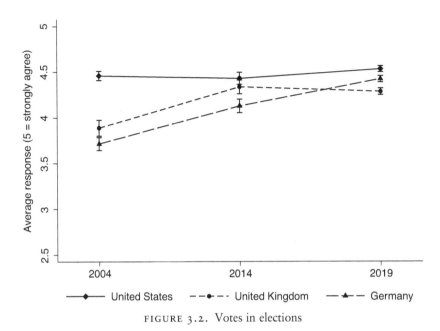

FIGURE 3.2. Votes in elections

the UK – increases significantly in Germany. This trajectory in Germany probably reflects recent events. The 2017 Federal Election produced major victories for the far right AfD as well as an embattled and weakened CDU-led coalition, followed by state elections that have seen increased turnout as well as support not only for the far right but renewed support for the left, specifically the Greens. This provides preliminary evidence that the character of democratic crisis matters.

Items one (obeyance) and two (voting) are procedural minimums for citizens in liberal democracies, and this is typically where a contractual or legalistic vision of citizenship begins and ends. But even here, Conover et al. suggest that context may make a difference in distinguishing these liberal understandings of citizenship, where the British maintain a more communal definition because liberalism is grounded in "the existence of the British welfare state," while US liberalism is based on a political culture "which is said to accent competition and individualism."[15] That said, we observe different trends in support for each over time. The rule of law and voting are highly valued, but their opposing trend lines suggest deeper issues at work. From here, we move to four elective components of civic obligation.

[15] Conover, Crewe, and Searing, "The Nature of Citizenship in the United States and Great Britain: Empirical Comments on Theoretical Themes," 804.

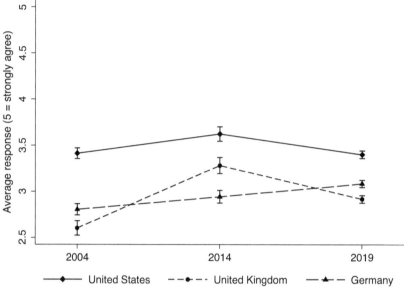

FIGURE 3.3. Active in social or political associations

3.4.3 A Good Citizen is Active in Social or Political Associations

Figure 3.3 shows this is among the lowest-rated citizenship norms. Both the US and the UK exhibit similar trends – increasing importance by 2014 and decreasing by 2019. While Alexis de Tocqueville observed that American democracy was unusually civic, standing out as a "nation of joiners," we see how that conclusion is borne out of comparison and not absolute support, and today we see a closing gap between the US, the UK, and Germany. Of note, we see that Germany's trend line diverges from the other two cases, where support for associational life is at its highest in 2019. The value of including lower-supported items like this, not only highlights within-item variance but also differences in support to other items. A "good citizen" doesn't "do all the things"; citizens pick and choose, and it varies cross-nationally and over time.

3.4.4 A Good Citizen Helps People Worse Off than Yourself

Figure 3.4 captures horizontal solidarity, and here, the three countries converge. It should also be noted that this is a fairly vague value; no commitment procedure for helping those worse off is specified. It is a

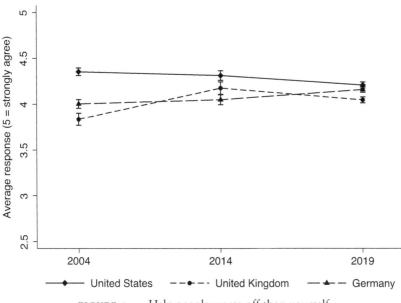

FIGURE 3.4. Help people worse off than yourself

value or belief in the truest sense, that a good citizen helps others. That this remains highly rated, and that countries are not changing much over time, suggests that community remains important in good and bad times. We might expect that citizens in European welfare states express more support for this item than Americans, but that is not what we see here. Moreover, to recall a point from Chapter 2, this is also an item disproportionately held by those on the political left versus the political right, being a programmatic aspect of progressive parties. It suggests there is a value to adding more conservative-leaning values (e.g., allegiance) for balance.

3.4.5 A Good Citizen Keeps Watch on Government

Alongside voting, vigilance is one of the most highly rated attributes in democratic hard times. Like obeying the law, "keeps watch on government" is an explicitly liberal value, encapsulating the belief that democracy requires a purposefully checked government and citizens should practice inherent distrust of government to avoid encroachment on individual autonomy. Dalton shows this type of civic norm is considered both

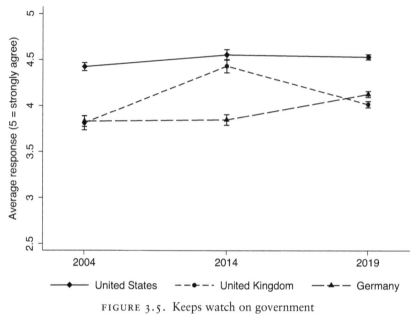

FIGURE 3.5. Keeps watch on government

a democratic duty and form of engaged citizenship,[16] so we can expect a broad coalition in support of this norm.

In Figure 3.5, we see differences across countries. Support for "keeping watch" in the US remains high and stable. Vigilance is rated slightly lower in the European cases, with trajectories that inversely mirror one another. The UK – having had a burst of government vigilance in 2014 – exhibits a steep decline to return to its 2004 levels. The spike in 2014 could be attributed to a number of political events, from local elections in 2013 that saw council seats won by the United Kingdom Independence Party (UKIP) to global surveillance disclosures, in which prominent British broadsheets like *The Guardian* were publishing documents leaked by Edward Snowden.

3.4.6 A Good Citizen Understands the Reasoning of People with Other Opinions

This item captures the liberal value of mutual tolerance. Figure 3.6 shows high valuation of tolerance across cases and time, with little change

---

[16] Dalton, "Citizenship Norms and the Expansion of Political Participation."

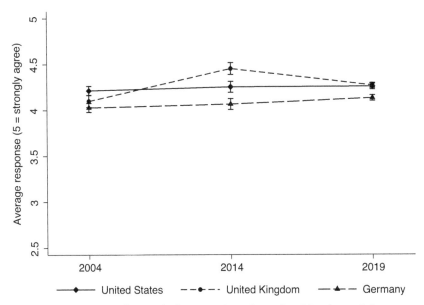

FIGURE 3.6. Understands the reasoning of people with other opinions

therein. This conveys a couple of pieces of information. First, high but stable importance could suggest that individuals who value tolerance are unaffected or unaware of democratic backsliding or polarization that may challenge it.

Second, tolerance – especially measured as understanding other opinions – may simply be a vague measure, so its value is not affected by democratic hard times because its meaning was also vague prior to the contemporary period. In other words, a good citizen who values understanding others' opinions may actually just be understanding information or all sides of a debate, and not as an act of tolerance or empathy. This suggests the need for other, more precise measures of liberal values, to get closer to the values that preserve cross-cutting social ties between citizens.

3.5 NEW ITEMS

My 2019 survey adds eight, novel questions for determining citizenship norms in democratic hard times: six original items on political liberalism (presented in Figure 3.7) and two on attributes of national belonging (presented in Figure 3.8). While one snapshot year cannot

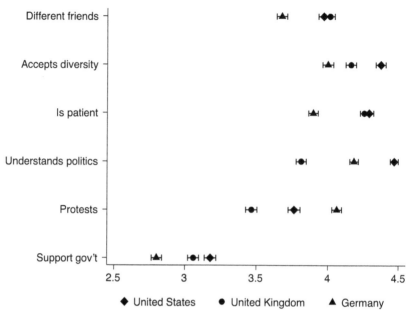

FIGURE 3.7. Six new items on political liberalism

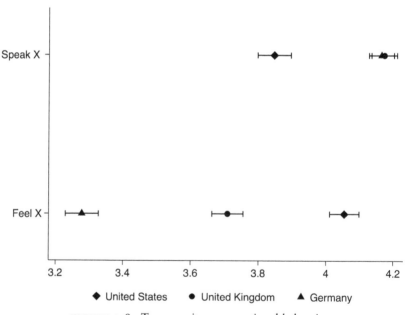

FIGURE 3.8. Two new items on national belonging

convey trends over time, we can observe cross-national patterns. I discuss each item in turn.

3.5.1 A Good Citizen Maintains Friendships or Ties with People Who Have Different Opinions than Yourself

This item ("Different Friends") is a second attempt to measure tolerance norms. Unlike the first item ("Understanding Others"), maintaining friendship is an explicit act of tolerance. It captures a practice of tolerance, and it is also an act of civility. And, in polarized times, these attributes may be especially hard to value and practice when connections beyond one's ideological or social silo are harder to maintain.

Consistent with other measures, we see that tolerance and civility measured through maintaining friendship is highly valued cross-nationally (near or above 4), with Germany posting weaker support.

3.5.2 A Good Citizen Accepts People of Diverse Racial and Religious Backgrounds

This third item on tolerance ("Accept Diversity") tests its expanse and limits by assessing disposition toward diverse racial and religious backgrounds. All three cases studied here are diverse and major immigrant-receiving states. As such, this is not a question about compositional preferences as much as it is a recognition of demographic reality. Among the three tolerance items, this is probably the hardest test as it makes explicit mention of nonideological outgroups.

Figure 3.7 shows high support for accepting racial and religious diversity as an attribute of a good citizen, by the US, UK and Germany in close but descending order – all at or above a mean of 4/5. Of course, these high scores may reflect social desirability bias. This, too, may also be an attribute associated more with the partisan left than the partisan right, so it is useful to add additional items on belonging (e.g., language, patriotism), which will enable a more rigorous test of the role of ideology in partisanship (compared to positional incentives).

3.5.3 A Good Citizen Has Patience, Recognizing that Sometimes Your Side Wins and Sometimes Your Side Loses

This measure of patience taps specifically into mutual tolerance (unlike the previous three items) and civility. Levitsky and Ziblatt refer to this behavior at the elite level as forbearance, in which one must be willing to practice restraint in their powers, recognizing the possibility that power could eventually change hands. Forbearance is highly valued, and necessary among political leaders, as it insures they play by and preserve the rules of the game for future iterations of play. However, we have no evidence about whether restraint – practiced by everyday citizens as patience and respect for the rules of the game – is valued or necessary among citizens in advanced democracies. Overall valuation is high; the US and UK boast similar scores, whereas Germany's is a bit lower on average.

3.5.4 A Good Citizen Understands How Government and Politics Work

A further behavioral norm of good citizenship is understanding how government and politics work ("Understand Politics"). The link between education and democracy is well-established,[17] but the correspondence between civic education and democracy is less so.[18] While there is evidence that civic education increases engagement,[19] and normative arguments about the role civic education should play in building a more vigilant and tolerant society,[20] there is a pervasive concern that democratic citizens today have low civic literacy. Looking at civic education, socializing processes, and other experiences, many fear that today's citizens simply do not know how to be citizens. This argument is widespread in the corridors of higher education,[21] Op-Ed pages of major

---

[17] Lipset, "Political Man: The Social Bases of Politics."

[18] Kenneth P. Langton and M. Kent Jennings, "Political Socialization and the High School Civics Curriculum in the United States," *American Political Science Review* 62, no. 3 (1968): 852–67; David E. Campbell, "Civic Engagement and Education: An Empirical Test of the Sorting Model," *American Journal of Political Science* 53, no. 4 (2009): 771–86.

[19] Paul Whiteley, "Does Citizenship Education Work? Evidence from a Decade of Citizenship Education in Secondary Schools in England," *Parliamentary Affairs* 67, no. 3 (2012): 513–35; Mikael Persson, "Education and Political Participation," *British Journal of Political Science* 45, no. 3 (2015): 689–703.

[20] Stephen Macedo, *Diversity and Distrust: Civic Education in a Multicultural Democracy.* Cambridge, MA:Harvard University Press, 2009.

[21] Michael B. Smith, Rebecca S. Nowacek, and Jeffrey L. Bernstein. "Don't Retreat. Teach Citizenship." *The Chronicle of Higher Education.* January 19, 2017. Available at www .chronicle.com/article/Don-t-Retreat-Teach/238923?cid=rclink

newspapers,[22] and vanity books by politicians.[23] But do ordinary citizens think that civic knowledge is important?

Americans rate civic knowledge as highly important and is found in other work to be a core obligation of civic duty.[24] The US valuation is followed closely by Germany. The gap between the UK and the US is more pronounced – about three-quarters of a point in difference. What accounts for the comparatively low prioritization of civic knowledge? One explanation is that civic education is only weakly institutionalized in the UK. Unlike the US, in which education has been the chief mechanism for nation-building,[25] where kindergarteners recite the Pledge of Allegiance," the UK only made citizenship a compulsory part of the national curriculum in 2002 (for England only and limited to pupils ages 11 to 16).

3.5.5 A Good Citizen Protests or Dissents When They Disagree with the Actions of Government

One of the most tangible ways for citizens to be seen and heard is through protest; protests are how democratic transitions often begin, and how a large, even unorganized group can signal preferences vertically to those who hold power. One of the most immediate manifestations of democratic hard times is protest – seeing it on the news, on your local Main Street, or in your state capitals. And marches for climate science, women's rights, Black Lives Matter, and against Brexit have been some of the strongest and largest protests since the 1960s.

Support for protesting as a citizenship norm is moderate, relative to other items. The data show that Germans value protesting as an act of good citizenship the most, followed by the US and the UK.

[22] Dana Goldstein. "Is the US a Democracy? A Social Studies Battle Turns on the Nation's Values." *The New York Times.* April 7, 2019. Available at www.nytimes.com/2019/04/07/us/usa-democracy.html?module=inline. Also Danielle Allen. "Here's One More Question Parents Should Think about During Back-to-School Season." *The Washington Post.* September 5, 2019. www.washingtonpost.com/opinions/we-need-civics-education-in-schools-to-build-effective-democratic-citizens/2019/09/05/3280dea4-cfe6-11e9-b29b-a528dc82154a_story.html

[23] Ben Sasse, *Them: Why We Hate Each Other – and How to Heal.* New York, NY: St. Martin's Press, 2018.

[24] André Blais, Carol Galais, and Danielle Mayer, "Is It a Duty to Vote and to Be Informed?," *Political Studies Review* 17, no. 4 (2019): 328–39.

[25] Amy J. Wan, *Producing Good Citizens: Literacy Training in Anxious Times* (Pittsburgh, PA: University of Pittsburgh Press, 2014).

3.5.6 A Good Citizen Supports Actions of Government

This question attempts to take a second look at the replicated question on vigilance (keep watch on government), which taps into inherent liberal distrust of government, as well as to balance out more liberal-leaning citizenship norms (e.g., social solidarity, accepting diversity) with a more conservative item like authority.[26] "Support government" refers not to system or regime support – which Rustow describes as a feature of national unity – but to government support, which changes with each election and governs over supporters and nonsupporters alike. Supporting government is deliberately ambiguous; citizens may support government because they are patriotic, because they are partisan, because they have generally positive and trusting dispositions toward governing institutions, because they value expediency and detest gridlock, because they are naïve, or because they are apathetic. Respondents may also interpret the term "government" variably; in parliamentary systems like the UK and Germany, it is a specific reference to the party or coalition in power versus an apparatus of power, which is closer to the US connotation.

Whatever the specific meaning, as a general marker of institutional support, the finding is clear: this is among the lowest valued citizenship norm. Respondents in the US, UK, and Germany exhibit moderate to low agreement that supporting government makes for a good citizen. This helps to confirm the descriptive findings for vigilance, as a healthy amount of skepticism and distrust is at the heart of liberal democracy.

The last two survey items pivot to look specifically at national belonging. A good citizen is not just a set of attitudes about behaviors and beliefs, but an identity or sense of belonging. There is a large literature on nationalism and national identity that plainly shows that some citizens are considered insiders (and others not) because of a variety of achievable (i.e., civic) or ascriptive (i.e., ethnic) characteristics, like religion, place of birth, or race. And, like supporting government, these two items may also associate with a more conservative citizen, and are therefore useful for obtaining ideological balance in citizenship norms and for testing positional incentives later on. Figure 3.8 presents these items: speaking [majority national language] and feeling [nationality].

---

[26] This intuition is grounded in moral foundations theory. See Martin V. Day et al., "Shifting Liberal and Conservative Attitudes Using Moral Foundations Theory," *Personality and Social Psychology Bulletin* 40, no. 12 (2014): 1559–73.

3.5.7 A Good Citizen Speaks [English/German]

Speaking English and German is highly valued in the UK and Germany, respectively, while speaking English is far less important in the US. There are two potential explanations for why linguistic proficiency is highly valued. First, support for speaking the national language may simply reflect ethnocultural preferences, where good citizens look or speak or behave in certain ways. Second, these responses may reflect preferences for civic proficiency. Linguistic integration is critical for immigrant incorporation. If a citizen can consume and understand political information in the national language, they may be more civically efficacious. The comparatively low priority of speaking English in the US reflects not only its multicultural demographic composition but also its law, as US federal law specifies no official language.[27] This is also reflected in language policy for citizenship, where the UK and Germany maintain far more difficult language requirements and tests than the US.

3.5.8 A Good Citizen Feels [American; British; German]

The final item asks if a good citizen feels or self-identifies with the national community. This may reflect innocuous patriotism, or it may be a deeper type of jingoism – when paired with other attributes – about what a respondent thinks "feeling American" (or British or German) actually means.[28] These different meanings are important and distinct. They may vary from person to person; they may also vary from context to context. For example, asking an individual if they think it is important to "feel American" on an average Tuesday is not equivalent to asking them if they "feel American" in the weeks following 9/11. Thus, one of the benefits of a capacious definition is that we can see how this item is rated alongside potential correlates, like accepting diversity. This context is useful in analysis, to adjudicate between types of patriotism. For example, feeling national pride in response to evidence of Russian interference in

---

[27] That said, English literacy is a requirement in US naturalization, and 32 out of 50 states have official state languages. See Deborah J. Schildkraut, *Press "One" For English: Language Policy, Public Opinion, and American Identity* (Princeton, NJ: Princeton University Press, 2005).

[28] Patriotism is ambiguous and open to interpretation. Robert E. Lane, "The Tense Citizen and the Casual Patriot: Role Confusion in American Politics," *The Journal of Politics* 27, no. 4 (1965): 735–60.

elections (what I would call "institution patriotism") is not the same as in response to information on immigration (which is closer to nationalism).

Interestingly, we see an inverse pattern to the language item in which Americans value feeling American the strongest and Germans value feeling German the least – with a substantial gap between the two. These results are certainly a historical product. Simply put, American patriotism remains relatively unstigmatized by history (though not unproblematically so), while British and German nationalism is associated not with pride but a type of colonial or ethnic nationalism that fueled respective historical experiences of global imperialism and the industrial genocide of the Holocaust. We can draw on the anecdotal observations of flag-waving practices as an example. In the US, the American flag is ever-present: in schools, courts, government buildings, shops, even on the bumpers of cars. In Europe, the British Union Jack[29] and German tricolor are reserved for government buildings and tourist shops, and usually only make public appearances during international sports competitions.

3.6 THE STRUCTURE OF DEMOCRATIC CITIZENSHIP IN HARD TIMES

As we see, good citizenship is nuanced and meaningfully varies across fourteen items, three cases, and over time. None of these attributes are rated as unimportant (1 or 2s), a bias reflecting costless support for costless beliefs, but there is variation, which justifies taking a purposefully capacious and inductive approach to identifying democratic norms. But is there a common, deeper structure to these survey responses? In this section, I use factor analysis to examine the interrelationships among these fourteen items and investigate the latent structure within the data. Since I theorize three dimensions of citizenship, I restrict the model to three factors. This allows the analysis to be theory-driven and exploratory, as it remains open to data-driven induction in terms of which items load together.

The results from a varimax rotated factor analysis for each country are in Table 3.1.[30] Table shading highlights those cells where the correlation

---

[29] Brexit has changed this practice. Country flags – like the St. George's Cross (England), St. Andrew's Cross (Scotland), and the Welsh Red Dragon – are also exceptions to this otherwise conservative practice.

[30] This approach makes factors as different as possible. Oblique models assume factors are related. Because of equal, but noisy, loading of some items, I also run an oblique model, which assumes factors are related. Results were comparable.

TABLE 3.1. *Dimensions of civic obligation*

Label:	United States			United Kingdom			Germany		
	Factor 1	Factor 2	Factor 3	Factor 1	Factor 2	Factor 3	Factor 1	Factor 2	Factor 3
	Belonging	*Belief*	*Behavior*	*Behavior*	*Belief*	*Belonging*	*Belief*	*Behavior*	*Belonging*
Obey laws	0.53	0.22	0.07	-0.10	0.28	0.45	0.26	0.04	0.38
Vote	0.17	0.17	0.53	0.40	0.19	0.23	0.21	0.35	0.12
Associations	0.08	0.25	0.45	0.56	0.13	0.10	0.30	0.33	0.18
Help people	-0.08	0.49	0.30	0.32	0.49	-0.10	0.39	0.30	0.03
Keep watch	0.06	0.13	0.70	0.68	0.15	0.08	0.08	0.68	0.17
Understand opinions of others	0.07	0.68	0.17	0.18	0.68	0.06	0.60	0.24	-0.11
Friends of different opinions	0.23	0.63	0.11	0.17	0.60	0.17	0.52	0.26	0.04
Accept diversity	-0.23	0.60	0.19	0.10	0.62	-0.24	0.72	0.01	-0.32
Patience	0.29	0.49	0.07	0.05	0.49	0.26	0.46	0.10	0.09
Support government	0.57	0.23	0.06	0.22	0.13	0.52	0.39	-0.01	0.34
Protest	-0.23	0.21	0.48	0.60	0.07	-0.13	0.03	0.51	-0.05
Understand politics	0.16	0.13	0.65	0.65	0.18	0.23	0.26	0.52	0.13
Feel X	0.79	0.06	0.10	0.09	-0.01	0.75	-0.17	0.09	0.74
Speak X	0.75	-0.12	0.01	0.08	-0.11	0.59	-0.15	0.14	0.60
Eigenvalue	3.08	1.93	0.90	3.01	1.51	1.05	2.51	1.68	0.69
Explained variance	0.36	0.33	0.31	0.35	0.34	0.31	0.41	0.30	0.29

Note: Table results are the varimax-rotated factor loadings. Factors are labeled where appropriate but preserved in the order of factor loading.

coefficients, or "loading," between each item (rows) and factors (columns) is significant at .30 or more.

The topline finding is that the fourteen items interrelate in such a way that the factor analysis provides construct validity for a theoretical model of citizenship as behavior, beliefs, and belonging. In all three cases, we observe comparable loading of similar items into three factors. First, voting, keeping watch, joining associations, protesting, and understanding politics all load to the *behavioral* dimension. These items all imply that good citizenship is expressed through active engagement, as opposed to expressions of belonging or the mere holding of beliefs. This behavioral dimension in the UK (eigenvalue of 3.01) and Germany (1.68) are substantially stronger than in the US (0.90).[31]

Second, helping others, understanding the opinions of others, having friends with different views, having patience, and accepting diversity all interrelate under the *liberal democratic beliefs* dimension. Two important observations follow. First, they all exhibit robust eigenvalues (US = 1.93, UK = 1.51; GER = 2.51), which defines them as a durable feature of democratic citizenship. Second, these liberal values do not group – or are not interrelated – with the more traditional proxies for liberal values that were replicated from previous ISSP surveys (e.g., obeying laws, watching government). To wit, "understanding others" is typically categorized as an item of "engaged citizenship" alongside other behavioral items, where voting and obeying the law are juxtaposed as "duty based."[32] Here, all three group separately. This only reaffirms the important caveat that dimensions are a function of the items included and excluded.

Obeying the law and supporting the government, along with feeling X and speaking X, load together on a third dimension, *national belonging*. The eigenvalues here differ greatly, being a robust dimension in the US and the UK (eigenvalues of 3.08 and 1.05, respectively) but weak in Germany (0.69). This value in Germany is below the cutoff, and looking at it closely we can see that two factors strongly load (speak German, feel German) while "obey laws" and "support government" are only weakly related. These two items also weakly load to the belief dimension, too. This does not mean these attributes of citizenship are

---

[31] Using the Kaiser criterion, eigenvalues < 1 should not be treated as a durable factor. Equal or greater to 1 means a factor explains more variance than a single observed variable or item.

[32] Dalton, *The Good Citizen*: 31.

TABLE 3.2. *Items of civic obligation, by dimension*

Behavior	Belief	Belonging
Always vote in elections	Understand otders	Obey laws
Keep watch on government	Have friends of different opinions	Support actions of government
Protest when in disagreement with government	Patience for winning and losing	Feel X
Understand politics	Accept diversity	Speak X
Active in associations	Help people	

unimportant; rather, German respondents who value obedience and government do not strongly associate them with values of belonging or beliefs.[33]

Inevitably, these loadings present some ambiguity, which contributes to some of these caveats in interpretation. Generally, the lower an item (especially below 0.4), the more noise there is. There are several items in Table 3.1 that load below this heuristic. Second, some items load similarly on multiple factors. This is especially true in the German survey; "active in associations" and "help people" load weakly with both behavior and belief, and "support government" loads weakly with belief and belonging. For ease of interpretation, I sort these items to mirror the British and American cases but proceed cautiously in interpretation. This is also why I only employ the factor analysis as a heuristic for confirming the theoretical dimensions of citizenship and as a device for identifying patterns in partisanship (Chapter 4) but not in experimental analysis (Chapters 5 and 6). In other words, I use each item as a dependent variable, and not an additive index by dimension. This trade-off chooses precision over parsimony.

Table 3.2 provides a summary of where each item is categorized by dimension. While confirmatory of theoretical dimensions, there is also empirical induction here. For example, "keeping watch on government" is considered a behavioral act of vigilance, not a liberal belief of

---

[33] Inductive factor analysis that allows for four factors, for example, may move these noisy items to other factors. Though, recall, support for government was a very low-rated item to begin with. This item loads more strongly to the belief dimension than belonging, though for the sake of comparability I present it alongside other belonging items but proceed with caution in analysis.

government distrust. In a second example, "helping people worse off than you" here resembles a belief, an ideal of solidarity and not an active behavior. In a third example, "supporting government" and "obeying laws" do not interrelate with other acts of political behavior, nor – as mentioned – are they categorized as liberal beliefs, but they load with items of national belonging, suggesting that these are more indicative of patriotism than participation.

To summarize, my 2019 survey confirms three dimensions of democratic citizenship, which vary in strength of interrelatedness across the three countries: behavior, beliefs, and belonging. The factor analysis shows that these dimensions are present in all three cases, providing empirical confirmation of the theoretical supposition. Yet the durability of these factors warrant caution in adopting a deductive approach to new cases. Democratic norms are not entirely generalizable, and these differences suggest that context-specific events – a result of history and nationally specifically political circumstances – may alter norms and how citizens think about obligation.

Further, these groupings illustrate how our understanding of citizenship will depend on what questions are asked. Of course, adding new items to a survey will affect how responses cluster with one another. But by expanding the battery of liberal norms, we discover that behavior previously serving as liberal norm proxies remain quite distinct from new, horizontal norms of civility, tolerance, and patience. We also see how adding dimensions of belonging load with law and order – especially in the US and UK, which combine to make for an allegiant and potentially illiberal dimension of democratic citizen.

The utility of these dimensions of civic obligation is in simplifying interpretation, where indices of behavior, beliefs, and belonging norms could theoretically be used instead of individual attributes in further research. For our purposes here, however, we want to know not only what clusters of obligation are affected by democratic crisis, but which items in particular. Flattening these differences into an aggregate misses the important difference by items. For example, we want to know if citizens think "protesting" in response to electoral interference is important instead of "behavior" more generally. Behavior could cover up important differences or be driven by theoretically irrelevant or substantively insignificant items, like joining associations. Still, these factors are a useful heuristic device for articulating hypotheses and for discussing clusters of findings and general trends.

3.7 DO NORMS PREDICT BEHAVIOR?

I conclude this chapter by exploring the link between norms and behavior. There is inherent value in understanding what everyday citizens believe their duty is. This tells us how citizens interpret their civic obligation, how they think they should be behaving when times get tough, but also what the shape of public opinion looks like in democratic crisis. Citizens view duties and responsibilities as a type of moral obligation,[34] and attitudes based on moral convictions have strong implications for political behavior. [35] Since Riker and Ordeshook first identified the important, normative role of "citizen duty" to explain voting behavior,[36] there is significant evidence pointing to norms as a motivation for political behavior.[37]

Understanding why citizens participate or not is critical for studying democracies, and, therefore, so are the antecedent determinants of those behaviors. Looking exclusively at behavior misses this underlying variation in norms. To invoke Hirschman's famous phraseology, we want to know who chooses "voice" and who "exits".[38] Democratic backsliding can occur in response to mass protests, or it can occur without. We want to know about who votes and protests, but we also want to know about the unobserved dispositions and norms of everyday citizens.

Are people who hold behavioral citizenship norms also active citizens? How do people who hold liberal citizenship norms behave? Are patriotic, belonging-oriented citizens active or quiescent? In this final section, I answer this question by examining whether civic obligation norms predict a variety of traditional political behaviors. To build an impression of this relationship, I use the three dimensions confirmed in the factor analysis to generate individual-level factor scores for each respondent.

---

[34] Conover, Crewe, and Searing, "The Nature of Citizenship in the United States and Great Britain: Empirical Comments on Theoretical Themes," 817.

[35] Linda J. Skitka, Christopher W. Bauman, and Edward G. Sargis, "Moral Conviction: Another Contributor to Attitude Strength or Something More?," *Journal of Personality and Social Psychology* 88, no. 6 (2005): 895–917.

[36] Riker and Ordeshook, "A Theory of the Calculus of Voting."

[37] For example, Bolzendahl and Coffé, "Are 'Good' citizens 'Good' participants? Testing Citizenship Norms and Political Participation across 25 Nations" present evidence where "well internalized" citizenship norms shape participation, such as voting and membership in associations.

[38] Albert O. Hirschman, *Exit, Voice, and Loyalty: Responses to Decline in Firms, Organizations, and States.* Vol. 25 (Cambridge, MA: Harvard University Press, 1970).

These scores capture the extent to which each respondent espouses behavioral, belief, or belonging-based concepts of good citizenship.

To capture political behavior, I used a series of variables corresponding to various forms of political participation. Respondents were asked the following: "There are different ways of trying to improve things in [COUNTRY] or help prevent things from going wrong. During the last 12 months, have *you* done any of the following?", which includes: contacted a politician, government or local official, worked in a political party or action group, worked in any political organization, displayed a campaign/issue sticker, signed a petition, took part in a lawful public demonstration, and posted or shared anything about politics online, like in blogs, email, Facebook or Twitter.[39] Individuals could answer "yes," "no," or "don't know."

Table 3.3 presents ordinary least squares regression analyses predicting participation (the dependent variables) based on different dimensions of civic obligation (the independent variables). The last column – Participation Index – combines the seven types of participation into a single measure. The independent variables correspond to respondents' predicted scores on the dimensions of citizenship discussed in the previous section. I present here regression models without controls.[40]

Across all three countries, behavioral norms are significant and positive predictors of reported political behavior. That is, individuals who hold behavioral citizenship norms also engage in almost every dimension of active citizenship.[41] This is consistent with a variety of scholarship that shows how beliefs in civic duty[42] and being informed[43] lead to higher levels of voter turnout. This also provides a useful validity check for my measure of a behavioral norms as not just an attitude but a credible commitment, where ideas are consistent with practice. In sum, support for behavioral norms of good citizenship is a good predictor of self-reported behavior.

---

[39] The order of these items was randomized.

[40] Basic demographic control models are on file with the author.

[41] One exception is Germany and "signing a petition," where active value holders are less likely to sign a petition. This finding is consistent with a variety of controls.

[42] Angus Campbell, Philip E. Converse, Warren E. Miller et al., *The American Voter* (Chicago, IL: University of Chicago Press, 1960); Campbell et al., "The American Voter."; Anthony Downs, "An Economic Theory of Political Action in a Democracy," *Journal of Political Economy* 65, no. 2 (1957).

[43] See, for example, David Dreyer Lassen, "The Effect of Information on Voter Turnout: Evidence from a Natural Experiment," *American Journal of Political Science* 49, no. 1 (2005): 103–18.

TABLE 3.3. *Predicting political behavior*

	Contact Politicians	Work for a Party	Work for an Organization	Campaign Display	Signed Petition	Attended Demonstration	Post Online	Participation Index
United States								
Behavior	0.19***	0.06***	0.05***	0.14***	0.16***	0.08***	0.16***	0.84***
	(0.01)	(0.01)	(0.01)	(0.01)	(0.01)	(0.01)	(0.01)	(0.04)
Beliefs	-0.02**	0.00	0.02**	-0.03**	0.00	0.02**	-0.03**	-0.03
	(0.01)	(0.01)	(0.01)	(0.01)	(0.01)	(0.01)	(0.01)	(0.04)
Belonging	-0.07***	-0.02**	-0.01	-0.04***	-0.08***	-0.09***	-0.05***	-0.35***
	(0.01)	(0.01)	(0.01)	(0.01)	(0.01)	(0.01)	(0.01)	(0.04)
N	2,640	2,642	2,645	2,649	2,635	2,641	2,635	2,571
United Kingdom								
Behavior	0.15***	0.06***	0.05***	0.10***	0.12***	0.08***	0.15***	0.71***
	(0.01)	(0.01)	(0.01)	(0.01)	(0.01)	(0.01)	(0.01)	(0.04)
Beliefs	0.02	-0.00	-0.00	0.00	0.06***	-0.01	0.04***	0.12***
	(0.01)	(0.01)	(0.00)	(0.01)	(0.01)	(0.01)	(0.01)	(0.03)
Belonging	-0.02**	-0.01	-0.00	-0.03***	-0.06***	-0.04***	-0.07***	-0.22***
	(0.01)	(0.01)	(0.01)	(0.01)	(0.01)	(0.01)	(0.01)	(0.04)
N	2,650	2,649	2,648	2,637	2,656	2,653	2,640	2,567
Germany								
Behavior	0.07***	0.03***	0.06***	0.04***	-0.16***	0.07***	0.11***	0.40***
	(0.01)	(0.01)	(0.01)	(0.01)	(0.04)	(0.01)	(0.01)	(0.06)
Beliefs	0.03***	0.01	0.02***	0.00	-0.01	0.01	-0.02**	0.12**
	(0.01)	(0.01)	(0.01)	(0.01)	(0.02)	(0.01)	(0.01)	(0.05)
Belonging	0.02*	0.01	0.00	-0.04***	0.07***	-0.05***	-0.07***	0.00
	(0.01)	(0.01)	(0.01)	(0.01)	(0.02)	(0.01)	(0.01)	(0.05)
N	2,524	2,518	2,521	2,526	1,349	2,530	2,509	1,253

* $p<0.10$, ** $p<0.05$, *** $p<0.01$

We observe more variation as we move to liberal beliefs. Liberal belief holders in the UK and Germany both exhibit a significant (and positive) participation index coefficient, where those who score strong liberal belief norms also exhibit higher political behavior. Drilling down into the items in the UK, those who score high on the beliefs dimension are more likely to sign a petition and post online. In Germany, this pattern is positive and significant but for a different set of behaviors: contacting a politician, working for a party, and working for an organization.[44] The US exhibits more mixed results. Liberal belief holders in the US are more likely to work for an organization and attend demonstrations, but less likely to contact politicians, display campaign information, and post online. Its participation index is also insignificant, with null results also for working for a party and signing a petition, meaning these behaviors are statistically unrelated to holding liberal beliefs.

What can we take from these results? They suggest we do not have a consistent prediction of how liberal value holders are going to behave. In aggregate, liberal value holders may be more participatory, but this is not always the case nor does this insight hold for all types of participation. It suggests liberal democratic citizens are biddable, mobilized in some areas and not others. And, in the US it remains an open question whether good citizens who uphold liberal democratic values are doing the work to support democracy.

Finally, in looking at the belonging dimension, we largely observe inactivity. These "allegiant" citizens value items of national belonging, obedience, and patriotism and are less likely to be politically active. De facto, these citizens are more quiescent and deferential to authority. In the US, allegiant citizens are significantly less likely to participate in almost every aspect of political participation.[45] In the UK, allegiant citizens are equally as passive. This is an important finding; citizens who value items of belonging are less participatory. Obedient and loyal citizens do not make demands; they stay home. But these invisible allegiants are not the same as the invisible apathetic. From the perspective of an aspiring authoritarian, they may all look the same in forming a part of the "silent majority," but we can distinguish the submissive from the fatigued by looking at norms.

---

[44] For German respondents, we see one negative result: The more individuals support liberal democratic norms of citizenship, the less likely they are to report participation in posting online.

[45] The exception is working for an organization or campaign, which posts a null finding.

Finally, in Germany, measures that comprise a "national belonging" dimension (using only "speak German" and "feels German") also relate to demobilization. These citizens are less likely to be politically visible (less likely to exhibit a campaign display, attend a demonstration, or posting online), but more likely to sign a petition and contact a politician (modestly significantly). One explanation is that these attitudes are publicly stigmatized. Therefore, private activism is considered more appropriate than public types.

What do we learn from this exercise? Citizens who value behavioral norms are active in real life. Norms may *predict* or *reflect* behavior (i.e., active citizens want to see themselves a "good citizens") but this model shows high correlation between the two, justifying norms as an internally valid wedge to look at the expectations and beliefs of citizens who may not participate. We want to know what democratic threat does to citizens, and we need a way to see what happens to those that do not participate in visible acts of citizenship. For example, those that see good citizenship as comporting to group identity are inactive. This inactivity, though, is not the same as that of a liberal democratic good citizen, which, in the US, is also inactive. In the UK and Germany, liberal belief holders are generally motivated to participate (though with a lot of individual null results), while in the US, results are evenly mixed (with its participation index posting a null result). It is a problem for democracy when liberal value holders stay home because the "soft guardrail" becomes implicit. It may be that democratic preservation requires more active behavior from these view holders.

Overall, these findings show the importance of maintaining a focus on norms – instead of behavior – in democratic hard times. If liberal viewholders are not participating, that creates one problem. And if citizens who believe national belonging is an important norm of good citizenship are, that's an entirely different problem. Participation alone is not a patch for democratic problems: the motivation and ideals behind it the participation matters enormously.

In this chapter, I operationalized, measured, and compared citizenship norms across fourteen items, using an original, three-country survey. In looking at change across time, we see that something is different about 2019. Obedience decreases, the importance of voting increases, while some norms – like helping others – withstand hard times. In looking at new measures of civic obligation, we see instances of similarity across liberal democracies regarding liberal norms, like tolerance, forbearance, and civility, but also differences when it comes to attributes of belonging.

We also saw that these norms thematically group together. Factor analysis identifies three dimensions of civic obligation – behavior, beliefs, and belonging – in the US, the UK, and Germany. Further, the behavior that corresponds to these norms reflects a variety of civic participants in democratic hard times. Behavior-based citizens use voice and belonging-based citizens express loyalty through exit. And the evidence is ambiguous for what liberal citizens do.

This descriptive overview of citizenship norms in 2019 lays the groundwork for the analysis in the rest of the book. Specifically, we see that by asking new questions – specifically on liberal values – we uncover a whole new dimension of citizenship, one that can intersect with belonging and behavior-based citizens. But what happens when only one political party believes good citizens adhere to liberal values? How much is good citizenship structured by partisan ideology? And what determines whether citizens turn to tolerance in democratic crisis versus hunkering down, turning inward, or turning off? The remaining chapters explore these questions by unpacking citizen responses to different types of democratic crisis.

4

Patterns of Partisan Citizenship

This chapter builds an important, descriptive bridge between the theoretical (Chapter 2) and the empirical (Chapter 3) insights of the preceding chapters and the testing of the role of positional incentives in citizens responding to threat in the subsequent chapters (Chapters 5 and 6). Specifically, it introduces the readers to the specific political parties within each case study and considers the extent to which the fourteen items of "good citizenship" are already partisan, that is, before introducing democratic threats. Chapters 2 and 3 signposted this possibility. In Chapter 2, I argued that democratic citizenship is not unitary or homogeneous but is composed of a variety of interests and cleavages. National citizenship serves as a foundation to democratic stability *because* it provides sufficient overlap in norms to sustain ties across diverse groups and interests in society. In Chapter 3, I flag what some of these possibilities may look like: liberal/left partisans support norms of social solidarity and engagement while conservative/right partisans support norms of belonging and system loyalty. This chapter systematically looks for these patterns. Before we examine how partisanship shapes a citizen's *reaction* to democratic crisis, we need to first look more closely at where differences and overlaps exist among citizenship norms by partisanship.

We have established so far that there are three dimensions to citizenship – behavior, beliefs, and belonging – and that there is variation in support of items within these dimensions both across countries and over time. With this foundation in place, this chapter examines variation *within* dimensions, specifically to the underlying partisan structure of civic obligation. I present evidence from the three-country survey to illustrate the partisan structure of everyday democratic citizenship. By "everyday" I mean quotidian citizenship norms that we can distinguish from citizenship norms *in response to* democratic threat. Do supporters of the right and left share quotidian commitments to liberal democratic norms as a part of everyday citizenship? Do both sides value participation? Do we see fewer differences in consensus systems than majoritarian systems?

Generally, we observe consistent patterns of partisan citizenship, even when controlling for demographic factors that might explain citizenship preferences. Supporters of left parties value protesting and solidarity-oriented beliefs like helping others; supporters of right parties strongly support allegiant items of belonging, from obeying laws to speaking X and feeling X. In majoritarian systems (US and UK), these patterns are strong and systematic. In Germany, a consensus system, we observe more agreement along more items in determining what it means to be a good citizen.

However, a crucial observation underlies these differences: There are *sufficient overlaps between the left and right* when it comes to liberal democratic beliefs and behavioral items of good citizenship. This "holding of the center" is critical. It suggests a strong base of agreement for preserving national unity and adequate ties for establishing common goals despite polarization in everyday politics. This is good news: Everyday citizenship provides a robust foundation for democratic stability. The central question then remains whether these overlaps hold in hard times. Do existing overlaps dissolve? By illustrating first both the entrenched role of partisanship *and* sufficient consensus in citizenship norms in our sample of advanced democracies, we are then able to assess what happens in response to democratic threat. This will tell us where divided citizenship may undermine democracy rather than strengthen it.

4.1 INTRODUCING POLITICAL PARTIES

I want to begin by taking a minute to orient readers to the major political parties in each of the three countries. Readers may be familiar with one – but not all – of the case studies or only with mainstream parties therein. The argument in this book takes seriously partisan attachment, because parties connect citizens to the stakes of the political process and threats to its integrity. To understand partisanship, it is helpful to look at where parties are located on the ideological spectrum and how they are positioned relative to each other, both within and across cases. Though ideology and partisanship have largely consolidated with one another in the US,[1] this is less so in our European cases, which offer more parties for individuals to choose from and, related, where individuals exhibit less attachment to particular parties.[2] I begin by introducing the political parties of each case.

The US is an effective two-party system, produced by a first-past-the-post, winner-take-all electoral system. The Republicans (abbreviated as GOP) are the major party of the ideological right; the Democratic party of the ideological left. These parties are heavily polarized, at both the elite and the mass level. The US also has a large and growing population that identifies as Independent. According to Gallup, in the summer of 2019 (June 19–30), 41 percent of a nationally representative sample identified as Independent (27 percent as Republican and 29 percent as Democrats). However, in a hyperpolarized system, where there is a stigma against being "political," many who claim to be independent are in fact "leaners," who consistently vote and identify with a partisan side.[3] In this study, I use a seven-point partisan identification measure throughout, to include leaners with their partisan side. The category of "Others" comprises supporters of myriad third parties as well as true Independents.

The UK combines a first-past-the-post electoral system with a multi-party system. Thus, the effective number of parties is higher than in the US,[4] though the electoral systems are similar. And, because it is a parliamentary system, national executive elections are embedded in – and therefore, simultaneous to – legislative elections. The Conservatives ("Tories," abbreviated as CON) are the main party on the right (led by Boris Johnson who, at the time of the survey, was newly elected as party leader) and the Labour party (LAB) the main party on the left (led then by Jeremy Corbyn, replaced after a failed General Election in 2019 by Keir Starmer).

There are a number of small and regional parties. Supporters of the Liberal Democrats ("Lib Dems"), a liberal third party, lie to the center-left. Between 2010 and 2015, the Lib Dems formed a coalition

---

[1] Levendusky, *The Partisan Sort: How Liberals Became Democrats and Conservatives Became Republicans.*

[2] Russell J. Dalton, *Democratic Challenges, Democratic Choices. The Erosion of Political Support in Advanced Industrial Democracies (Comparative Politics).* UK: Oxford University Press, 2004).

[3] Samara Klar and Yanna Krupnikov, *Independent Politics* (New York: Cambridge University Press, 2016).

[4] Markku Laakso and Rein Taagepera, "'Effective' Number of Parties: A Measure with Application to West Europe." *Comparative Political Studies* 12, no. 1 (1979): 3–27.

government with the Conservatives, under David Cameron's premiership, and in the 2017 General Election won 12 seats in parliament. Regional parties include the Scottish National Party (SNP; Scotland), the Democratic Unionist Party (DUP; Northern Ireland), Sinn Fein (SF; Northern Ireland), and Plaid Cymru (Wales). These parties span the ideological spectrum and are defined by their positions on the national question. Finally, there is the United Kingdom Independence Party (UKIP). A small party (they held no seats in the House of Commons) with an enigmatic if controversial leader (Nigel Farage), it exerted an outsized influence on national politics, pinching the Tories from the right enough that former PM David Cameron thought a national referendum on British membership to the European Union would quiet the right flank in his party. Cameron did not anticipate – along with most political observers – that the UK would narrowly vote to support the referendum, ushering in a drawn-out period of a British exit ("Brexit"). Once Brexit was accomplished, support for the group waned even further. Additional splintering of UKIP support by the breakaway Brexit Party in 2018 also reduces overall support, but has not diminished the salience of Euroskeptic, anti-immigrant politics.[5]

Finally, Germany is a multiparty, parliamentary system that uses a mixed-member proportional representation electoral system. Unlike a traditional PR system, each voter gets two votes: one to choose a representative from their single-seat constituency (using FPTP) and one for a political party, filling in the remainder of parliamentary seats to achieve proportional results (e.g., a party that gets 25 percent of the vote gets 25 percent of the seats). In Germany's last federal election (2017), six parties gained seats in the Bundestag: the Union Party, comprised of the Christian Democratic Union (CDU) and the Christian Social Union (CSU), the Social Democrats (SPD), the Alternative for Germany (AfD), the Greens, the Left (Die Linke), and the Free Democratic Party (FDP). The CDU is the main party on the right. At the time of the survey (from 2005 until 2021), the CDU was led by Chancellor Angela Merkel. The CDU is traditionally supported by its more conservative Bavarian sister party, the CSU, which often moves the CDU further to the right. For example, they often disagree on policy – frequently when it comes to refugees.

---

[5] Brexit Party was not included as a political party choice. However, one respondent indicated they voted Brexit Party.

The traditional, main left party is the SPD, though they only captured 21 percent of the vote in the 2017 federal election. Other left parties like Die Linke and the Greens proved successful at picking off their voter base, having both received around 9 percent in that same election. Explanations for the SPD's decreased support at this time are several, ranging from a participation penalty from their long-time cooperation with the CDU in a grand coalition (*Große Koalition*, or GroKo),[6] the costs of convergence,[7] to the changing structural foundation of social democracy.[8] By 2020, support for SPD plummeted to 16 percent[9] but they ultimately rebounded by the 2021 election, capturing nearly 26 percent of the vote, enough to form a new coalition government. The FDP is an economically liberal (pro-free market), socially liberal party, which in Germany's political system makes them a centrist party. For instance, they often cooperate with Social Democrats and Greens in regional coalitions, but also considered joining Merkel's national coalition in 2017. A small party, it failed to clear the 5 percent threshold in 2013 and lost its seats in the Bundestag. Last, the AfD entered the Bundestag for the first time in the 2017 election, becoming the third largest party with 12.6 percent of the vote. The AfD is a far right, Euroskeptic, anti-immigrant party.

To assist the reader, Figure 4.1 shows where these political parties from the US, UK, and Germany fall on the ideological spectrum, intersecting economic values (x-axis) and social values (y-axis). These data come from Norris's Global Party Survey (2019),[10] which relies on party and election experts to code party ideological orientation, issue positions, and rhetoric. For economic values, those on the economic left are described as "want[ing] government to play an active role," where those on the right "favor a reduced role for government." For social values, those with liberal values (lower scores on the y-axis) "favor expanded personal freedoms, for example, on abortion rights, same-sex marriage, and democratic participation" while those with conservative values

---

[6] Heike Klüver and Jae-Jae Spoon, "Helping or Hurting? How Governing as a Junior Coalition Partner Influences Electoral Outcomes." *The Journal of Politics* 82, no. 4 (2020): 1231–42.

[7] Berman and Kundnani, "The Cost of Convergence."

[8] Giacomo Benedetto, Simon Hix, and Nicola Mastrorocco, "The Rise and Fall of Social Democracy, 1918–2017." *American Political Science Review* 114, no. 3 (2020): 928–39.

[9] Forsa Poll, fielded 8/31/20 to 9/4/20 (N = 2,503). See national poll average http://europeelects.eu/germany (accessed September 7, 2020).

[10] Pippa Norris, "Global Party Survey, 2019." Harvard Dataverse, 2020, www.globalpartysurvey.org/.

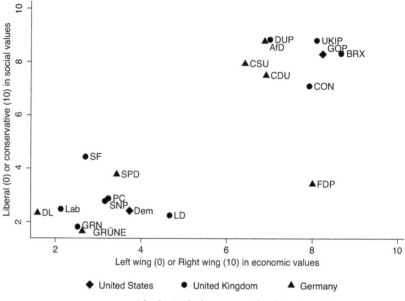

FIGURE 4.1. Ideological placement of political parties

(higher scores) "reject these ideas in favor of order, tradition and stability, believing that government should be a firm moral authority on social and cultural issues."[11]

We see a very clear clustering where, programmatically, there are two groups: parties on the right (clustered in the upper-right-hand corner) and parties of the left (clustered in the lower left). For parties on the right, there is more variation in economic values than social values, and we see mainstream (GOP/Republican, CON/Conservative, CDU/Christian Democrats), small or regional (DUP/Democratic Unionist, CSU/Christian Social), and far right (AfD/Alternative for Germany; UKIP/UK Independence Party, BRX/Brexit). Note that the US Republican party clusters tightly with far right parties on both economic and social dimension, and not with mainstream center-right parties in Germany or the UK.

We see a looser clustering of parties on the left, with large gaps along economic values. Some left parties are far more economically centrist (Dem/Democrats, LD/Liberal Democrats) than others (DL/The Left, Lab/Labour), while some are more socially conservative (SPD/Social

---

[11] From the Global Party Survey Questionnaire.

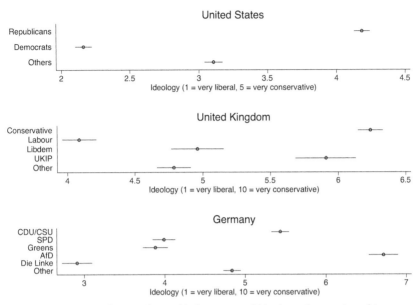

FIGURE 4.2. Respondent self-placement of ideology, by partisanship

Democrats) than others (GRN/Greens). Along this vertical dimension, we can see how the Greens in Germany manage to differentiate themselves from the SPD, positioning themselves as more inclusive on social issues. In this left cluster, we also locate Sinn Fein (SF), offsetting its regional competitor (DUP), as well as the Scottish National Party (SNP). Note that, as a whole, right parties hover closer to the social conservative pole (a value of 10) than left parties to the liberal pole (a value of 0).

Given that overview, I want to connect ideological structuring of partisanship at the macro-level to individual self-placement. How do survey respondents place themselves on a left–right ideological scale, and does it correspond to these larger patterns? While a unidimensional scale necessarily flattens differences between economic and social placement, it gives us a good impression of how individuals think about their political ideology and partisan identity. Figure 4.2 maps ideological self-placement by partisanship. Ideology in the US is measured on a 5-point scale, and on a 10-point scale in the UK and Germany. Note that these scales are not equivalent, prioritizing interpretation of within-case comparisons rather than across cases.

We see individual self-placement consistent with party positioning from Figure 4.1. In the US, Republicans locate on the extreme right (where the maximum conservative score is 5), while Democrats are in a more moderate left position. Others include Independents and supporters of third parties and are located in the middle. In the UK, we see Conservative voters in a moderately conservative position (6.3/10) and Labour in a moderately progressive position (4.1/10). Liberal Democrats here self-place as more conservative than Labour (consistent with Figure 4.1). UKIP is located just to the left of the Conservative Party, highlighting how the unidimensional nature of the self-placement scale may be a crude measure for one-issue parties. Regional parties are grouped together in the "other" category. Last, we see more convergence in Germany than in the UK, where parties are more polarized. Specifically, the CDU is more moderately right, and the SPD is more moderately left. Greens supporters self-place near the SPD supporters and, consistent with programmatic positioning and philosophical commitments, Die Linke is located on the far left and the AfD on the far right.

This introduction to political parties in our three cases establishes variation in partisanship and ideology, but also consistency between individual self-placement and macro-level party positioning by experts. This lets us use the language of "left versus right" to speak cross-nationally about parties (where party names are nationally specific) and to derive general observations about how individuals value different citizenship norms across the political spectrum. To this, we now turn.

4.2 THE PARTISAN STRUCTURE OF CITIZENSHIP NORMS

Do citizenship norms have an inherently partisan structure to them? Studies locate liberals as exercising a more active, engaged citizenship while conservatives focus on cultural dimensions and duty.[12] Van der Meer et al. find ideological preference is a strong predictor of political action across 20 Western democracies.[13] Ypi describes value alignments as a means for activating political commitment, in which individuals "care about the public good and actively seek to promote it, making one's efforts and ideas of social change part of a joint project shared with

---

[12] Coffé and Bolzendahl, "Partisan Cleavages in the Importance of Citizenship Rights and Responsibilities"; Dalton, *The Good Citizen: How a Younger Generation Is Reshaping American Politics.*

[13] Van der Meer, Van Deth, and Scheepers, "The Politicized Participant: Ideology and Political Action in 20 Democracies."

others."[14] In other words, partisanship draws individuals into democratic politics.

The premise of democratic citizenship is that it can contain disagreement, so long as there are overlaps to establish national unity in common values and group goals. In fact, factions are inevitable (to quote James Madison, they can only be cured by "destroying the liberty which is essential to its existence" or "giving every citizen the same opinions, the same passions, and the same interest") but only tenable when democracy supersedes these divisions. Giovanni Sartori discusses this feature as a "parts-of-a-whole"[15] problem; the interests of democracy ("whole") must take precedence over – but nevertheless will be pursued through – parties ("parts").

So what are the parts? In investigating the partisan structure of citizenship norms, I present predicted outcomes – support for the 14 items of democratic citizenship norms – across major political parties in two different ways per country. The first aggregates the 14 items of citizenship, using factor scores predicted from the factor analysis in Chapter 3 to rate respondents along the categories of behavior, liberal beliefs, and national belonging. The x-axis shows the range of factor scores produced by the factor analysis. This view presents, in broad brush strokes, the extent of partisan citizenship across the three theoretical dimensions of obligation.

The second view drills down to show support for each of the 14 items of civic obligation by partisanship. In this second view, the x-axis includes outcomes that vary from 1 (least supportive) to 5 (most supportive), corresponding to the scale in which respondents were asked whether each item reflects an attribute of a "good citizen." In both analyses, I control for the following demographics: race (or immigrant-heritage in the case of Germany), gender, age, education, income, and region. Each figure presents predicted values based on the regression coefficients, averaged over the observed values of the demographic covariates, enabling me to compare predicted levels of support across parties while accounting for other demographic differences.

---

[14] Lea Ypi, "Political Commitment and the Value of Partisanship." *American Political Science Review* 110, no. 3 (2016): 601. Also see also see Eric W. Groenendyk and Antoine J. Banks, "Emotional Rescue: How Affect Helps Partisans Overcome Collective Action Problems." *Political Psychology* 35, no. 3 (2014): 359–78.

[15] Sartori, *Parties and Party Systems: A Framework for Analysis.*

A word on interpretation: some of these differences between parties are significant but appear subtle. For example, there may be statistically significant differences between two parties on an item, but those predicted scores appear close together, for example, Party A values an item at 4.3/5 and Party B at 4.6. One might argue these differences are statistically significant but substantively insignificant. I take a different position. We see strong support for certain items, and partisan differences exist *even given that strong support*. I can detect those subtle differences in otherwise broadly popular items and, by controlling for a variety of factors, identify that those difference are partisan in origin.

4.3 THE UNITED STATES

Beginning with the US, we see meaningful differences in everyday citizenship norms by partisanship. Figure 4.3 shows partisan citizenship by norm dimensions. There are statistically significant differences between Democrats and Republicans when it comes to all three dimensions of civic obligation. Looking at both behavior and beliefs, Democrats are more likely to value these dimensions compared to Republicans. When it comes to the belonging dimension, we see the opposite. Republicans value this

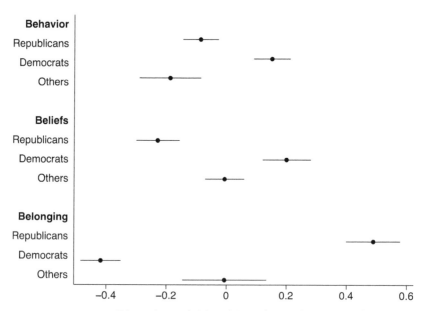

FIGURE 4.3. Dimensions of citizenship in the US, by partisanship

aspect of citizenship much more than do Democrats, with independents and others in the middle. These differences are large and significant, illustrating how partisanship consolidates around different meanings of "good citizenship." In other words, Democrats and Republicans maintain different understandings about what it means to be a good citizen in their day-to-day lives.

Partisanship, of course, is not the only factor that structures different definitions of good citizenship. Looking at the demographic control variables, we find that women, for example, are more likely to support liberal democratic norms and are less likely to support behavior relative to men.[16] Black, Hispanic, and Asian respondents (pooled) are more likely to value liberal, solidarity items compared to White respondents. Arguing that citizenship is partisan does not undercut these observations. Rather, it identifies that partisanship is a central cleavage that shapes civic identity and arguably, the most pernicious one for thinking about how citizens respond to democratic threats.

Moving from this aggregate view of good citizenship dimensions, we can look at each of these categories to see *which individual items* are most highly valued across parties – where is there consensus and where is there difference? Figure 4.4 presents predicted valuations of each item of good citizenship, where five is most supportive.

This 14-item view offers more nuance, and, with it, we see that some of the aggregate patterns are misleading. Beginning with behavior, the large differences visible in aggregate appear to be driven by the high value Democrats place on protesting (relative to Republicans, $\beta = 0.77$, $p = 0.00$). But for other items of behavior, like voting or being informed, we find no statistical difference between Democrats and Republicans. We can conclude, then, that outside this single dimension of political behavior, citizens on a day-to-day basis think similarly about the behavioral norms of citizenship. In other words, behavioral norms represent a meaningful overlap and dimension of consensus.

Moving to liberal democratic beliefs, we again see overlap between Republicans and Democrats. There is no statistical difference in "understanding the opinions of others," "having friends with different views," and "have patience, recognizing that sometimes your side wins and sometimes it loses." These items are really the core of mutual tolerance and, thus, it is a good sign that there are not statistically significant

---

[16] On file with author.

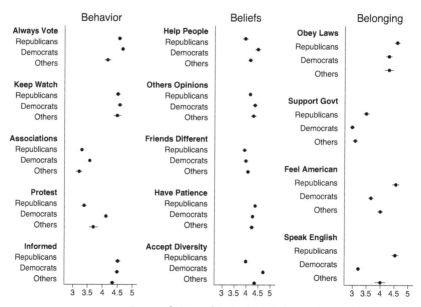

FIGURE 4.4. Items of citizenship in the US, by partisanship

differences by partisanship when it comes to liberal democratic norms. There are two items where we do see difference: Democrats are more likely to value helping people and accepting diversity as items of good citizenship. This is consistent with expectations discussed in Chapter 3.

Where behavior and beliefs offer several items of consensus, we see the largest difference between the two major parties when it comes to items of belonging, with statistically significant differences between the two parties along all four items. Republicans are more likely to support all four items of the belonging dimension: obeying the law, supporting government, "feeling American," and speaking English (the largest difference relative to Democrats). The margins between the two parties here are large, consolidating a strongly allegiant and ascriptive character to good citizenship for Republicans that does not exist for Democrats. Like liberal beliefs, it is a normative problem for liberal democracy if one political party and its supporters define good citizenship as a matter of belonging above all else. Not only is this a problem in immigrant-receiving contexts, but in hard times more generally, when uncertainty strengthens in-group solidarity.

This also casts doubt on whether messages of patriotism are reparative and unifying in polarized times. Levendusky shows that priming

Americans about shared national identity reduces partisanship, specifically how individuals feel about members of the opposite political party.[17] While any evidence of reducing partisan discord is encouraging, this finding overlooks a deeper concern, evidenced here, that partisanship leads individuals to hold different definitions of national belonging in the first place. If some value cultural homogeneity and others tolerance, diversity, and deliberation, a polity may be unable to establish meaningful national unity in the first place, much less construct the necessary civic coalitions or establish the cross-partisan comity needed to solve problems.

Most citizens do not think about their citizenship; that someone on the right thinks speaking the national language is a dimension of good citizenship more than someone on the left may be true but irrelevant to how an individual operates in most contexts. These differences exist but are usually inactive. Uncovering these modest differences in everyday understandings of good citizenship helps us to characterize continuity or change when met with crisis.

4.4 THE UNITED KINGDOM

Now we will move to British respondents, Figure 4.5 presents predicted scores for the three dimensions of good citizenship by partisanship among four national parties.[18] In this view, we observe patterns that mirror the US. Like the US, the partisan left (Labour and Liberal Democrats) values behavior more than the Conservatives on the right. Note that on this dimension, UKIP resembles the partisan left more than the ideologically adjacent Conservatives. We can attribute this to the party's unique and outsized mobilization tactics that raised their profile as a viable challenger party. There are also statistically significant differences between the left and right on the liberal democratic beliefs dimension, though this gap is much narrower than in the US. Unsurprisingly, UKIP supports are the most illiberal on this dimension. Last, we see the partisan right (both the Conservatives and UKIP) as predictably more supportive of the belonging dimension of good citizenship, compared to Labour and Lib Dem.

Moving to individual items of good citizenship, Figure 4.6 shows predicted support for each of the 14 attributes of democratic citizenship.

---

[17] Matthew S. Levendusky, "Americans, Not Partisans: Can Priming American National Identity Reduce Affective Polarization? ." *The Journal of Politics* 80, no. 1 (2018): 59–70.
[18] Regional parties in Wales, Northern Ireland, and Scotland are pooled together with those that designate "other."

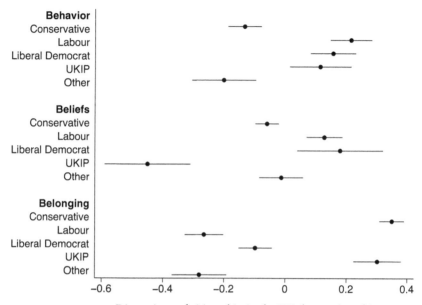

FIGURE 4.5. Dimensions of citizenship in the UK, by partisanship

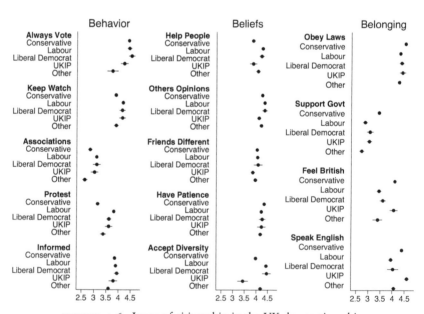

FIGURE 4.6. Items of citizenship in the UK, by partisanship

Starting with behavior, we see areas of similarity and difference. There are no significant differences by partisanship on being informed and voting, establishing a core, overlapping value. And there is the expected difference between the partisan left and right when it comes to protesting. But Labour and Liberal Democrats are more likely to value joining associations and keeping watch on government (vigilance). These are deeper partisan differences than we saw in the US when it comes to items of behavior.

Moving to liberal democratic values, we see the same pattern as exhibited in the US, in which a liberal democratic "core" of mutual tolerance remains intact alongside predictable partisan differences. Specifically, the partisan left and right exhibit similar support for items like understand the opinions of other, maintaining friends of different views, and having patience, while left supporters report stronger support for "helping people" and "accepting diversity," which is broadly consistent with their ideological and policy platform. Finally, as with US Republicans, Conservatives exhibit stronger support than left party supporters on all four items of national belonging: obey laws, support government, feel British, and speak English. For these last two items, Tory supporters exhibit similar predicted probabilities to UKIP supporters, an explicitly xenophobic party. Last, note that UKIP departs from the Conservatives in expressing a low valuation of government support, similar to Lib Dems, and consistent to their status as challenger party[19] and system outsider.

Reflecting on the US and UK, we observe similar partisan schisms when it comes to citizenship norms. The good news is that both left and right are united by a baseline of behavioral (voting, being informed) and liberal democratic (understanding others, maintaining friend with different views) norms. This is reassuring for democratic stability, as these are some of the very characteristics that democracy scholars argue citizens need. The bad news is that there is a durable cleavage around the issues of community and solidarity. The partisan left in both cases exhibit more care and inclusion (help others, accept diversity) while the partisan right in both cases support an allegiant and homogenous type of national belonging as a feature of a good citizen. It is an obvious problem when these competing visions of community are distinctly held by parties on the opposite side of the political aisle.

---

[19] Catherine E. De Vries and Sara B. Hobolt, *Political Entrepreneurs: The Rise of Challenger Parties in Europe* (Princeton, NJ: Princeton University Press, 2020).

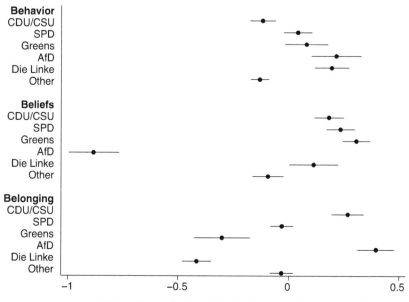

FIGURE 4.7. Dimensions of citizenship in Germany, by partisanship

4.5 GERMANY

Like the UK, Germany also has multiple parties, but has a consensus-style political system. Not only do elections use proportionality to translate votes into seats, German democracy requires consensus through governing coalitions. Grand coalitions (composed of parties on the left and right) are a near-consistent feature of contemporary German federal politics.[20] Merkel's first CDU/CSU + SPD coalition was formed in 2005, as part of her first cabinet (2005–2009), and renewed in 2013 (third cabinet) and again following the 2017 elections (fourth cabinet). Merkel's second cabinet governed through a coalition with the free market FDP. Per Chapter 2, consensus systems should incentivize more overlaps by structuring politics as a series of positive-sum exercises. To examine this, Figure 4.7 investigates the three dimensions of good citizenship among five major national parties: the Union party (CDU and CSU) and Alternative for Germany (AfD) on the right and the Social Democrats

---

[20] (West) Germany's other notable grand coalition in the post-Weimar period was Kurt Kiesinger's (CDU) cabinet, which controlled over 90% of the Bundestag by joining CDU and the SPD. It lasted from 1966 to 1969.

(SPD), Greens, and the Left (Die Linke) on the left, pooling any additional responses into the Other category.

Compared to the British and US cases, we see more, well, consensus. Beginning with behavior, there is consensus support for a behavioral interpretation of good citizenship across the political spectrum; parties on the left exhibit higher levels of support than the center-right CDU, but differences are substantively smaller than in the UK or the US. Like UKIP, we see AfD look like other small parties on the left, valuing behavioral citizenship as a feature of a challenger party to compete against (and outflank) the CDU on the right.

We also find partisan consensus on the liberal democratic dimension of good citizenship, where there are no statistical differences between democratic parties. This dimension is rated highly among all parties except for the far right illiberal AfD. This is the strongest evidence of consensus, and revealing of a strong base of mutual commitment to liberal democratic norms, valuable not only for offsetting AfD illiberalism (perhaps even a product of a type of rallying effect to offset the strength of the AfD), but also as a reflection of Germany's careful protection of liberal democracy in the postwar period.

Belonging is where we continue to see variation across parties. Recall this dimension for Germany is only comprised of the two items on "feeling German" and "speaking German." AfD unsurprisingly exhibits the strongest support for this dimension of citizenship, followed in descending order by the center-right CDU, the center-left SPD, the Greens, then Die Linke. In this dimension only, partisan differences in Germany's consensus-based system resemble the partisan differences found in the UK and the US.

Moving to individual items of good citizenship in Figure 4.8, we can see how similar partisans are in more detail. First, in looking at the behavioral items, we see that the aggregate result – like the other cases – is driven by differences in protesting. This aligns the partisan left in Germany with the other two cases, suggesting that support for this dimension of civic obligation is a feature of the partisan left, regardless of institutional setting. High support for this item overall, however, echoes the student protests of 1968 (the "68ers"), in which students on the left became increasingly disillusioned with the political establishment when (among many catalysts) the SPD joined the Grand Coalition with the CDU. While the student movement did not produce broad political change, it did solidify protest culture in German politics. But, beyond protesting (and much like the majoritarian systems), there appears to be

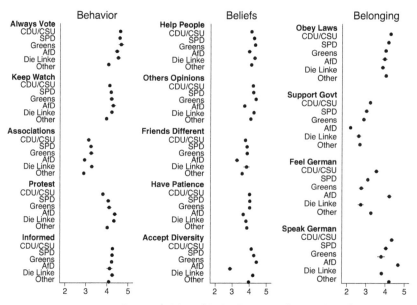

FIGURE 4.8. Items of citizenship in Germany, by partisanship

strong consensus when it comes to behavioral citizenship norms. That is, partisans of the left and right broadly evaluate attributes of behavior similarly. This is not the case for an outsider party like the AfD. It is an outlier for protesting ($\beta = 0.56$, $p = 0.00$), as it relies on protesting as a challenge party, having effectively used this as a messaging and mobilizing instrument and piggybacking off alliances with PEGIDA and their marches. The AfD also stands out as being weakly supportive of associational activity ($\beta = -0.26$, $p = 0.00$).

We also see little in the way of partisan differences when we turn to liberal democratic beliefs. Mainstream parties on the left and right are statistically indistinguishable across most items – both the "core" of mutual tolerance items (understanding others, friends that are different, and having patience) and even on items traditionally associated with left politics, namely, "help people" and "accept diversity." On this last item, Greens exhibit a modest amount of support than the CDU/CSU, but the latter is in line with the SPD and Die Linke. On each of these items, support from members of the illiberal AfD is lower. This is internally consistent; supporters of illiberal parties should not uphold liberal norms of good citizenship. Last, along with the AfD, Die Linke also expresses less patience, consistent with their status as a far left challenger party.

Finally, like in the British and the US case, items of belonging exhibit the most variation across party. On "feeling German," the CDU/CSU rank it as highly important, though – predictably – AfD members support this item even more, where anti-immigrant policies are a center-piece of their far right platform. By contrast, the SPD and Greens value this item of patriotism and belonging at a much lower level of import-ance. Moving to "speaking German," this has higher support across the board. The order of support (CDU, SPD, Greens) is the same, but all rate it at nearly an order of magnitude more important than "feeling German." The AfD also rates this item at a statistically higher rate than the CDU. "Support for government" is relatively low among all parties, and especially low for the AfD. Even among governing parties (CDU/CSU and SPD), supporters rate this norm as only moderately important. Last, the Greens, AfD, and Die Linke are all statistically less likely than the CDU to value "obeying laws." Recall that these last two items did not load strongly with other belonging items in the factor analysis in Chapter 3. That suggests it is more accurate to interpret these items as dispositional measures toward government as opposed to a characteristic of national belonging.

Having identified the partisan structure in citizenship norms cross-nationally, we see some generalizable patterns. First, the partisan left is more community- and solidarity-oriented; the partisan right values items of national belonging as more important than the partisan left. Second, we see more prominent partisan differences in the US and UK compared to Germany. Third, challenger parties on the left and right stand out for valuing protest as a norm of good citizenship. Last, and perhaps the most important for preserving democratic stability, there are behavioral and liberal democratic norms that endure across these differences. Essential commitments to behavioral items as well as norms of mutual tolerance prevail, which suggest a strong core of national unity in confronting democratic hard times.

4.6 PARTISANSHIP STRUCTURE OVER TIME

Our last descriptive task is to consider whether these areas of overlap and disagreement are a function of ideology or incumbency. In other words, how much of this partisan structure is a function of ideology or positional incentives? Parties in power may be less likely to support norms that recognize threat and disrupt the status quo, while parties out of power may be less supportive, tolerant, and patient of status quo practices. For example, system "losers" are more likely to think their vote makes a difference,[21] so they may also value voting as an attribute of good citizenship. More generally, citizens are likely to be more motivated to action when they face a government that espouses opposite views to their own.[22] Therefore, it is possible that some of the differences we observe in the 2019 survey data are not products of partisanship but in- versus out-of-power dynamics. Are these differences programmatic or a product of incumbency advantage? We can test this by looking at a time when the party in power is reversed, that is, when each of the case studies had a left government in power. Do we see similar patterns?

The longitudinal nature of ISSP data allows us to partially investigate this. As a point of comparison, I look at the 2004 Citizenship survey. In 2004, both Germany and the UK had left governments. Germany was led by Chancellor Gerhard Schröder of the Social Democrats (SPD), who led the federal government in coalition with the Greens. The UK was led by Labour Prime Minister Tony Blair. The US is the only case that does not have an ideologically different government. In 2003, Republicans controlled the executive branch (George W. Bush) and both legislative houses. While hyperpartisanship has made the Republican Party more conservative today than it was two decades ago, we can leverage comparisons to the UK as a hard test for positionality.

Comparison is also limited by availability of questions. Though we cannot go back in time and add questions (e.g., test whether patience is an incumbency attribute), the available items asked in 2004 cover all three dimensions. Thus, we can examine whether there is an underlying partisan structure or in/out government dynamics on behavioral (always vote, keep watch on government, join associations), beliefs (help people, understand opinions of others), and even belonging (obey laws), though this is a very weak dimension of belonging (especially for Germany) and excludes core items on national identity.

Figure 4.9 presents the predictive ratings of citizenship norms by party, conditional on other covariates. We observe neither a partisan structure nor an in/out structure across the six items of good citizenship. The only partisan difference that we observe in citizenship norms is in helping people worse off than you. Across the US, UK, and Germany, this is the

---

[21] Anderson et al., *Losers' Consent: Elections and Democratic Legitimacy*, 40–7.

[22] John R. Hibbing and Elizabeth Theiss-Morse, *Stealth Democracy: Americans' Beliefs About How Government Should Work* (New York, NY: Cambridge University Press, 2002).

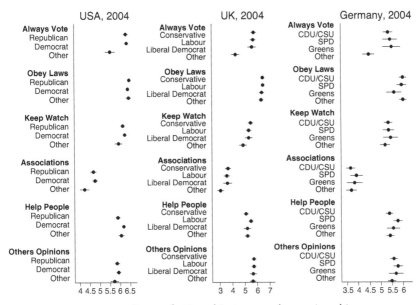

FIGURE 4.9 Items of citizenship in 2004, by partisanship

only significant difference between parties on the left (more likely) and right (less likely). While there are more differences in the 2019 data – due in no small part to the addition of more items – we see the same differences replicated from 2004. Therefore, we can rule out that partisan citizenship is simply or only a function of government positionality. Instead, it points to something far more concerning, which informs the next several chapters: there is something fundamentally different about citizenship in hard times, that is, when citizens are confronted with democratic threat.

4.7 CONCLUSION

In this chapter, consistent with our understanding of citizenship, we saw strong and consistent partisan differences held together by common principles, where both the partisan left and right in all three cases embrace core values as part of everyday citizenship. This is good news: the liberal democratic core, as well as a handful of behavioral dimensions of good citizenship, is widely shared by a state's citizenry. With this core in place, we may view the inevitable differences that result from partisanship to be less threatening or divisive and, indeed, a natural feature of diverse and democratic societies.

There are several lessons to take away from these observations. First, if we look beyond protesting, there are few differences between the left and right when it comes to engaged citizenship. This suggests that the traditional view of citizenship that only focuses on behavior would miss important differences between citizens and across advanced democracies, differences that may matter for how citizens confront hard times. Second, there is a deep core of agreement when it comes to liberal democratic values. Commitments to core values uphold cross-cutting ties. Mutual tolerance requires *mutuality;* both sides must be at the table as part of an intentional practice of forbearance. These are the "soft guardrails" that keep democracy in line. That they are present in everyday citizenship is encouraging and suggests polarization may not be as corrosive as pundits or politicians fear.

However, we must balance these areas of agreement with partisan disagreements. While a mutual tolerance core prevails, we observe stark differences when it comes to community-oriented values. Across systems, the partisan left values helping others and accepting diversity and the partisan right embraces allegiant values of national belonging. These differences add up to a problematic baseline for national unity in any circumstance. Further, it identifies a tinderbox issue that strongly divides citizens along partisan lines and can be strategically invoked to mobilize partisan support. In short, in all three cases, the main difference between citizens is about identity. The implications are troubling. Simply put, it leaves open the possibility that politicizing diversity or immigration at any point can exacerbate existing divisions.[23] It also means any issue – from economic inequality to racial injustice – can easily slip into a question of belonging where there are already clear differences between sides. Political conflicts become fused with questions of "who belongs" and deservingness.

We see the fewest differences overall in Germany, consistent with the proposition that a consensus-based system is better at reining in partisanship when it comes to core system values. On items of behavior and beliefs, where gaps exist, they are much smaller between the CDU and SPD than between the Republicans and Democrats or between the Conservatives and Labour. This is an extension of positive-sum games, which reduces dissensus through multiple iterations and greater mutual gains.

---

[23] Sara Wallace Goodman, "Immigration Threat, Partisanship, and Democratic Citizenship: Evidence from the US, UK, and Germany." *Comparative Political Studies* (2021), Online first, https://doi.org/10.1177/0010414021997165.

But what does this tell us about democratic hard times? If the latent structure of good citizenship is where partisan differences coexist but are held in check by a liberal democratic and behavioral core, what happens when partisanship gets activated? In normal circumstances, we seldom see these differences because civic obligation is composed of latent attitudes – intermittently activated to solve community problems or during elections. But when a democratic crisis is added to the story, these differences can become stark, or the core could corrode. What happens if differences become amplified or, even worse, if the liberal core weakens? It is to these central questions that we now turn.

5

The Threat of Polarization

How does democratic threat affect citizenship norms? What we have seen in Chapter 4 is that citizenship is structured in distinctly partisan ways, while bound together by an overlapping core of behavioral norms and mutual tolerance. Specifically, while the partisan left expresses greater support for helping people and accepting diversity and the partisan right expresses support for belonging items, these differences are balanced by a shared set of overlapping commitments to citizenship norms. This overlap is integral for democratic stability (Chapter 2). And while difference are part and parcel to everyday citizenship, they are also costless and latent. What happens when citizens are confronted with democratic threat? Do partisan differences endure? Do new ones emerge? Does the center of overlapping values hold?

Here we pivot to the context of democratic crisis directly, to examine the consequences of partisan citizenship in hard times. I embedded a vignette survey experiment in each national survey to see how citizens' views of obligation changes when we focus their attention on democratic threat. A block-randomized subset of each sample received a vignette about two types of democratic threat – polarization and foreign interference in elections. Variation in type of threat captures vital differences for testing the effects of positional incentives on citizenship norms. First, it varies citizen agency, where polarization is a type of problem a citizen can do something about while foreign interference affects distant institutions. Second, it also captures variation on status quo framing, for example, an election has explicit partisan winners (status quo beneficiaries) and losers (status quo challengers), while polarization relies on inferred status quo benefits.

These vignettes were followed by the fourteen items on what it means to be a 'good citizen.' In the broadest terms, we see that partisanship affects how individuals interpret and respond to both types of democratic threat. Individuals define citizenship norms by whether it benefits their side or not, mediated by institutional contexts that either encourage winning and losing or compromise. And, across both types of threats, it is status quo challengers that respond the most.

In this chapter, we look directly at polarization as a democratic threat. Polarization is the ideological distance between parties and factions, or the clustering of discernable groups on opposing sides. It can refer both to structural distance in the positions of political parties, or dispositions between individuals. Both usages recognize polarization as a feature of politics today that makes partisan identity a powerful one, though it makes societies more divided, and it, arguably, makes polities more susceptible to democratic erosion.

Polarization is a critical test for thinking about the role of positional incentives in democratic hard times. First, the positional incentives itself are unclear. It is unlike an election, where the winners and losers are evident. As such, this is a crucial case for citizens to identify status quo benefits or costs in responding to threat. Second, while it is a type of agentless problem (who causes polarization? Who is to blame?), it is one in which citizens can experience a high amount of agency in addressing. Polarization exists *among* citizens; recognizing and responding to the threat is not an exercise in futility. Third, polarization can be a slow-moving, protracted problem without a seeming cause and in which culpability can be diffuse or ignored. The point at which the condition of polarization *becomes* a threat or crisis may not be discernable *a priori*. It may be perceived not as a problem of democratic politics but a feature. This necessitates a strong threat frame for the experiment, to convince ordinary citizens that this condition presents real problems for democracy.

Here, I turn the lens around to invite citizens to reflect on the condition of polarization directly. Do citizens think polarization is a threat? Does it impact how they define good citizenship? Do we see individuals respond as democratic citizens or as partisans? We find respondents who receive the polarization treatment are significantly more vigilant ("watches the government") than the control group in all three countries. A disaggregated analysis by partisanship reveals that the effects of the polarization treatment differ between the left and right. In highly polarized, winner-take-all contexts, polarization may be framed as a shared problem, but only partisan left challengers mobilize to repair it. There are differences in *how* they respond across cases, but we only see significant changes to citizenship norms within this subset of respondents.

In the US, Democratic challengers support liberal democratic values more compared to Republicans, including the formerly shared items of mutual tolerance. Democrats also express greater importance in obeying the law and vigilance. Republicans, by comparison, do not lean into liberal democratic norms. Instead, they reduce support for obeying the law and associational life. These represent a turn away from the problem, not an effort to resolve it. Last, polarization does not mobilize either side to embrace other behavioral items of good citizenship, nor items of national belonging. This is consistent with an assumption of correspondence that citizens will respond to problems with appropriate solutions.

In the UK, the polarization treatment also induces an uneven response, though Labour challengers emphasize a different panel of items than the US. While challengers value mutual tolerance, they also are more likely to value items of national belonging, including support-ing government, speaking English and – along with Conservative sup-porters – feeling British. Labour supporters are also more likely to devalue accepting diversity. We see similar patterns of response if we look at Remain versus Leave as a salient political cleavage, where Remainers (system challengers) embrace mutual tolerance, vigilance, and items of national belonging. In this cleavage, Leavers (status quo beneficiaries) respond by devaluing diversity in response to polarization.

Last, Germany portrays the least asymmetry in citizen responses. This stands to reason; Germany is the least polarized of the three cases. Yet while the polarization treatment had no effect on belonging, it has small effects on liberal norms and substantively large effects on active citizen-ship. These findings are exhibited across the political spectrum. Supporters of parties both in and out of government are likely to increase the importance of vigilance and items of mutual tolerance. This is consist-ent with our expectation of how positive-sum systems work; they mitigate the likelihood of deep polarization by necessitating consensus, where and shared responses are less "costly." Looking specifically at partisanship, we can leverage the SPD – a left party in coalition government – to separate party ideology with system position. We see the left SPD and the right CDU – both in government – supporting items like 'understanding others' and protesting. We also see the SPD express distinct impatience with their long, costly position in government by rating items like 'obeying the law,' 'supporting government,' and 'voting' as less important in response to a polarization threat. Meanwhile, other left parties (Greens, DL) are highly mobilized on liberal democratic items along with the CDU.

In all, an analysis of the consequences of polarization in times of democratic crisis provides evidence that citizenship norms are filtered through the positional incentives offered by partisanship, even when the status quo incentives are not obvious. Uneven responses in majoritarian systems only exacerbate the conditions and dangers of polarization further. When only citizens on the left prioritize liberal values (US, UK), it reveals a worrying erosion of that cross-cutting, overlapping core of liberal values that is vital for preserving national unity and – as an extension – democratic stability. There seem to be few incentives for system incumbents and partisan right winners to alleviate the corrosive conditions of polarization. This may be good for their political allies, but bad for democracy. It also suggests that there are substantial obstacles in restoring national unity in hard times, a precondition for rebuilding a healthy democracy.

5.1 POLARIZATION AS A DEMOCRATIC THREAT

Democracy is inherently conflictual and competitive. However, increasing polarization has been found to decrease the likelihood that those of opposing viewpoints work together,[1] which is necessary for well-functioning democracy.[2] Under such circumstances, polarization is characterized not only by political difference, but also ingroup attachment and outgroup antipathy.[3] Democracy depends on the underlying norms that enable meaningful exercise of procedures of competition and participation. Thus, declining support for liberal norms among citizens erodes the foundation of democracy.

---

[1] Nicholas A. Valentino et al., "Is a Worried Citizen a Good Citizen? Emotions, Political Information Seeking, and Learning Via the Internet," *Political Psychology* 29, no. 2 (2008).

[2] Robert Dahl, *Pluralist Democracy in the United States: Conflict and Consent* (Chicago: IL Rand McNally, 1967).

[3] Iyengar, Sood, and Lelkes, "Affect, Not Ideology: A Social Identity Perspective on Polarization"; Mason, *Uncivil Agreement: How Politics Became Our Identity.*

Polarization is not always partisan; oftentimes, it is a coalescence of opinion-based differences, like over the Vietnam War,[4] Brexit,[5] or immigration. Polarization can occur around any issue-based axis, but partisanship is among the more threatening for democratic stability. This is because parties are the source of elite cueing and a coordinating device that channels individuals into participating in the political process.

Polarization is also not always inherently negative. When parties take distinct, nonoverlapping positions on issues, it makes choices clearer for citizens. This may fuel more participation, more engagement,[6] and it can be a "surprising" source of institution-building in new democracies.[7] Polarization is also useful if a political system contains nondemocratic or illiberal actors, as mainstream parties have the opportunity to distance themselves from far right parties as much as possible. Although, evidence suggests this does not happen. One of the more concerning pieces of evidence to emerge in European studies is that even left parties have found electoral gains in moving *toward* – instead of away from – far right actors.[8]

Putting polarization front and center means taking seriously its "pernicious" effects.[9] First and foremost, by increasing ingroup solidarity, polarization diminishes outgroup tolerance. This is consistent with the literature on the origins of affective polarization, which draws heavily on social identity theory.[10] This literature positions social group membership as a source of pride and identity. The strengthening of ingroup identification precedes intergroup differentiation between 'us' and 'them,' which, in

---

[4] Marc J. Hetherington, "Putting Polarization in Perspective," *British Journal of Political Science* 39, no. 2 (2009).

[5] Sara B. Hobolt, Thomas Leeper, and James Tilley, "Divided by the Vote: Affective Polarization in the Wake of the Brexit Referendum," Ibid. (2020).

[6] Nancy L. Rosenblum, *On the Side of the Angels: An Appreciation of Parties and Partisanship* (Princeton, NJ: Princeton University Press, 2010).

[7] Adrienne LeBas, "Can Polarization Be Positive? Conflict and Institutional Development in Africa," *American Behavioral Scientist* 62, no. 1 (2018).

[8] Jae-Jae Spoon and Heike Klüver, "Responding to Far Right Challengers: Does Accommodation Pay Off?," *Journal of European Public Policy* 27, no. 2 (2020). On the right, see Winston Chou et al., "Competing for Loyalists? How Party Positioning Affects Populist Radical Right Voting," *Comparative Political Studies* (2021), Online first, https://doi.org/10.1177/0010414021997166.

[9] McCoy and Somer, "Toward a Theory of Pernicious Polarization and How It Harms Democracies: Comparative Evidence and Possible Remedies."

[10] Tajfel et al., "Social Categorization and Intergroup Behaviour"; Tajfel and Turner, "An Integrative Theory of Intergroup Conflict"; John Turner and Henri Tajfel, *Social Identity and Intergroup Relations* (Cambridge, UK: Cambridge University Press, 1982).

turn, informs social comparison and competitive understandings of social relations.

Second, with diminished tolerance for outgroups, polarization severs the cross-cutting ties necessary to sustain democratic institutions; that is, it does not simply *distinguish* but *distances* "us" and "them." This affects several liberal democratic norms, by vacating a middle ground where compromise and consensus are possible. Democracy is based on disagreement, but only survives when sustained by cross-cutting avenues that *lower the stakes* of disagreement. If citizens exist in ideological silos where they only interact with other like-minded citizens and consume media that reinforces their existing worldviews, reconciling disagreement may be impossible. Citizens cannot confront evidence and opinions that may persuade them to change their views, making cooperation less likely.[11] As Bermeo describes, "when political actors polarize, the common ground required for democratic procedures and policy-making erodes." Thus when, for instance, social media networks function as siloing mechanisms, they are bad for democracy.[12] The most extreme consequence of this isolation was predicted early on by Seymour Lipset, that group conflicts might "solidify to the point where they threaten to disintegrate society."[13]

Last, polarization is not just the separation of groups while vacating the middle but the moralization of these differences as "good" versus "evil."[14] In other words, disagreement has become dislike. Again, democracy allows for and even thrives on disagreement, but not the vitriolic encampment of individuals "into several highly antagonistic groups."[15] Democratic crisis is likely where there is "limited consensus, deep cleavages" and, pointedly, "*suspicion* between leading participants"[16] (italics mine). In short, polarization threatens democracy,[17] and amounts to a democratic threat by reducing a citizen's willingness and, eventually,

---

[11] Giovanni Sartori, *Parties and Party Systems: A Framework for Analysis* (Cambridge: Cambridge University Press, 1977).

[12] David Runciman, *How Democracy Ends* (New York: Basic Books, 2018).

[13] Lipset, "Political Man: The Social Bases of Politics," 83.

[14] For this and further problems of polarization, see McCoy and Somer, "Toward a Theory of Pernicious Polarization and How It Harms Democracies: Comparative Evidence and Possible Remedies."

[15] Dahl, *Polyarchy: Participation and Opposition*, 105.

[16] Juan José Linz and Alfred C. Stepan, *The Breakdown of Democratic Regimes* (Baltimore, MD: Johns Hopkins University Press, 1978), 28.

[17] Achen and Bartels, *Democracy for Realists: Why Elections Do Not Produce Responsive Government*.

ability to work together to fend off authoritarian power grabs.[18] This, then, creates opportunities for leaders with authoritarian aspirations to mobilize around dividing cultural cleavages[19] and seize power.[20]

The evidence is overwhelming. Polarization is a real threat to democracy. Citizens may experience this in their day-to-day and believe it is normatively undesirable, but feel that the problem is intractable, a concern for elites, or that it has become a lasting feature of politics around which we adapt. Yet it is a democratic problem born of citizen (and elite) interactions and, thus, something that citizens can theoretically do something about.

5.1.1 Polarization in the US, UK, and Germany

Polarization is endemic to advanced democracy, but not all democracies experience the same *type* of polarization. The amount and specifics of polarization necessarily vary across cases. In terms of amount, the comparative literature on affective polarization reveals each of our case studies as experiencing decreasing degrees of polarization. (The US is highly polarized, the UK is moderately polarized, and Germany is negatively polarized.[21]) These differences create three possibilities. First, that we will see more concern for polarization in more polarized states. This may also suggest that responses to polarization will, in itself, be polarized and asymmetrical. Second, that more polarized states are more saturated and inured in polarization and thus unlikely to generate a substantively new reaction to this context as a threat, that is, reject the suggestion that the status quo constitutes a democratic threat. And third that polarization occurs along many dimensions – partisanship being but one – and that there is more variable polarization in each case than affective polarization by partisanship might show. Since the amount of polarization provides for these indeterminant predictions, we can flag this variation as a motivation for inductive analysis.

Moving from amount of polarization to specifics, each case has strong instances of different types of polarization. In the US, partisan

---

[18] Bermeo, *Ordinary People in Extraordinary Times: The Citizenry and the Breakdown of Democracy.*
[19] Norris and Inglehart, *Cultural Backlash: Trump, Brexit, and Authoritarian Populism.*
[20] Levitsky and Ziblatt, *How Democracies Die.*
[21] Boxell, Gentzkow, and Shapiro, "Cross-Country Trends in Affective Polarization."

polarization is ubiquitous.[22] It is quintessentially affective, resulting in mass-level animosity, incivility, loathe of opponents, distrust, and a decline of cross-cutting social identities.[23] These negative attitudes toward others reflect a dislike of opposing party support by strong partisan identifiers and, from the US's growing number of Independents, a dislike of partisanship more generally.[24] Outside of politics, affective polarization influences social interactions, including friendships and economic behavior.[25] Affective polarization makes it more difficult for citizens to collaborate and dialogue,[26] limits people's exposure to diverse opinions by creating partisan echo chambers,[27] and, therefore, inhibits people's ability to make decisions with multiple points of view and without prejudice.[28] For these reasons, partisan polarization in the US directly undermines pluralism, liberal norms, and democratic institutions.[29]

Outside of the US, we see opinion-based polarization that goes beyond partisanship, especially as party attachment is weaker. Americans are not unusually polarized in magnitude, they are just divided along a different cleavage to that of Western Europe.[30] In the UK, the sharpest political division during the time of the survey was the opinion-based cleavage between Leave and Remain.[31] These Brexit positions cut across party identification. A Pew Research Center poll in 2019 – three years after the referendum vote and during the still-ongoing, protracted Brexit

---

[22] Levendusky, *The Partisan Sort: How Liberals Became Democrats and Conservatives Became Republicans.*

[23] Mason, *Uncivil Agreement: How Politics Became Our Identity*; Iyengar, Sood, and Lelkes, "Affect, Not Ideology: A Social Identity Perspective on Polarization."

[24] Samara Klar, Yanna Krupnikov, and John Barry Ryan, "Affective Polarization or Partisan Disdain?: Untangling a Dislike for the Opposing Party from a Dislike of Partisanship," *Public Opinion Quarterly* 82, no. 2 (2018).

[25] For more, see Shanto Iyengar et al., "The Origins and Consequences of Affective Polarization in the United States," *Annual Review of Political Science* 22 (2019).

[26] MacKuen et al., "Civic Engagements: Resolute Partisanship or Reflective Deliberation."

[27] Levendusky, *How Partisan Media Polarize America.*

[28] Valentino et al., "Is a Worried Citizen a Good Citizen? Emotions, Political Information Seeking, and Learning Via the Internet."

[29] Levitsky and Ziblatt, *How Democracies Die*; Jennifer McCoy, Tahmina Rahman, and Murat Somer, "Polarization and the Global Crisis of Democracy: Common Patterns, Dynamics, and Pernicious Consequences for Democratic Polities," *American Behavioral Scientist* 62, no. 1 (2018).

[30] McCoy and Somer, "Toward a Theory of Pernicious Polarization and How It Harms Democracies: Comparative Evidence and Possible Remedies."

[31] Sara B. Hobolt, Thomas Leeper, and James Tilley, "Divided by the Vote: Affective Polarization in the Wake of Brexit," *American Political Science Association, Boston* (2018).

proceedings – Conservative party supporters voted 60 percent to Leave (29 percent Remain), while 20 percent of Labour supporters voted to Leave (53 percent Remain), and Lib Dem supporters voting Leave at 12 percent (70 percent Remain).[32] Support for Leave was not cleanly tied to party, but rather to attitudes toward immigration and national sovereignty, as well as a variety of economic and regional factors.[33]

In proportional representative and multiparty systems, we expect high issue polarization (where parties hold distinct and distant positions on policy) but low political polarization, as their system requires consensus and coalition-building to govern. The SPD commitment to the grand coalition, despite declining support related to its participation, is no better evidence of the effects of the culture of consensus on reducing polarized outcomes. As compromise among traditional parties of the left and right creates a type of structural convergence instead of polarization, it undermines democracy in other ways. In this sense, reducing polarization decreases the distinctiveness of party positions and platforms. On the one hand, this creates opportunities for parties like the Greens to pick up supporters but, at the same time, this also means radical parties can credibly compete on the left (Die Linke) and the right (AfD), moving into unoccupied issue areas.[34] In fact, where one observes issue polarization, like immigration or the environment, for example, smaller parties like the Greens and the AfD can gain a real foothold.[35] This, arguably, creates more polarization, as party positioning becomes more distinct and issues like migration make both the left-wing and right-wing extremes even stronger.

In Germany, we can also talk about polarization to discuss social dimensions, where division is seen as a grave risk to social solidarity

---

[32] Pew Research Center. "Brexit Divides the UK, but Partisanship and Ideology Are Still Key Factors", available at https://www.pewresearch.org/fact-tank/2019/10/28/brexit-divides-the-uk-but-partisanship-and-ideology-are-still-key-factors (accessed February 8, 2021). For Leave vote in my sample, I have Conservative voters at 65 percent (N = 720); 30 percent of Labour voters (N = 297); 20 percent of Lib Dem voters (N = 54), and 85 percent of UKIP voters (N = 187).

[33] Sara B. Hobolt, "The Brexit Vote: A Divided Nation, a Divided Continent," *Journal of European Public Policy* 23, no. 9 (2016).

[34] Jae-Jae Spoon and Christopher J. Williams, "'It's the Economy, Stupid': When New Politics Parties Take on Old Politics Issues," *West European Politics* 44, no. 4 (2021): 802–24.

[35] In fact, issue ownership has been a key explanation for the decline in mainstream party support. Jae-Jae Spoon and Heike Klüver, "Party Convergence and Vote Switching: Explaining Mainstream Party Decline across Europe," *European Journal of Political Research* 58, no. 4 (2019).

and *sozialer Zusammenhalt*, or social cohesion. According to a study by Bertelsmann Foundation, social cohesion in Germany is strong but at risk, particularly in poor areas with high unemployment and lower levels of educational attainment.[36] This threat to social cohesion is most comparable to the status quo of polarization in other cases, but reflects a concern that is salient to the German mass public. Perhaps this sentiment is best reflected in German President Walter Steinmer's 2018 Christmas speech:

"Wherever you look – especially on social media – we see hate; there is shouting and daily outrage. ... I feel that we Germans are spending less and less time talking to each other. And even less time listening to each other ... What happens when societies drift apart, and when one side can barely talk to the other without it turning into an all-out argument, is all too evident in the world around us. I believe it's good for us to engage in debate; it's good for us to talk to each other. If I had one wish for our country, then it would be: Let's have more debate."[37]

Thus, the problem of polarization can be effectively characterized as a problem of weak social ties, threatening to unravel a fabric of cohesion across different groups. It does not exist to the extent we see in the US or UK (consistent with comparative studies and the decreasing scales of polarization), but it is on the horizon and a problem familiar to Germans.

5.1.2 Theoretical Expectations

Moving to theoretical expectations, a citizen-centered theory of democratic instability would predict individuals respond to polarization as partisans, adjusting their expectations of what they should do based on positional incentives. The substance of these responses may vary according to the type of threat, but the predicted responses should be overall consistent with power incentives and institutional context.

However, unlike an election or a far right populist party surge, it is not entirely predictable who the "winners" and "losers" of polarization are. No side is explicitly "called out" to feel defensive about polarization, though each side is likely to blame the other for becoming more extreme.

---

[36] Bertelsmann Foundation. "Radar Gesellschaftlicher Zusammenhalt". Available at www.bertelsmann-stiftung.de/fileadmin/files/BSt/Publikationen/GrauePublikationen/GP_Radar_Gesellschaftlicher_Zusammenhalt.pdf (accessed November 18, 2020).

[37] Deutsche Welle, "Frank-Walter Steinmeier: Our Democracy is as Strong as We Make it." Available at www.dw.com/en/frank-walter-steinmeier-our-democracy-is-as-strong-as-we-make-it/a-46849802 (accessed November 4, 2020).

Nor does polarization inevitably produce partisanship.[38] Both sides may feel aggrieved by division, especially if individuals are strongly committed to liberal democratic values (as we saw cross-nationally in Chapter 3), but not all parties may see incentives in repairing divisions. But polarization is not just a condition that keeps citizens apart. In hollowing out the middle ground of overlapping values, polarization makes cooperation harder. Thus, it is not just a democratic problem; it makes existing problems worse by limiting the range of reparative responses. When incumbent costs and challenger benefits are not obvious, we can expect status quo incentives to predominate.

But how does this account align with explanations for how citizens respond to polarization more generally? The wider literatures on polarization and tolerance offer useful evidence for thinking about theoretical prediction along the dimensions of citizenship norms. First, a decline in democratic norms like tolerance[39] and fairness[40] traditionally coincide with xenophobia and outgroup discrimination. This finding is consistent in fields that examine group conflict, from race and ethnic politics to immigration studies.[41] Overall, group threat leads individuals to "hunker down," preferring their own ingroup over others.[42] Moreover, this process is self-reinforcing—polarization begets more polarization. While exposure to diversity can moderate tolerance[43], perception on its own

---

[38] Hetherington, "Putting Polarization in Perspective."

[39] Michael Tesler, "The Return of Old-Fashioned Racism to White Americans' Partisan Preferences in the Early Obama Era," *The Journal of Politics* 75, no. 1 (2012); Nazita Lajevardi and Marisa Abrajano, "How Negative Sentiment toward Muslim Americans Predicts Support for Trump in the 2016 Presidential Election," *The Journal of Politics* 81, no. 1 (2018); John Sides, Michael Tesler, and Lynn Vavreck, *Identity Crisis: The 2016 Presidential Campaign and the Battle for the Meaning of America* (Princeton, NJ: Princeton University Press, 2018).

[40] David C. Wilson and Paul R. Brewer, "The Foundations of Public Opinion on Voter Id Laws: Political Predispositions, Racial Resentment, and Information Effects," *Public Opinion Quarterly* 77, no. 4 (2013); Jacob Appleby and Christopher M. Federico, "The Racialization of Electoral Fairness in the 2008 and 2012 United States Presidential Elections," *Group Processes & Intergroup Relations* 21, no. 7 (2018).

[41] For early work in these fields, see Herbert Blumer, "Race Prejudice as a Sense of Group Position," *Pacific Sociological Review* 1, no. 1 (1958); Lincoln Quillian, "Prejudice as a Response to Perceived Group Threat: Population Composition and Anti-Immigrant and Racial Prejudice in Europe," *American Sociological Review* 60, no.4 (1995): 586–611.

[42] This insight dates back to early psychology work that shows threat-induced anxiety produced dogmatism and intolerance. Milton Rokeach, "The Open and Closed Mind," (1960); Sullivan, Piereson, and Marcus, *Political Tolerance and American Democracy*.

[43] George E. Marcus et al., *With Malice toward Some: How People Make Civil Liberties Judgments* (New York, NY: Cambridge University Press, 1995).

induces negative outgroup attitudes, like xenophobia[44], which produces further isolation from those groups.

The very suggestion that polarization needs to be addressed may be perceived as threatening to ingroup status, forcing status quo beneficiaries into defensive positions.[45] This is particularly the case in majoritarian systems, which inevitably produces "sideism" on most issues. But group threat accounts would typically attribute this defensive response to cultural majorities more generally when the outgroup is immigrant or minority groups. It becomes more difficult to parse when the problem is shared between citizens and the outgroup is defined by partisanship. Here, out-of-power partisans may rally, taking the shape of more liberal democratic values or more acceptance of diversity, while status quo preservers may exhibit the opposite, in which belonging attributes become more important. But a response can be an ingroup defense of values without being nationalistic. These are not necessarily the same thing.

Thus, we expect status quo challengers to become more activated to address problems of polarization, elevating the importance of liberal norms like mutual tolerance (understanding the opinions of others or maintain ties with friends with different political views). While this may include items of national belonging, we primarily expect status quo challenger citizens to respond to polarization, when framed as a democratic threat, with more liberal democratic values (consistent with the assumption of rational correspondence). Evidence of this, while beneficial as a short-term solution to polarization – meeting the problem of intolerance with more tolerance – is deeply problematic in the long-run, as this type of asymmetric response suggests a weakening of the core of values of *mutual* tolerance vital to democratic stability.

Finally, we would expect weakly polarized contexts to produce active norms that cross political and social identities. If the scenario itself does not *a priori* define status quo winners and losers, then citizens are less likely to take defensive or offensive positions. In contrast, hyper-polarized scenarios may lead to different response according to partisan or issue-based identities, where individuals not only object to polarization as a problem but "double down" by overcompensating in quiescence, that is, allegiant, patriotic norms in defense of their positional advantages.

---

[44] Daniel J. Hopkins, John Sides, and Jack Citrin, "The Muted Consequences of Correct Information About Immigration," *The Journal of Politics* 81, no. 1 (2019).
[45] Mason, *Uncivil Agreement: How Politics Became Our Identity.*

5.2 DATA AND METHODOLOGY

To test the effects of polarization on citizenship norms, I embedded a survey experiment into the three country surveys, using a vignette on polarization to prime respondents to think about its democratic implications. Vignette experiments manipulate the *salience* of democratic crisis in the minds of survey respondents. This purpose is important: polarization in itself is a fact of life and a type of ambient condition, so raising the salience of this threat is less of a traditional manipulation (i.e., to convince or change one's mind) than it is a means to focus a respondent's attention on a real-life event. It does so not only by providing a random sample of respondents the opportunity to read about polarization but also by presenting it as a democratic threat, utilizing elite framing to highlight specific implications for democracy.

Respondents were randomly assigned into four groups. One group received a vignette that discussed polarization, another on foreign interference in national elections (Chapter 6), a third group received a vignette on immigration,[46] and a control group received an apolitical vignette about diet and exercise.[47] To reinforce each vignette for the respondents, they were subsequently asked to "Please spend 30 seconds discussing the topic you just read" in an open-ended question. Respondents also were given a multiple-choice attention check to see that they had absorbed the content of the vignette. These were followed by the randomized, fourteen questions on attributes of a "good citizen." Thus, compared to the control group, which evaluates items of good citizenship in an everyday, apolitical context, each treatment group rated items in the context of a specific threat.

There is a trade-off involved in designing cross-national survey experiments. To make cross-national inferences, each vignette should be as close

---

[46] For more on this, see Goodman, "Immigration Threat, Partisanship, and Democratic Citizenship: Evidence from the US, UK, and Germany."

[47] US control: "Doctors recommend eating a healthy diet and exercise. The basics of a healthy diet include a mix of proteins, carbohydrates, and fats, plus enough vitamins and minerals for optimal health. Healthy choices include vegetables, fruit, whole grains, fat-free or low-fat dairy products. Unhealthy foods that should be limited include food with added sugar, saturated fats, and salt. Regular exercise can help you lose or maintain weight. If you do not have time to exercise, try parking farther away from work and walking, or using the stairs instead of an elevator." British control changes "parking farther away" to "getting off public transport a stop early" and "elevator" to "lift." German control is translated to German.

to one another as possible.[48] But, as discussed, the nature of polarization is context-specific. For vignettes to be effective, one must balance cross-national similarity with describing scenarios that are realistic and contextually appropriate. This means, at the same time, if we are to learn from comparisons across countries and if the goal is to prove the generalizability of findings, vignettes need to be consistent with one another, controlling for as much as possible. Erring on the side of treatments that are politically meaningful and nationally resonant, each polarization vignette shares a similar framework of describing the (nationally specific) problem, followed by a shared elite framing for why polarization contributes to a democratic crisis. But the details of the polarization vignette match the specific national context.

To test the effects of polarization as a crisis, I use the following three nationally salient polarization scenarios: the polarized partisan cleavage between Republicans and Democrats in the US, the polarized Brexit cleavage of Leave versus Remain in the UK, and nonpartisan concerns over social polarization and social cohesion in Germany. Imposing a binary, polarizing cleavage on Germany is not appropriate or as self-evident in the absence of an event to define it (e.g., Brexit, an election). The approach I take here, then, is not to force a division but to allow several potential divisions of social cohesion to play out. This makes Germany the most inductive case of the three.

In all, national differences require the vignettes about polarization to vary in type. For the US, the domestic democratic threat vignette on polarization reads as follows:

Political polarization – the wide and growing gap between liberals and conservatives – is a critical problem in the United States. Lawmakers are increasingly unable to reach bipartisan compromise. The public, too, is growing intolerant of opposing views – reading news and maintaining social ties that confirm their beliefs, rather than exposing them to differences of opinions.

---

[48] There are not many examples of cross-national experimental research, but for some examples, see: Scott Blinder, Robert Ford, and Elisabeth Ivarsflaten, "Discrimination, Antiprejudice Norms, and Public Support for Multicultural Policies in Europe: The Case of Religious Schools," *Comparative Political Studies* 52, no. 8 (2019): 1232–55; Maria Sobolewska, Silvia Galandini, and Laurence Lessard-Phillips, "The Public View of Immigrant Integration: Multidimensional and Consensual. Evidence from Survey Experiments in the UK and the Netherlands," *Journal of Ethnic and Migration Studies* 43, no. 1 (2017); Jennifer L. Merolla and Elizabeth J. Zechmeister, "Threat and Information Acquisition: Evidence from an Eight Country Study," *Journal of Experimental Political Science* 5, no. 3 (2018).

Many experts fear these developments undermine our country. As the chief researcher at the National Policy Institute (a leading, bipartisan think tank) states, "Polarization has made our nation into tribes, unwilling to debate and ready to win at any cost. This is a democratic crisis for our country."

The second paragraph includes expert framing to specifically convey the relevant effects of polarization for democracy, as opposed to other consequences of polarization. Elite framing highlights integral components of the passage and invokes a psychological process that invites individuals to deliberately think about the issue at hand.[49] Moreover, while the passage includes references to both politicians and experts, Alberston and Gadarian find that politicians are rated like experts in times of crisis,[50] thus mitigating concerns that individuals are responding not to the threat but expressing attitudes about politicians more generally.

The UK vignette begins similarly, changing the axis of polarization from partisanship to issue-based Leave/Remain, but adds more detail on the nature of Brexit as seen through the lens of polarization (i.e., gridlock in Parliament, politicians enriching themselves, intimations of the rise of the Brexit party). Brexit – on its own – may be interpreted simply as incompetence or mendacity. But the challenge here was to describe how the problems of "delivering" Brexit reflect a democratic threat, reinforced by the elite framing in the second paragraph:

Political polarisation – like the wide and growing gap between Remainers and Leavers – is a critical problem in British politics. Politicians are increasingly unable to reconcile differences and legislate, with Westminster in unprecedented chaos. The public, too, is growing intolerant of opposing views – reading news and maintaining social ties that confirm their beliefs, rather than exposing them to differences of opinions. And as political elites put their needs before those of the nation, everyday citizens are coming to distrust traditional parties and seek out more extreme alternatives.

Many experts fear these developments undermine our country. As the chief researcher at the National Policy Institute (a leading, nonpartisan think tank) states, "Polarisation has transformed our nation into tribes, reflecting sharp divisions in core values. In this environment, we are unwilling to debate or reach a middle ground, and ready to win at any cost. This is a democratic crisis for our country."

---

[49] Thomas E. Nelson, Zoe M. Oxley, and Rosalee A. Clawson, "Toward a Psychology of Framing Effects," *Political Behavior* 19, no. 3 (1997).
[50] Albertson and Gadarian, *Anxious Politics: Democratic Citizenship in a Threatening World*.

Finally, the German prompt bears a strong similarity to the British vignette. It reads (in translation[51]):

Political polarization and the breakdown of social cohesion is a critical problem in German politics. Political parties are no longer interested in consensus, stability, and compromise. The public, too, is growing isolated and intolerant of opposing views—reading news and maintaining social ties that confirm their beliefs, rather than exposing them to differences of opinions.

Many experts fear these developments undermine our country. As the chief researcher at the Federal Institute for Policy Research (a leading, nonpartisan think tank) states, "Polarization has transformed our nation, reflecting sharp divisions in core values. In this environment, we are unwilling to debate or reach common ground, and are ready to win at any cost. That puts social cohesion at risk. This is a democratic crisis for our country."

In what follows, I present statistical analyses to test the effect of a polarization crisis on civic norms. The baseline (OLS) models regress a binary indicator for the polarization treatment T on outcome Y. To improve efficiency, I also estimate extended statistical models that adjust for the following pretreatment variables: age, race (or, in the case of Germany, immigrant-origin), gender, region, and level of education.[52] I estimate robust standard errors throughout.

The dependent variables in each model are the fourteen items of good citizenship ("How important is it for a good citizen to...?"), as presented in detail in Chapter 3. Higher values correspond to more support for that

[51] Die politische Polarisierung und der Zerfall des sozialen Zusammenhalts sind kritische Probleme in der deutschen Politik. Politische Parteien interessieren sich nicht mehr für Konsens, Stabilität und Kompromiss. Auch die Bevölkerung isoliert sich zunehmend und wird weniger tolerant gegenüber Andersdenkenden: man liest Nachrichten und pflegt Kontakt mit denen, die eigenen Meinungen bestätigen, anstatt sich mit Andersdenkenden auseinanderzusetzen.

Viele Experten befürchten, dass unser Land dadurch geschwächt wird. So meinte der leitende Wissenschaftler des Bundesinstituts für Politikforschung, eines der führenden unabhängigen Forschungsinstitute: "Die Polarisierung hat unser Land umgestaltet und tiefe Spaltungen entlang unserer grundlegenden Werte entblößt. In diesem Klima sind die Menschen immer weniger bereit, miteinander zu diskutieren oder Gemeinsamkeiten zu finden, und wollen stattdessen um jeden Preis ihre eigene Meinung durchsetzen. Der Zusammenhalt in Deutschland ist gefährdet. Das ist eine Krise der Demokratie für unser Land."

[52] Adjustments follow the recommendations in Lin Winston Lin, "Agnostic Notes on Regression Adjustments to Experimental Data: Reexamining Freedman's Critique," *The Annals of Applied Statistics* 7, no. 1 (2013), with every model taking the form of a regression of Y on T, X, and $T * X$, where X is a set of mean-centered covariates $(X_i - \bar{X})$. Income was excluded as it reduces the overall sample size by 10% (of respondents who "prefer not to say" their income). As a control, its effect is largely captured by education, and including does not change the results (on file with author).

item of good citizenship. While these variables can be shown to reflect distinct factors or dimensions of democratic citizenship (e.g., behavioral, belief, and belonging), I study them here individually so we can observe the norms that are important in the face of democratic threat. Recall also that we have general expectations that citizens respond like partisans in hard times per side incentives, but also of correspondence, where *threat type* may produce differences in the size and substance of those responses. This necessitates a granular look at citizenship norms.

Each figure in the results section presents coefficient plots for the covariate adjusted effects of receiving the polarization treatment on norms for each of the fourteen items.[53] The rows present items by grouping them within general dimensions of citizenship – behavior (acts of good citizens), beliefs (commitments to a variety of liberal democratic norms), and belonging (attributes of allegiance and membership) – as a heuristic aid for thinking conceptually and categorically. These figures plot the treatment effects estimated from the OLS regressions in the extended models. The dot represents the regression coefficient, and the horizontal line maps its 95% confidence interval. Each dot thus compares respondents who received the treatment to the control group. Recalling that the dependent variable varies along a scale of 1–5, the x-axis measures the difference in average responses between the treatment group and the control group.

5.3 RESULTS

Polarization threat reveals strong differences in how the partisan right versus partisan left interprets civic obligation in hard times. Consistent with theoretical expectation, we see an unevenness in citizen response, where status quo challengers update citizenship norms in response to threat, while incumbent status quo beneficiaries withdraw or remain unaffected. Overall, we observe the partisan left in the US and UK increase their valuation of liberal democratic norms, while in Germany

---

[53] Baseline summary statistics available in Appendix I. I report here covariate-adjusted models. I analyzed the results using both unadjusted and adjusted regression because there was an imbalance in the treatment assignment by age in Germany. Further information on balance in experimental assignment (assessed by a multinomial logistic regression) is available with the author. As parties are noncomparable across samples, adjustment is by gender, age, region, and amount of college education. Unadjusted results are on file with author but are broadly consistent with adjusted results. Full models and robustness checks on file with author.

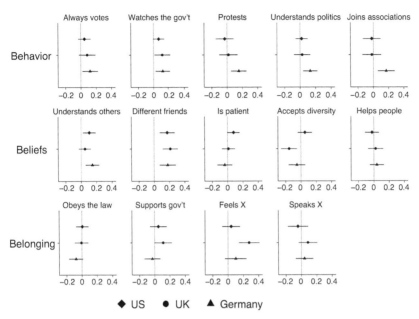

FIGURE 5.1. Polarization treatment effects

we observe this uptick from a plurality of respondents supporting both in- and out-of-government parties. By comparison, we observe much more asymmetry in our majoritarian case studies. As a caveat, we may not be able to infer from one consensus-based case that positive-sum politics *produce* a shared response, but we can infer from comparison that different positional incentives (with zero-sum games) produce more asymmetry in citizenship responses.

Beginning with aggregate results, Figure 5.1 presents general results for the US (diamond point; top row of each plot), the UK (dot point; middle row), and Germany (triangle point; bottom row). We see that the polarization vignette significantly affects citizenship norms in aggregate, that is, before we look at responses by partisanship. First, across the three countries, polarization makes individuals on average increasingly value vigilance ("watch the government") and tolerance (valuing "friends with different opinions"). This is an important finding. Polarization is, at its core, a problem of liberal democracy – the straining of cross-cutting ties. That, citizens provide a rational response to democratic threat by emphasizing key attributes of liberalism is evidence of internal validity of the experiment, as well as it illustrates the correspondence assumption of the theory. This is what democratic citizens are supposed to do and *can* do.

But, substantively, it is worth noting that polarization not only motivates citizens to value tolerance, but that within-group or horizontal tension sensitizes people to vertical distrust. This is an unequivocally liberal response to crisis in all three cases – but, importantly, one oriented away from fellow citizens and toward democratic institutions.

Beyond these similarities, we see major differences cross-nationally. Beginning with the US, in addition to "watches government" and "different friends," we see two other items of mutual tolerance activated in response to the polarization threat. That "understanding others" and "is patient" also become statistically significant is strong evidence that polarization increases the importance of mutual tolerance values. This appears encouraging: being made aware of political polarization as a problem activates the shared, overlapping core of liberal democratic values.

We see specific differences between the UK and Germany. In the UK, effects of polarization on citizenship norms are wider and more varied across behavioral, belief, and belonging-based citizenship norms. While valuing vigilance and tolerance, British respondents also offset this with illiberalism (devaluing acceptance of diversity and feeling British). Finally, the effects of polarization in Germany look different to the majoritarian cases, where in addition to two items of mutual tolerance becoming significant ("understanding others" and "different friends"), information on social polarization in a low-polarized context leads to a strong, behavioral norm response. All five engaged citizenship variables are statistically significant. Moreover, none of the major items of belonging are significant, despite a framing of polarization as a problem of declining social cohesion.[54]

What do these aggregate results look like when we consider partisanship and status quo incentives? Do the effects endure across groups, or are they driven by one group versus another? I now turn to explore each of these cases in more detail, examining the role of positional incentives in responding to democratic threat by disaggregating responses by partisanship and opinion-based cleavages.

5.3.1 United States

The aggregate results indicate that American respondents embrace a liberal democratic citizenship in response to polarization, in which items

---

[54] Note: "Obeying laws" approaches significance in the negative direction for Germany ($p = 0.10$), a puzzling result in aggregate.

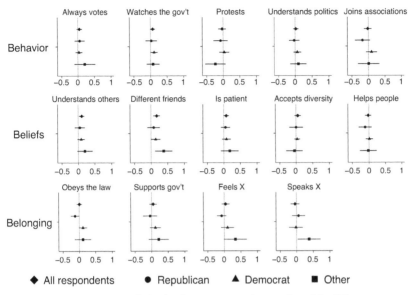

FIGURE 5.2. Polarization treatment by partisanship, US

of mutual tolerance feature prominently. However, when disaggregating these effects by partisanship, we see that these effects are entirely driven by non-Republicans (i.e., Democrats and others). In other words, all the liberal attributes significant in aggregate are driven by positional outsiders. In Figure 5.2, we see Democrats statistically significant on the items of vigilance ("watches the government," p = 0.04), two items of mutual tolerance (also significant among the category of others), and – interestingly – in "obeying the law." That is, information on polarization not only makes status quo challengers more likely to support watching government but also makes them increasingly value obeying the law. Thus, in Democratic responses, we see two dispositions increase: mutual tolerance and system, or vertical affect.

These last two items of vertical affect – "watching the government" and "obeying the law" – are a good illustration of divided responses by partisanship. Where status quo challengers (Democrats) increase in vigilance in response to threat, polarization has no significant effect on status quo beneficiaries (Republicans). And where Democratic outsiders are more likely to value obeyance in response to polarization (p = 0.08), Republican incumbent supporters express the opposite sentiment (p = 0.04). This expression is a type of hunkering down, but we do not see changing support for any other attributes associated with homogenous preferences (e.g., speaking English, rejecting diversity).

Overall, we see little effect of polarization on evaluation of civic obligation among status quo winners in the US. That is, there were two possible predictions for how status quo incumbents would react: defensively or not at all. This appears to confirm the latter. And while MacKeun et al. hypothesize that aversion elicits allegiant sentiment,[55] it has instead produced a series of null results, suggesting that citizenship for Republicans is stable in a status quo environment, despite framing that highlights the corrosive, regime-level consequences of polarization. Again, it is not to say that belonging or liberal dimensions of citizenship do not matter but that status quo beneficiaries are not uniquely moved by the problem of polarization.

There is a further test we can conduct to see whether partisan winners experience differential treatment effects, where they reject the premise of the prime altogether. I conducted an objection analysis to assess whether respondents agreed with the treatment. Recall that just after exposure to the polarization vignette, respondents were given thirty seconds to "discuss the topic" they just read. Again, on a functional level, this served to reinforce the vignette by encouraging them to concentrate for an extended period of time on polarization as a democratic threat. But these open-ended responses also provide an opportunity to assess their views of the treatment.

Open-ended responses were coded based on two categories: attention (whether the respondent could recall the topic of the vignette) and objection (whether the respondent objected to polarization as a democratic crisis, or whether they objected to the fact of polarization as a condition of, in this case, American political life).[56] Open-ended responses echoed overwhelming agreement. In fact, only 12 percent of Republican supporters objected to the vignette (N = 33), while only 8 percent of non-Republican (including Democrats, Democratic leaners, third-party supports, and others) respondents in total objected to polarization (N = 42). One respondent agreed, "Never have I seen the country so divided. Everyone has their own opinion, and for them, they are not bending or

[55] MacKuen et al., "Civic Engagements: Resolute Partisanship or Reflective Deliberation."
[56] Each respondent was coded three times, randomized across a team of thirteen coders. For attention, coders agreed in 89.5 percent of the cases (Kappa = 0.620). For objection, coders agreed in 81.8 percent of the cases (Kappa = 0.572).

listening." While many respondents were quick to blame one side or the other ("Democrat party has shown over and over again they have no interest in bipartisan solution" and "Republican voters vote with their racist views, instead of the good of the country"), blame was a feature of acknowledging the problem, not part of a treatment objection. Other responses reflect the difficulty of solving this problem; where some called for centrism ("we need neutral parties and candidates that neither lean hard right or left"), others rejected it ("politically responsible citizens should strive to take in viewpoints from other sides. At the same time, it can be dangerous to insist on centrism and to draw a false equivalency between two sides").

Reflecting on citizenship norms patterns, we can conclude that polarization is less threatening – and therefore less consequential – to everyday partisan winners. Or, more worrying, perhaps status quo recipients have become habituated to hyper-partisanship and no longer see polarization as an imminent democratic threat. By contrast, we see status quo challengers respond to threat by increasing the importance of both mutual tolerance and system skepticism.

5.3.2 United Kingdom

In the UK, given that the axis of polarization is Brexit, we look at citizenship norms by both partisanship and voter choice on Brexit. Beginning with partisanship, in Figure 5.3 we see a similar pattern to the US, in that the mobilizing effects of polarization are largely visible among the political left. Labour supporters, along with other status quo challengers, drive the aggregate finding on tolerance ("different friends"). But we also observe a notable – and concerning – difference: These same partisan outsiders are *also* driving the significant decrease in support for diversity and increase in items of national belonging. At the partisan level, we see Labour supporters devaluing diversity, an increased importance in speaking English, and feeling British. "Support government" is also significant (p = 0.04), which could either be an expression of positive system affect (like in the US case) or, because of strong significance for other belong items, another correlate of belonging, suggesting an allegiant citizen is important in response to polarization.

What do we make of this? Polarization makes Labour supporters and other non-Conservatives both tolerant (to insiders) and intolerant (to diversity). While the principle itself may seem contradictory, we can

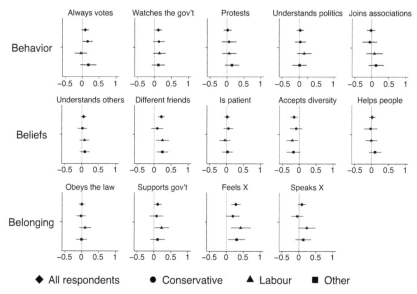

FIGURE 5.3. Polarization treatment by partisanship, UK

reconcile these differences as a type of liberal chauvinism: tolerance for other insiders (e.g., British) but intolerance for outsiders. This is not only consistent with the unique, European bundling of liberal politics with exclusionary immigration attitudes but specifically resonant of the positions of Jeremy Corbyn, which have been characterized as populist[57] and radically anticapitalist.[58] Last, this strong ethnocentrism on the political left and right is highly characteristic of "Brexitland" Britain. Not only is ethnocentrism a core feature of political conflict in postwar Britain, as Sobolewksa and Ford detail, the referendum itself represented a "moment of awakening," mobilizing identity along new cleavages including divides in education, age, and ethnicity.[59]

Turning to partisan right winners, Conservative supporters exhibit two significant changes. "Feeling British" (p = 0.07) is significant, alongside status quo challengers, as well as the importance of voting (p = 0.05). It is

---

[57] Jake Watts and Tim Bale, "Populism as an Intra-Party Phenomenon: The British Labour Party under Jeremy Corbyn," *The British Journal of Politics and International Relations* 21, no. 1 (2019).

[58] Paul Whiteley et al., "Oh Jeremy Corbyn! Why Did Labour Party Membership Soar after the 2015 General Election?," Ibid.

[59] Maria Sobolewska and Robert Ford, *Brexitland: Identity, Diversity and the Reshaping of British Politics* (Cambridge UK: Cambridge University Press, 2020), 3.

notable that where we saw Americans respond to polarization with liberal democratic norms, we see British respondents react with national identity items, and a comparatively muted liberal response. Positional incentives account for *who* responds, but the *contents* of that response seem to reflect a type of preoccupation with identity that predominates during hard times. This is especially the case in European countries, where immigration and identity are durable features of party politics.

But, in addition to these asymmetric results, we also see a lot of null results. They are not altogether surprising, considering Brexit is an issue area that cuts across traditional party lines. As Hobolt et al. note, there is a large and growing body of literature on determinants of Brexit voting behavior, but "we know very little about the way in which the vote has divided people."[60] This requires looking at Brexit vote as a second, opinion-based cleavage driving polarization responses in the UK. It could be that citizens interpret positional incentives in response to addressing Brexit-related polarization not by supporting in-power versus challenger parties, but by whether they identify as issue winners or losers. The Brexit referendum occurred in 2016 but the process of "Brexiting" was ongoing at the time the survey was in the field. The protracted nature of Brexit may have increased the salience of this identity as a winner versus loser issue.

In Figure 5.4, Remainers (including abstainers) look like partisan left challengers – supporting vigilance, mutual tolerance, and items of allegiance. Likewise, Leavers look like partisan right winners, prioritizing "feeling British." Unlike the previous view of the partisan left, we do not see the anti-diversity effect among Remainers, though we do see it among Leavers. This observation stands out as an important departure from partisanship. Where Brexit positions are more mixed by partisanship, this view triangulates to support the argument that civic response to threat is about positional incentives, and not programmatic dimensions of partisanship.

Moreover, where a partisan lens revealed intolerance of diversity as a type of systemic factor of the majoritarian system structure, here we see this effect is prominent only among Leavers (issue insiders), consistent with widely acknowledged motives for voting for Brexit.[61] Unlike Leavers, who attribute their pro-referendum vote to motives like "regaining control" and "limiting immigration," British voters against

---

[60] Hobolt, Leeper, and Tilley, "Divided by the Vote: Affective Polarization in the Wake of Brexit."
[61] Hobolt, "The Brexit Vote: A Divided Nation, a Divided Continent."

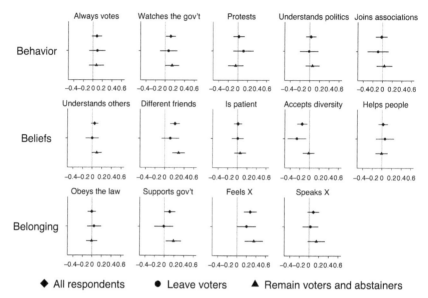

FIGURE 5.4. Polarization treatment by Brexit vote, UK

the referendum point to other factors, like the economy.[62] This is surprising because it also suggests there is not a ceiling effect in place for diversity intolerance.

Finally, I test whether polarization yields a differential treatment effect among British respondents who objected to the vignette.[63] Only 8 percent of respondents objected to polarization as a democratic crisis, and it was evenly divided between Leavers and Remainers. Further, citizenship norms were unaffected by objection. (All results were statistically insignificant.)

In looking more carefully at open-ended responses, blame attribution features prominently among Leavers. Accusations range from blaming Remainers ("The problem we are experiencing is that the Remainers are behaving like spoilt children. Once we leave they will have to accept the democratic result.") to experts and politicians ("Most people are just fed up with the politicians in general because they have not done what the

---

[62] Matthew Goodwin and Caitlin Milazzo, "Taking Back Control? Investigating the Role of Immigration in the 2016 Vote for Brexit," *The British Journal of Politics and International Relations* 19, no. 3 (2017).

[63] Coding was randomized across a team of seven coders. For objection, all three coders agreed in 85.09 percent of the cases (Kappa = 0.610). Full results are on file with author.

'people' voted for in leaving the EU.").[64] Other objects to polarization exhibit less emotion ("Although causing conflict, it's a sign of democracy if anything – people have a right to their own personal opinion, are aware of that right and exercise it.").[65]

5.3.3 Germany

Last, the effects of social polarization in Germany produce a distinctly different picture to that of the US and the UK. In aggregate, citizens that support parties both in and out of power are mobilized by threat. Citizens, in aggregate, express increased importance for every single behavioral item of good citizenship (voting, keeping watch, joining associations, protesting, being informed) and more commitment to mutual tolerance (understanding the opinions of others, friends of different opinions). From both positional and partisan perspectives, we see this response is not driven by one side but by both sides.

Looking first to positionality, Figure 5.5 presents effects of polarization on citizenship norms by whether an individual supports a party in versus out of government. Consistent with the composition of the governing coalition in 2019, "in government" combines supports of the mainstream right (CDU/CSU) and left (SPD) parties, so it cross cuts ideology in a way US and UK analysis cannot. Outsiders comprise all other citizens. That the problem of polarization is not about politics *per se* but social cohesion makes this a hard test for positional incentives. If we see significance, controlling for other factors, we can be confident that they play an important role in shaping citizenship norms.

By organizing positionality explicitly by governing role, we see a few ways in which incumbent versus challenger incentives break through, but also how consensus institutions reduce differences. Figure 5.5 shows several important findings. First, we see large similarities in active citizenship norms – where both "sides" become more likely to value active citizenship in aggregate. Status quo challengers increase the value of every single dimension of engaged, or active citizenship.

---

[64] A third object of blame is people in general: "There is an excess of stupidity in the UK and that is the main problem. Unfortunately the stupid have the same voting rights as anyone else."

[65] And some are uniquely expressive: "it a load of cod wallap" [sic].

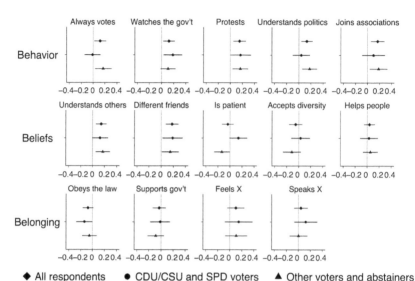

◆ All respondents   ● CDU/CSU and SPD voters   ▲ Other voters and abstainers

FIGURE 5.5. Polarization treatment by coalition participation, Germany

But incumbents also express support for behavioral items, including vigilance and protesting.

Further, both "sides" become more likely to value mutual tolerance (understanding the opinions of others, having friends with different opinions). This is a strong endorsement of the liberal democratic core, and the only case of the three in which both sides increase their support of liberal democratic norms in the face of polarization. On patience, we see a unique pattern: incumbent power holders express that patience is more important in the face of polarization while status quo challengers value patience as less importance. One possibility worth flagging is that forbearance is a type of incumbent luxury. As this was not significant in either of the other cases, we can test this claim using a second threat in Chapter 6. Finally, none of the belonging attributes become significant according to positionality. Obeying the law becomes significant and negative (p = 0.05), which is a surprising result outside of theoretical expectations and one we can probe further by looking at partisanship directly.

With that, Figure 5.6 looks at the effects of polarization treatment on citizenship norms by partisanship. Two caveats here. First, partisanship in Europe – and in multiparty systems – is generally weaker than in bipartisan settings. The emergence of new parties, party splintering, coalition configurations, issue salience, and de-alignment more generally makes

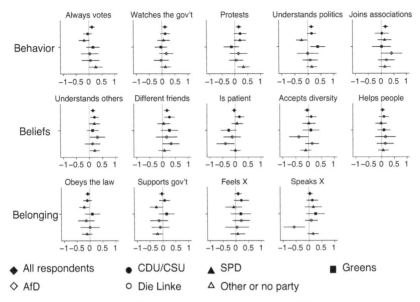

FIGURE 5.6. Polarization treatment by partisanship, Germany

citizens more malleable and less loyal in their partisan support.[66] Second, because Germany is composed of multiple parties, the statistical power of the experiment is necessarily reduced when subsetting by an increasing number of groups (in this case, parties). One would need either a much larger sample size or to proceed with caution in interpreting results. As such, I look at this as a hard test of partisanship.

In looking at Figure 5.6, we see a lot of variation. We can begin by looking at behavioral norms. Recall the in-versus-out of government finding – out of government was significant on all five items and in government along two – we see here that these results are largely dissipated across partisan groups. Yet, moving through each item, we see some significance. For voting, while significant and positive in aggregate, SPD (the left party coalition party) decreases support for this norm (p = 0.07). For protesting, both in-government groups (CDU/CSU and SPD) rate this as positively significant. For "understanding politics," we see that where some rate this as more important in the face of polarization (CDU/CSU and Greens), the SPD again devalue behavior, where being informed becomes less important (p = 0.03). In this, there is a significant

---

[66] Dalton and Wattenberg, *Parties without Partisans: Political Change in Advanced Industrial Democracies.*

takeaway. We can observe a kind of frustration in SPD supporters: they perceive both voting and being informed as less important. For a long-time coalition member, this demobilizing effect is not surprising. It gives insight into some of the long-term effects not on parties but on party-supporting citizens, and how decline effects an intrinsic sense of civic duty.

Moving to liberal democratic beliefs, measures of tolerance ("understanding the opinions of others") in response to the problem of polarization are statistically significant for almost every party – even the AfD! The importance of having friends with different opinions is also statistically significant for several groups (CDU/CSU, Greens, Die Linke). For patience, consistent with the positionality perspective of Figure 5.5, we see CDU/CSU voters express support for more patience in response to threat, but not supporters of the SPD. Greens (p = 0.10) and Die Linke (p = 0.03) think forbearance is less important. This is additional evidence in support of the idea that patience is an incumbency luxury. This outsider, partisan left might also reflect the exasperation of left party voters with the mainstream left's role in coalition (SPD), who post a null result on this item. Last, accepting diversity becomes significantly less important for the AfD only (p = 0.04) in response to the problem of declining social cohesion, and likely drove the previous result for out-of-government party supporters. "Helps people" shows no statistically significant results. As a reminder on interpretation, that is not to say that social solidarity is not an important attribute of good citizenship, just that it is not uniquely activated in hard times. Social solidarity remains a structural feature of the welfare state, and a central component of the EU Charter of Fundamental Rights.

Last, no attributes of national belonging change in response to declining social cohesion, which speaks to a strong dissociation between obligations of citizenship and concepts of membership, or national belonging – even if the treatment alludes to immigration and diversity. Though, again, we observe frustrations among SPD supporters, where obeying the law and support for government becomes statistically significant in the negative direction. We also see Die Linke come out strongly against German language as a feature of good citizenship.

In the end, these results are broadly similar to governing positionality; both sides are mobilized, tolerant, and nonnationalist in response to threat. The details vary slightly, but these results align to theoretical expectations about the role of consensus-based institutions in lowering incentives for zero-sum competition. Because there are so many political

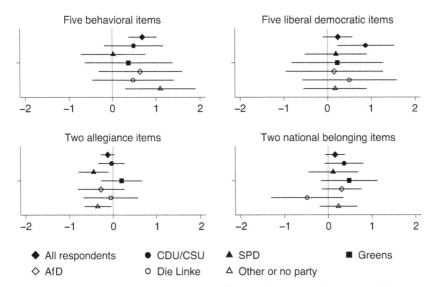

FIGURE 5.7. Aggregate dimensions of citizenship norms by partisanship,
Germany

parties in Germany and given the reduced power as a result of subsetting,
Figure 5.7 offers a second look at the effects of declining social cohesion
on citizenship norms by partisanship, this time grouping each of the
fourteen items into additive indices by dimension. Recall from the factor
analysis in Chapter 3 that German responses produced different dimensions of citizenship norms: behavioral, liberal democratic beliefs, and a
more limited definition of belonging (speaking Germany, feeling
Germany). There were also two remaining items that did not load on to
any dimension – support government and obey the law. I group them here
together as "allegiant" items.

Here we see two important findings. In aggregate, the CDU/CSU
supporters are highly responsive to polarization, increasing the importance of liberal democratic values in total. That the status quo beneficiaries
are significantly affected by threat to change expectations of good citizenship is evidence in support of how different institutional design contexts
alter the incentives to respond. Specifically, positive-sum systems reduce
the costs and consequences of status quo beneficiaries to recognize and
respond to democratic threat. At the same time, the second important
finding here is that the SPD expresses a real frustration, where obeying the
law and supporting government were not only significant and negative on
their own, but also together in the "allegiant" category (and alongside

those that identify as "others" and of "no party"). The compromise required to support a conservative-led coalition may signal lower political polarization, but it could also exacerbate polarization among those that feel like their issues are no longer being heard and drive support for smaller parties.

Finally, I test whether polarization produced a differential treatment effect among German respondents who objected to the treatment.[67] Effects for objections are statistically significant, and comprise 4 percent of the respondent pool, but this only amounts to 25 respondents in total, divided evenly across partisan groups, so interpreting results does not provide much analytical purchase. Despite the treatment not being explicitly about political polarization, some of the open-ended responses assigned blame to specific political divisions ("German democracy is particularly endangered by the left-wing Green *Gutmenschen* mafia, which divide society and immediately push dissenters into the right corner."), while others disagreed with the treatment in principle ("The fact that politicians do NOT believe in compromise or general consensus is not true. On the contrary, Mum [Angela Merkel] tries to balance everything out."). Many responses referenced migration – though it is implicit in the text – while most discussions were generic (and even-keeled): "Many citizens are dissatisfied with politics, democracy and the federal government. But basically, this is always the case. There is always something to complain about. I wouldn't overestimate that now." Last, instead of clearly positioning themselves as in agreement or objection, some respondents expressed discontent more subtly by using subjunctive quotation marks to express doubt or by adding the word *angeblich* (English: alleged) to their statement.

5.4 CONCLUSION

In this chapter we saw that citizens see their obligation according to partisan incentives. These incentives are sharpened in majoritarian systems, where partisan right incumbents are largely demobilized or unresponsive to polarization. While status quo winners appear largely indifferent to information about polarization, we see a strong response among partisan left challengers, who are more likely to embrace liberal norms (especially in the US) and value keeping a watch on government

---

[67] Coding was randomized across a team of six coders. For objection, all three coders agreed in 95.5 percent of the cases (Kappa = 0.721).

(Democrats, Remainers). While we see this turn toward liberal democratic norms, we also observe in the UK an illiberal undercurrent, where partisan left challengers turn away from diversity and toward national belonging norms. These differences between status quo beneficiaries and challengers are mitigated in a consensus-based political system like Germany, where we see both the partisan left and right, both in and out of government, responding to polarization with changes in civic norms.

This is an important caveat for interpreting existing work on polarization, which argues from a US-case perspective that polarization facilitates more informed and engaged political participation among citizens overall.[68] We see here these activated norms are largely confined to positional outsiders, while behavioral dimensions only become shared practice in contexts with comparatively low polarization, like Germany. Moreover, we see strong asymmetry in the US and the UK in terms of who responds by invoking core, overlapping liberal democratic values. While both the left and right highly value items of mutual tolerance in everyday citizenship, we only see left challengers increasing support for these norms in response to threat. This uneven response to threat within core items is worrying.

In addition to partisan patterns, we also observe opinion-based and status cleavages dividing respondents in how they understand civic obligation in democratic hard times, consistent with the varying nature of polarization itself. In the UK, Leavers versus Remainers exhibited important divisions in the effects of polarization on liberal norms, while retaining similar support for patriotism. These results usefully triangulate a partisan perspective, where status quo of governing advantage – not issue position – reveals similar problems for overcoming deep polarization from Brexit in a majoritarian system. In Germany, coalition insiders – which constitute supporters for both mainstream left and right parties – came to value both vigilance and patience in the face of polarization. And, as the German case helpfully illustrates, these insider and outsider positions transcend ideology. We see partisan left parties both inside and outside government taking positions that align more strongly with their positional incentives as coalition partner versus challenger. This leads us to conclude that while partisanship connects citizens to politics, it is *how*

---

[68] Alan I. Abramowitz and Kyle L. Saunders, "Ideological Realignment in the US Electorate," *The Journal of Politics* 60, no. 3 (1998); Fiorina and Abrams, "Political Polarization in the American Public."

parties experience incentives in politics that determines what individuals think they should be doing in response to hard times.

Where does that leave us? Some partisans lean toward active and tolerant citizenship, others are indifferent, and some veer away from liberal democratic ideals. That polarization begets polarization is not surprising, but it portends chilling consequences. Polarization is something that citizens can do something about. When only one side identifies obligation, or when one side feels attacked, it further entrenches the problem and politicizes any potential response. In abstract, American citizens on both the left and the right respond with an obligation for mutual tolerance in the face of polarization, but once we take partisanship into account, this common tie breaks apart. There is also ample evidence that moving from a generic discussion of polarization to the experience of polarization makes compromise – even overlaps in what it means to be a good citizen – more costly. It is hard to imagine how democracies rebuild tolerance from deep division and distrust.

6

Foreign Interference in Elections

No institution is more critical to the functioning of a democracy than an election. Whether that election is free, fair, and frequent is a key yardstick by which political scientists measure democratic quality. Thus, interference in an election – by foreign or domestic actors – directly undermines the integrity and independence of the process and, by extension, the democracy itself. Interference can not only manipulate the results of an election but can also reduce participation and institutional trust for future elections. Advanced democracies have often interfered in elections abroad, but only recently have the integrity and vulnerability of their own elections come into question.

In Chapter 5, we observed a pattern of uneven citizenship, in which status quo challengers responded to polarization, where status quo beneficiaries did not. These patterns emerged despite polarization being the type of democratic problem without clear winners and losers. Foreign interference is a very different type of democratic threat. First, there are clear winners and losers to elections, so there are clear benefits and costs in recognizing and responding to interference. The raison d'être of elections is picking winners and losers. So, unlike polarization, interference is a "most likely" case for where we should see positional incentives predict how citizens interpret obligation.

But there is a second major difference that makes foreign interference a challenge for observing effects on citizenship norms. Polarization is a type of threat that exists at a citizen's level, so individuals can exercise agency and feel like they are accomplishing something by participating in the potentially costly process of civic engagement. Unlike polarization, citizens may recognize foreign interferences as a real problem for democracy but feel like the problem is so distant that they can't really do anything about it. Average citizens can do almost nothing about foreign interference. Citizens participate in elections – and even volunteer in voting centers – but generally have little effect on their overall integrity and fairness, much less an ability – even in coordination – to sanction interfering countries or counteract instances of interference in any meaningful way. In that sense, foreign interference in elections may be a serious democratic threat, but not one that citizens find threatening or that rouses citizens to mobilize in any meaningful way. Thus, examining the effects of foreign interference on citizenship norms is also a "hard test," in which we should expect more muted responses from citizens overall to what amounts to a distant threat.

This type of variation in democratic threat enables a broader test of a citizen-centered theory of democratic instability. And there are few threats more likely to destabilize a democracy than directly undermining one of its core practices. So, how do citizens respond to information on electoral interference in their country? In the case of foreign interference, we again see individuals taking distinct positions on civic obligation that correspond to partisanship. Like polarization, we see status quo challengers respond to threat. Unlike polarization, they respond not with norms of liberal democratic beliefs but with behavior – that is, expectations of a more active, engaged citizenry. This illustrates the correspondence assumption that citizens respond rationally to threat.

Moreover, we also observe a strong status quo bias, in which winners of the election in question generally do nothing. Where norms are affected for citizens supporting incumbent power holders, we observe impatience (US) and demobilization (UK). Meanwhile, the partisan left – as governing outsiders and losers of the elections in question – are more likely to value vigilance, that is, watching the government (US, UK) and understanding how politics and the government work (UK, Germany), alongside other active, engaged citizenship attributes. Evidence of interference in majoritarian systems, compared to Germany's consensus political system, produces stronger partisan differences. Comparisons between different types of elections (presidential, Brexit referendum, and a federal election) enable different tests for status quo cleavages and the role of partisanship. As each of the cases has a right-wing government in power and left wing challengers, I again leverage insights from looking at Brexit as a secondary cleavage and the effects of threat on SPD supporters in Germany to adjudicate between positional incentives and ideological characteristics of political parties. In other words, to show that challengers update norms because it is in their interest, not because it is a programmatic characteristic of supporting a left party.

Last, like in Chapter 5, I include objection analysis to study how the treatments worked. Foreign interference is a particularly unique democratic threat because it is so heavily politicized. Despite robust evidence, interference has typically gone unchecked by incumbent governments (i.e., the perpetrator has faced little in the way of sanctions) and victimized states have done little to shore up defenses against further attacks. This was the case in both the US and the UK. In fact, in the US, foreign actors felt so unchecked and emboldened after interfering in the 2016 presidential election that they attempted to do so again in the 2020 election. Testing for objection allows me to consider heterogenous treatment effects, and the extent to which the threat itself is recognized as threatening.

6.1 FOREIGN INTERFERENCE AS A DEMOCRATIC THREAT

Foreign governments frequently interfere in elections, and Russia and the United States are frequent perpetrators.[1] Corstange and Marinov write of two types of intervention: partisan (to support one party) and process (to "support the rules of democratic contestation, irrespective of who wins").[2] This distinction is important. The latter is interference in support of institutions, ensuring robust participation and competition (and typically in nascent and recently transitioned democracies). This is different from the former, which picks winners and losers and, by meddling with democratic fairness, clearly undermines the integrity of an election. What makes contemporary election interference unique is that advanced democracies have become a target of partisan interference.

Foreign interference represents an external threat that undermines the core democratic institution of free elections, which citizens in all three of the case studies recognize as essential to a healthy democracy. In the 2019 Pew Global Attitudes Survey, a large majority of citizens in each country responded that "honest elections" were very important (US – 84 percent; UK – 78 percent; Germany – 70 percent), versus lower levels in

[1] Dov H. Levin. "When the Great Power Gets a Vote: The Effects of Great Power Electoral Interventions on Election Results." *International Studies Quarterly* 60, no. 2 (2016): 189–202.
[2] Daniel Corstange, and Nikolay Marinov. "Taking Sides in Other People's Elections: The Polarizing Effect of Foreign Intervention." *American Journal of Political Science* 56, no. 3 (2012): 655–70.

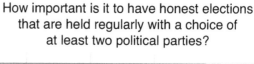

How important is it to have honest elections
that are held regularly with a choice of
at least two political parties?

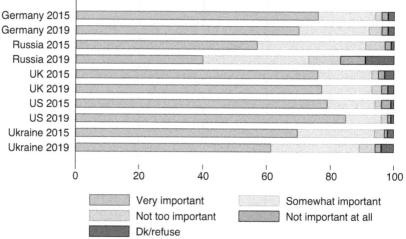

FIGURE 6.1. Percentage support for honest elections in five states, 2015 and 2019

recent democracies like Ukraine and non-democracies like Russia (included in Figure 6.1 for purposes of comparability), who have also experienced electoral interference. Also, of note, between 2015 and 2019 support went up in the US, remained relatively similar in the UK, and slightly declined in Germany.

We know relatively little about how citizens respond to foreign interference in elections, partially because the phenomenon is so new in advanced democracies. Of course, the "democraticness" of an election is often compromised from within, through barriers like voter suppression, which decreases turnout and increases protesting.[3] But among the few studies that have examined the effects of external electoral interference, there is evidence that partisan electoral intervention contributes to polarization and political instability,[4] as well as distrust.[5] In a study of Lebanon's

[3] Pippa Norris. *Why Electoral Integrity Matters* (New York: Cambridge University Press, 2014); Elizabeth Iams Wellman, Susan D. Hyde, and Thad E. Hall. "Does Fraud Trump Partisanship? The Impact of Contentious Elections on Voter Confidence." *Journal of Elections, Public Opinion and Parties* 28, no. 3 (2018): 330–48.

[4] Dov H. Levin. "A Vote for Freedom? The Effects of Partisan Electoral Interventions on Regime Type." *Journal of Conflict Resolution* 63, no. 4 (2019): 839–68.

[5] Tomz, and Weeks. "Public Opinion and Foreign Electoral Intervention."

parliamentary election of 2009, Corstange and Marinov find that "one-sided intercessions" in an election produce a partisan response, dividing voters in their attitudes toward the intervening power.[6] In a study of the 2004 Ukrainian president election, Shuman and Bloom show that citizens disapproved of interventions by both Russia and the US, concluding that interfering with a central aspect of the state "risks unleashing a backlash fueled by citizens jealously guarding their national autonomy and national identity."[7] Tomz and Weeks use the 2016 US presidential election to illustrate the polarizing effects of intervention, where "both Democrats and Republicans were far more likely to condemn foreign involvement, lose faith in democracy, and call for retaliation."[8]

These works are largely drawn from the field of international relations, and accordingly cover attitudes toward the intervening state and the interference directly. These studies do not examine how interference affects citizenship norms. That is, interference may erode trust in elections, but what does a citizen think they should do about it? This question matters because the consequences of foreign interference are not limited to the election in question. Beyond institutional trust and system disposition, threats to electoral integrity can have wide reverberations on civic attitudes, behavior, and agency. Moreover, these studies focus on individual countries, which limits our ability to draw generalizable conclusions from them. By examining patterns in how citizens respond across countries and considering the rules that structure electoral competition (winner-take-all versus proportional representation design), a comparative approach helps us make broader generalizations about democratic citizenship.

6.1.1 Interference in the US, UK, and Germany

All three case studies were subject to Russian meddling in recent elections. Details vary on the extent of interference, influence, and damage, but for

---

[6] Corstange, and Marinov. "Taking Sides in Other People's Elections: The Polarizing Effect of Foreign Intervention." Similar polarizing responses can be found in other areas of foreign interference, such as endorsements. See Sarah Sunn Bush, and Amaney A. Jamal. "Anti-Americanism, Authoritarian Politics, and Attitudes About Women's Representation: Evidence from a Survey Experiment in Jordan." *International Studies Quarterly* 59, no. 1 (2015): 34–45.

[7] Stephen Shulman, and Stephen Bloom. "The Legitimacy of Foreign Intervention in Elections: The Ukrainian Response." *Review of International Studies* 38, no. 2 (2012): 470.

[8] Tomz, and Weeks. "Public Opinion and Foreign Electoral Intervention."

none of these cases is the *idea* of interference hypothetical. Russia's interference in the 2016 US presidential election is widely known and well-documented, most significantly by a bipartisan Senate intelligence committee.[9] The intelligence report recognized outright that "Masquerading as Americans, [Russian] operatives used targeted advertisements, intentionally falsified news articles, self-generated content, and social media platform tools to interact with and attempt to deceive tens of millions of social media users in the United States ... and was part of a foreign government's covert support of Russia's favored candidate in the U.S. presidential election."[10]

Russia also targeted electoral infrastructural vulnerabilities at the state and local levels, including hacking into the Democratic National Committee (DNC) database, data exfiltration of voter registration information, and disinformation campaigns on social media sites, such as Facebook ads for anti-immigrant rallies. The aim of this meddling was to weaken the campaign of Democratic candidate Hillary Clinton, undermine citizen confidence in the electoral system, inevitably supporting the election of Republican candidate Donald Trump. Russia was also connected to the Trump campaign directly, cultivating relationships with key Trump aides like Roger Stone. This interference became a feature of politics during the Trump Administration, in which high-profile investigations – from the report by Special Counsel Robert Mueller to Trump's impeachment hearing – questioned the administration's role in Russian interference and what measures are being taken to prevent it in the future.

In response to interference, and accusations of complicity, prominent Republicans and Trump himself drifted in messaging from denying that any interference took place, to denying Russia was responsible ("It also could be somebody sitting on their bed that weighs 400 pounds, OK?"), to recognizing there was interference but that it wasn't consequential ("Russia, Russia, Russia! That's all you heard at the beginning of this Witch Hunt Hoax. ... And now Russia has disappeared because I had nothing to do with Russia helping me to get elected").[11] It should come as no surprise, then, that the lackluster sanctions placed on Russia following

---

[9] See for example the redacted intelligence report of the Select Committee on Intelligence of the US Senate. www.intelligence.senate.gov/sites/default/files/documents/Report_Volume1.pdf

[10] www.intelligence.senate.gov/sites/default/files/documents/Report_Volume2.pdf

[11] *The Hill.* "Trump's Evolving Remarks on Russian Election Interference." June 1, 2019. Available at https://thehill.com/homenews/administration/446392-trumps-evolving-remarks-on-russian-election-interference (accessed October 1, 2020).

2016 would not be a productive deterrent. The National Intelligence Council released a community assessment in March 2021, confirming that Russia (as well as Iran) attempted to influence voters in the 2020 election. In the case of Russia, this included "influence operations aimed at denigrating President Biden's candidates and the Democratic Party, supporting former President Trump, undermining public confidence in the electoral process, and exacerbating sociopolitical division in the US."[12]

Russia also interfered in the Brexit Referendum of 2016. While in 2017, then-Prime Minister Theresa May claimed Russian propaganda had "no direct successful influence" on the Brexit vote, though, in the same breath, warns Russia that "We know what you are doing. And you will not succeed."[13] To wit, there were a number of problematic inconsistencies that had come to light since. Cambridge Analytica's services were "donated" to the Leave.EU campaign; they were not declared and were later found in violation of election laws by the UK Electoral Commission. There was ample evidence of Kremlin-backed acts of disinformation, cyber hacking, social media campaigns, bribery and corruption. For example, Arron Banks[14] – the biggest Leave campaign donor – was offered investments in a Russian gold mine and later lied about his entanglements before a Parliamentary committee hearing. Nigel Farage, the head of UKIP and Brexit champion, held deep ties to Russia, eventually coming under the radar of Mueller's investigation. The British Intelligence and Security parliamentary committee ultimately published a complete report on Russian-government-sponsored activities during the referendum in October 2019,[15] though Boris Johnson refused to release the publication, citing timing in the run-up to his own general election on December 12. Ultimately, the Russia Report was released in July 2020, which stated plainly that Russian influence is "the new normal," that the UK was a "top Western intelligence target" and the government "badly

---

[12] Unlike 2016, they did not see cyber efforts to gain access to electoral infrastructure. National Intelligence Council. "Foreign Threats to the 2020 US Federal Elections", available at www.dni.gov/files/ODNI/documents/assessments/ICA-declass-16MAR21 .pdf (accessed March 11, 2021).

[13] Karla Adam, and William Booth. "Rising Alarm in Britain over Russian Meddling in Brexit Vote." *Washington Post*, November 17, 2017.

[14] www.theguardian.com/politics/2018/jun/09/arron-banks-russia-brexit-meeting

[15] Caroline Harper, Richard Kerbaj, and Tom Wheeler. "Revealed: The Russia Report." *The Sunday Times*, November 17, 2019.

underestimated the response required to the Russian threat, and is still playing catch up."[16]

Finally, Russia made attempts to influence the German Federal Election of 2017 through disinformation campaigns. These steps were less penetrative than British and American efforts, but were still consequential, directed at undermining the effectiveness and cohesiveness of democratic institutions. The most significant difference was not the meddling *per se* but the response and, ultimately, the system vigilance that resulted. In May 2015, German officials discovered individuals had broken into the internal server of the Bundestag and stole volumes of data, including emails and personal contact information.[17] It was later revealed to be Russia-linked hackers, in an operation that resembled – and, indeed, foreshadowed – similar jobs against the DNC a year later as well as Emmanuel Macron's campaign in France.[18] In publicly condemning the infiltration and data theft, Merkel remarked there was "hard evidence that Russian forces are involved."

The release of these hacked emails was anticipated, but – puzzlingly – never materialized.[19] What *did* occur was a public conversation focusing on preparedness, with Bruno Kahl, the head of the Bundesnachrichtendienst (Germany's foreign intelligence) warning that Russians may attempt to interfere in the 2017 election. By preemptively discussing it publicly, and explicitly attributing cyber-attacks to Russia, Merkel put the country on guard, habituated Germans to vigilance: "We have to inform people, and express our political convictions clearly. ... You just have to know that there's such a thing and learn to live with it."[20] By contrast, American discussion were much quieter, where then-

---

[16] BBC News. "Russian Report: UK 'Badly Underestimated' Threat, Says Committee." July 21, 2020. Available at www.bbc.com/news/uk-politics-53484344 (accessed March 24, 2021).

[17] Deutsche Welle. "Data Stolen during Hack Attack on German Parliament, Berlin Says." May 29, 2015. Available at www.dw.com/en/data-stolen-during-hack-attack-on-german-parliament-berlin-says/a-18486900 (accessed January 18, 2021).

[18] www.euronews.com/2020/05/13/merkel-says-germany-has-hard-evidence-of-russian-hacking

[19] Zeit Online. "Merkel und der schicke Bär." May 10, 2017. Available at www.zeit.de/2017/20/cyberangriff-bundestag-fancy-bear-angela-merkel-hacker-russland (accessed January 18, 2021).

[20] *The Guardian.* "German Spy Chief Says Russian Hackers Could Disrupt Elections." November 29, 2016. Available at www.theguardian.com/world/2016/nov/29/german-spy-chief-russian-hackers-could-disrupt-elections-bruno-kahl-cyber-attacks (accessed January 18, 2021).

President Barack Obama perceived any public discussion of the election as a type of partisan bias.[21]

In the end, Russia's main target was not voting machines but the minds of voters, in which both extreme-left and right-wing media outlets helped to forward Russian narratives, both disinformation and propaganda. One example of disinformation stands out: "Our Lisa," the alleged raping of an underage German girl of "Russian origin" in January 2016 by three "Muslim" refugees.[22] Originally broadcast by a Russian TV station and disseminated by outlets such as RT (formerly Russia Today), it soon gained coverage in the German press. The report was quickly debunked, but Russian officials including Foreign Minister Sergei Lavrov maintained the veracity of the story. This was another wake-up call for building-up German vigilance ahead of 2017. Of course, with a large Russian-speaking community, Germany was already attentive to Russian efforts to infiltrate this population and gain a toehold in German politics. Still, Kremlin-backed media served as a fitful vehicle to distribute favorable coverage of the AfD, reaching millions of German homes by satellite.

These are not the first global elections in which the Russians interfered; 2004 in Ukraine is a notable example. What makes this round of attacks on democratic elections remarkable is the documented scope, bipartisan recognition, and – most disturbingly – the little that incumbent governments have done to prevent their recurrence in the US and UK, suggesting that strong status quo effects play an overriding role in confronting democratic threat.

6.1.2 Theoretical Expectations

So, how do individuals define citizenship norms in response to foreign interference in a national election? Recalling the central argument (Chapter 2), we have three expectations to work from, the first two pivoting around the central observation that electoral winners experience

---

[21] Miller, Greg, Ellen Nakashima, and Adam Entous. "Obama's Secret Struggle to Punish Russian for Putin's Election Assault." *The Washington Post*, June 23, 2017. Available at www.washingtonpost.com/graphics/2017/world/national-security/obama-putin-election-hacking (accessed June 2, 2019).

[22] Deutsche Welle. "Man Found Guilty of Abusing Russian-German Teenager Who Fabricated Rape Story." June 20, 2017. Available at www.dw.com/en/man-found-guilty-of-abusing-russian-german-teenager-who-fabricated-rape-story/a-39328894 (accessed January 12, 2021).

different attitudinal effects than losers.[23] The specifics of these hypotheses will vary; that is, the substance of these responses may differ across the 14 items as a function of the *type of threat*, but the predicted responses should be overall consistent with positional incentives and institutional context.

First, electoral winners *qua* status quo beneficiaries will want to preserve their position. This may produce a demobilizing response, hunkering down and rallying around the flag, repudiating liberal norms like tolerance, or even denying the threat altogether. Suggesting electoral results are illegitimate, or accusing one side of corruption or complicity, for example, may trigger further conflict and animus, even if both sides value rule of law and honest institutions.[24] In this case, partisans may disagree with or otherwise discount the treatment itself. These "sore winners" may not only object to interference evidence but *double-down* on partisanship, exhibiting allegiant values of "law and order" and patriotism.

Second, electoral losers identify incentives by their challenger position. This may include mobilization, inclusionary norms (widening the tent and coalition of support) and supporting liberal democratic institutions and values. Partisan challengers should be inclined to agree to both that foreign electoral interference happened and that it constitutes a democratic threat. Unlike status quo winners, challengers incur fewer costs. From this group we might expect more vigilance[25] and information gathering, consistent with the literature on anxiety.[26] These are not traits expected of status quo winners, in which anger – as opposed to anxiety – inhibits information gathering.[27] Specifically, anxiety produces deliberate

---

[23] Anderson, et al. *Losers' Consent: Elections and Democratic Legitimacy*; Anderson, and Guillory. "Political Institutions and Satisfaction with Democracy: A Cross-National Analysis of Consensus and Majoritarian Systems."

[24] Donald E. Stokes. "Spatial Models of Party Competition." *The American Political Science Review* 57, no. 2 (1963): 373.

[25] Consistent with findings that fear influences participation. e.g., Abraham Aldama, Mateo Vásquez-Cortés, and Lauren Elyssa Young. "Fear and Citizen Coordination against Dictatorship." *Journal of Theoretical Politics* 31, no. 1 (2019): 103–25; Wendy Pearlman. "Narratives of Fear in Syria." *Perspectives on Politics* 14, no. 1 (2016): 21–37.

[26] Albertson, and Gadarian. *Anxious Politics: Democratic Citizenship in a Threatening World*; Merolla, and Zechmeister. "Threat and Information Acquisition: Evidence from an Eight Country Study."

[27] Pavlos Vasilopoulos. "Terrorist Events, Emotional Reactions, and Political Participation: The 2015 Paris Attacks." *West European Politics* 41, no. 1 (2018): 102–27. Vasilopoulos also finds that anger inhibits information-gathering.

citizens who seek out information and compromise, whereas anger creates partisan citizens who behave with allegiance and seek out information that confirms priors.[28] Further, we expect challengers to become more patriotic, in a stand of solidarity with democratic institutions. This type of patriotism ("feeling [nationality]" or "supporting the government") in the face of a foreign threat is distinct from the kind of nationalist fervor expressed outside of this context. Rallying around the flag is different when the opponent is foreign versus domestic. It is also an important reminder to look at items inductively and interpret in context.

Third, incentives for challengers to respond and status quo beneficiaries to ignore threat are greater in majoritarian systems, which structures competition through a series of zero-sum games. The preceding predictions make the most sense in a situation where there are clear winners and losers from an election – particularly the case of winner-take-all, plurality elections in presidential or Westminster systems. When there is no "side," that is, proportional representative *qua* multi-sided systems (e.g., Germany), the anticipated effects of information about electoral interference should not break down so neatly. I therefore leave open the possibility that individuals across the political spectrum value active citizenship to preserve electoral integrity (consistent with the consensus valuations seen by Germans on behavioral items in Chapter 4), as more players stand to gain in what is fundamentally a frequently iterative, positive-sum game. It follows also, then, that the incentives to ignore or deny threat are also lower. Testing the expectations using the German case should also be considered a conservative assessment of the effects of interference on citizenship, given the comparatively minimal nature of interference experienced.

6.2 DATA AND METHODOLOGY

To study the effects of foreign interference on citizenship norms, I employ the same research design specified in Chapter 5, replacing the polarization treatment with the election treatment. Recall that a randomized quarter of respondents received a vignette on electoral interference as a threat to democracy. To reinforce each scenario, vignettes were followed by an open-ended question to reinforce the content of the prime (e.g., "Please spend 30 seconds discussing the topic you just read") and a multiple-

---

[28] MacKuen et al. . "Civic Engagements: Resolute Partisanship or Reflective Deliberation."

choice attention check about the content of the vignette. These were followed by the randomized, fourteen questions on attributes of a "good citizen."

But, why Russian interference? There are numerous democratic threats taking place in these case studies – arguably, the simultaneity of multiple threats is both a sign and consequence of democratic backsliding. However, I want to leverage the important differences that characterize threat for predicting how partisan citizens respond. Foreign interference in elections is an external threat that undermines institutional integrity. It also makes partisan incentives clear, where the election determines system "winners" and "loser" challengers. This is a most likely case for testing partisan citizenship, where individuals evaluate obligation per party incentives and given constraints of institutional design. Other democratic threats are equally important and threatening, but incentives are less clear.

Russian meddling in national elections is a common threat to each advanced democracy under study, though there is variation in the magnitude and success of that interference. Given that methods of meddling were similar, we can use an identical vignette script to describe it. For each of the three countries, the vignette read as follows:

Western democracies have recently come under attack, with hostile foreign governments like Russia interfering in national elections, including those in the [United States/United Kingdom/Germany]. Tactics include accessing voter databases, running a campaign of disinformation through social media (like Facebook and Twitter) to spread false information about candidates and issues, and breaking into email accounts of political parties. Russia has also been found to illegally filter money to candidates they support.

Many experts fear actions like these undermine our country. As the chief researcher at the National Policy Institute (a leading, [bipartisan/nonpartisan] think tank) states, "Foreign interference like this compromises the fairness and independence of our elections. This is a democratic crisis for our country."

Like the vignette experiment in Chapter 5, the second paragraph provides framing for a respondent who may need assistance in connecting how foreign interference in an election affects democracy more generally. Russian electoral intervention is a direct threat to free democratic institutions, yet publics generally express low levels of fear toward Russia. In a study by the European Council on Foreign Relations,[29] Russia was rated

---

[29] European Council on Foreign Relations. "What Europeans Really Want: Five myths debunked". April 16, 2019. Available at www.ecfr.eu/specials/what_europeans_really_want_five_myths_debunked (accessed September 18, 2020).

the lowest threat in democracies like Germany (2 percent) and Italy (under 1 percent), compared to Poland (15 percent). By contrast, a fear of radical Islam and immigration predominates in each of these cases. Therefore, the elite framing helps focus the reader to the goal of the passage.

Moreover, as Russian electoral interference had deliberately partisan objectives, the vignette framing is also careful to make clear that interference presents a threat to the election and those participating in it, as well as to democracy and therefore the country. Vignettes were as nonpartisan as possible – not mentioning election winners and losers explicitly. Invoking partisan frames or mentioning winners triggers motivated reasoning, where "if a frame is sponsored by a party people feel attached to ... [they] pay closer attention to frame content and assess it more favorably."[30] However, because these vignettes reference real-life events, and the winner of elections are plainly known, we may expect motivated reasoning in any case. For example, US Republicans may reject the foreign interference prime altogether if they conclude that it challenges the legitimacy of the 2016 election outcome. So, too, may British Leave supporters and far right voters in Germany. This is consistent with the well-known phenomenon of biased information processing: individuals perceive events and information based on their preexisting orientations.[31] This is why the open-ended question and objection analysis is valuable, as it allows for expressions of disagreement without explicitly soliciting it.

In what follows, I present statistical analyses to test the effect of the electoral interference vignette on citizenship norms. I employ the same methods specified in Chapter 5. The dependent variable in each model is the fourteen questions on attributes of civic obligation ("How important is it for a good citizen to...?").

6.3 RESULTS

The regression analysis reveals strong differences in how partisans interpret civic obligation in the face of democratic crisis. Contrary to expectations from the threat literature that external events unify citizens, we see here that partisan differences are made worse, where only some – namely, the partisan "losers" of elections and those who support parties out of

---

[30] Rune Slothuus, and Claes H. De Vreese. "Political Parties, Motivated Reasoning, and Issue Framing Effects." *The Journal of Politics* 72, no. 3 (2010): 632.
[31] Campbell et al. "The American Voter."

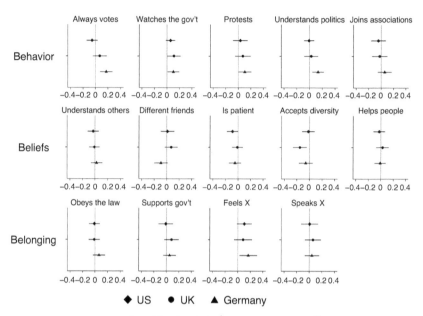

FIGURE 6.2. Foreign interference treatment effects

power – mobilize in response to threat while the "winners" withdraw or reject the frame that interference is threatening (or, in the case of several US respondents, even took place).

Beginning with general results, Figure 6.2 shows the US (diamond point; top row of each plot), the UK (dot point; middle row), and Germany (triangle point; bottom row). There is clear variation across countries and indicators. Beginning with the US, the treatment positively affected patriotism ("It is important that good citizens feel American," p = 0.08) and negatively affected patience ("good citizens have patience, recognizing that sometimes their side wins and sometimes it loses," p = 0.05). That is, in general – specifically, *without taking partisanship into account* – Americans significantly and positively respond to interference with greater patriotism, while becoming significantly more negative toward patience, or forbearance. It is useful to note here that the absence of significance for most outcomes does not mean these attributes of civic obligation are unimportant – recall the high ratings that the Americans gave these dimensions of good citizenship in Chapter 3 – just that they are not significantly affected by the vignette treatment relative to the apolitical control. This is also consistent with our baseline assumption about rational responses; as interference in elections is a more distant threat from a citizen's everyday than polarization, we expect a more muted response overall.

The effects of foreign interference in the UK were similarly limited, with support for "keeping watch on the government" significant and positively signed (p = 0.04) and "accepts diversity" significant and negative (p = 0.01). This is strong evidence of support for ingroup homogeneity in response to crisis, though none of the belonging items become significant. It is worth recalling, however, that British respondents also became less accepting of diversity as an attribute of good citizenship in response to the polarization threat. To summarize, Americans became more inclined to define good citizenship as more patriotic and less patient in response to foreign interference, while British respondents valued vigilance more and accepting diversity less.

In Germany, we see a different pattern in aggregate. Not only does foreign interference affect more citizenship norms in Germany than in the US and UK, it affects different norms. First, in contrast to the other two cases, German respondents exhibit a strong behavioral norms response to foreign interference, including the increased importance in voting, keeping watch on government, protesting, and understanding how government works. This, too, looks a lot like the aggregate result in response to the polarization threat. Indeed, it appears that German citizens under threat become engaged. Germans also become more likely to value "Feeling German" (p = 0.02), and the effect of foreign threat on valuing the importance of friends with different views – a measure of mutual tolerance – approaches significance (p = 0.10). Together, these could add up to an illiberal undertone to an otherwise strong behavioral turnout. But, rallying around the flag need not amount to exclusionary nationalism, rather an expression of institutional pride, particularly in the face of outsider meddling in national elections. In fact, strong feelings of German national pride and an intrinsic civic duty to vote are documented to go hand-in-hand.[32] This interpretation is context-dependent and merits a closer examination by partisanship.

How might we explain this aggregate difference between Germany and the other two cases? We can first look at the transparent discussion and vigilant response taken by the German government, who framed this issue

---

[32] Aram Hur. "Is There an Intrinsic Duty to Vote? Comparative Evidence from East and West Germans." *Electoral Studies* 45 (2017): 55–62.

as a communal problem. Hans-Georg Maassen, head of the domestic intelligence agency, was quoted as wanting to get ahead of misinformation campaigns: "When people realize that the information that they are getting is not true..., then the toxic lies lose their effectiveness."[33] That we observe a communal response is a predictable consequence of this proactive government behavior.

But these results only look at aggregate responses. One interpretation of these results is that evidence of foreign interference as a democratic crisis did not move citizens very much to define their obligations differently. In other words, the modest aggregate effects of the foreign interference treatment may suggest interference does not affect citizenship norms. A second interpretation may be that the prime did not work. But, recall, our hypotheses are not for aggregate responses but for partisans navigating positional incentives of costs and rewards. For partisan winners, acknowledging foreign interference potentially undermines the legitimacy of the elections themselves and may evoke a type of illiberal backlash, "cancelling out" mobilizing or information-gathering patterns expressed by challengers. A closer analysis supports this intuition, that these aggregate results mask important treatment effect heterogeneity by partisanship. I examine these in turn.

6.3.1 United States

In aggregate, Americans became more patriotic and impatient in response to foreign interference. Looking directly at effects by partisanship, we see a different picture. Figure 6.3 presents the effects of the foreign interference threat, separating respondents by partisanship (grouping leaners with stronger partisan identifiers). Here we see two key findings. First, the effect of foreign interference treatment on impatience is statistically significant but only for Republicans. This finding is consistent with our theoretical expectation that incumbents face few incentives to respond to threat that upends the status quo and even respond by recoiling from obligation and engagement. Recall from earlier chapters that the luxury of incumbency enabled Republicans to express more patience than

---

[33] Reuters. "Germany Alarmed About Potential Russian Interference in Election: Spy Chief." November 16, 2016. Available at www.reuters.com/article/us-germany-election-russia/germany-alarmed-about-potential-russian-interference-in-election-spy-chief-idUSKBN13B14O (accessed Sept 2, 2020).

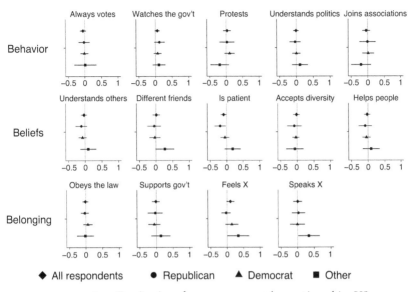

FIGURE 6.3. Foreign interference treatment by partisanship, US

challenger party supporters when it comes to everyday citizenship. Here we see the limits of this patience.

Second, there are no statistically significant effects of foreign interference for Democrats. The other significant aggregate finding – "feeling American" – is only significant at the partisan level for Democrats when grouped with Others, which include self-professed Independents (non-leaners) and third- party supporters, that is, as a more generic "challenger" cleavage. In fact, the "Others" category responds more than Democrats, becoming more likely to express strong support for citizenship norms of feeling American, speaking English, and "having friends with different political opinions." While this is a type of confirmatory evidence for our hypothesis – challengers rally and incumbents disengage – it is limited evidence overall. We do not find evidence that foreign interference increases vigilance or the importance of being informed or other behavioral attributes per the literature on external threat. And the effects of the foreign interference treatment are only statistically significant among Independents and Others. Independents eschew politics more generally,[34] but why do Democrats remain unaffected?

[34] Klar, and Krupnikov. *Independent Politics.*

One possibility is the timeline of interference in the US election. The DNC was first notified by the FBI that their servers were being hacked in September 2015,[35] in a breach dating back to July of that year. Crowdstrike, an information security firm, identified a second data breach in April 2016, in which Russian intelligence stole thousands of documents and DNC data.[36] Data theft and misinformation campaigns became well-known facts about the 2016 election by way of a series of bipartisan acknowledgments, Congressional reports, and intelligence community findings that not only documented interference but connections between Russia and the Trump campaign. And with the exception of expelling some Russian diplomats and imposing light sanctions, there were no real consequences.

The second, and related, potential explanation for the muted effect for Democrats is fatigue. By 2019, when the survey was in the field, Democratic respondents undoubtedly confronted this vignette with a type of fixed resignation, perhaps even cynicism, knowing that nothing *was* done at the institutional level to address foreign interference, and knowing that nothing *could* be done until the next election in 2020. (This is different in parliamentary systems like the UK and Germany, where votes of no confidence and snap elections inherently increase a citizen's sense of agency.)

The *fact* of interference was well-known for years, deeply politicized, and saturated American political life. In a 2018 YouGov poll, 78 percent of Democrats believed Russia interfered with the 2016 elections, while only 31 percent of Republicans answered affirmatively.[37] The notion that Democrats might be newly mobilized to update citizenship norms by a vignette that highlights its democratic relevance is already a tall order.

Yet, *because* interference was so heavily politicized, it suggests there may be differential treatment effects where some respondents are convinced by (or "take") the vignette while others object to the premise.

[35] Permanent Select Committee on Intelligence, US House of Representatives. "Interview of Yared Tamene Wolde-Yohannes." August 30, 2017. Available at https://intelligence .house.gov/uploadedfiles/ty54.pdf (accessed May 8, 2019).

[36] Crowdstrike Blog. "Crowdstrike's Work with the Democratic National Committee: Setting the Record Straight." June 5, 2020. Available at www.crowdstrike.com/blog/ bears-midst-intrusion-democratic-national-committee (accessed February 20, 2021).

[37] YouGov. "Reviewing Russia's Role in 2016 While Getting Ready for 2018." July 27, 2018. Available at https://today.yougov.com/topics/politics/articles-reports/2018/07/27/ reviewing-russias-role-2016-while-getting-ready-20 (accessed May 12, 2019).

Therefore, I proceed to test for whether we observe differences between objectors and non-objectors.

To test for treatment objection (as a refresher to the procedure from Chapter 5), respondents were given thirty seconds to "discuss the topic" they just read in an open-ended response following the treatment and control. On a functional level, this served to reinforce the vignette by encouraging them to concentrate for an extended period of time on foreign interference as a democratic threat. But these open-ended responses also provide me with an opportunity to assess how respondents reacted to the treatment. Open-ended responses were coded as objection if they disagreed with the facts of the frame or the premise that foreign interference was a threat. To test the conditional hypothesis that effects obtain differently between respondents that do and those that do not object to the treatment, I subset the data, running separate analyses for the subset of respondents that objected to the treatment and for the subset that did not.

Here is an example of a statement coded as "objection": "I believe the position shows a total liberal bias. It is an attempt to discredit the Trump Victory in the last election." Objections typically lay the blame on someone else (Democrats, the media, immigrants) or discredit the claim in general ("Sounds like a conspiracy to me"). Here is an example of a statement coded both as an "objection" and "emotional": "This crap is totally exaggerated. The REAL foreign interference in our elections is non-citizens being allowed to vote." Among those who objected to the treatment, 15.1 percent were also emotional (75 out of 496), so they are not particularly correlated. Again, respondents were not instructed to agree or disagree with the foreign interference treatment, so this is a natural – if conservative – estimate of opinion.

This test reveals important findings among objectors. We can confirm there were differential treatment effects, where 18 percent of the total treatment group expressed objection (compared to 10 percent objecting to polarization). Looking only at Republicans, objection rate goes up to 33 percent. In other words, out of all the Republicans that received the vignette, a full third objected to foreign interference (either the fact of it or that it is a democratic threat). This is much larger than Republican objection to polarization (12 percent). For Democrats and Others, objection rate is much lower (at 9 percent), and close to the objection rate of polarization (8 percent). This gap between Republican and Democratic objection invites us to look at objection separately.

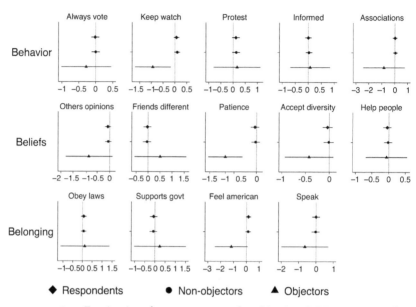

FIGURE 6.4. Foreign interference treatment by objection, US Democrats only

Beginning with Democratic objection, Figure 6.4 portrays citizenship norms among Democrats who received the foreign interference treatment, sorted by all Democrats (diamond point; top row), Democrats who did not object (dot point; middle row), and Democrats who objected (triangle point; bottom row). The Y-axis represents the effect of the treatment on each dependent variable. We see a sizable difference in response to threat between objectors and non-objectors. Democrats who objected to the foreign interference vignette respond by becoming less likely to value vigilance/keeping watch (p = 0.02), patience (p = 0.00), and patriotism (p = 0.07). This is a small group of objectors. But, importantly, once you filter out those that objected to the treatment, you begin to see significant effects of foreign interference on citizenship norms for Democrats, including vigilance keeping watch (p = 0.09). This is promising, but of course not strong evidence on its own of a citizen responding to challenger incentives. I take seriously the effects of politicization, saturation, fatigue, and the nature of the threat itself to account for muted effects. Foreign interference is not a hypothetical, but due to these concerns, it was always going to be a hard test. There are only so many times one can fire up the outrage machine.

Moving to Republican objectors (not pictured), the only statistically significant difference is that they become more likely to value

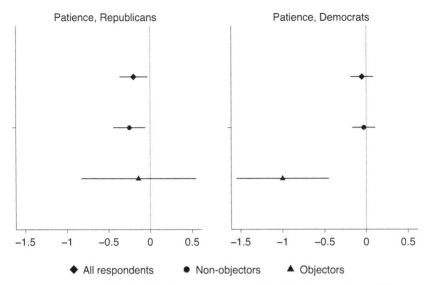

FIGURE 6.5. Foreign interference treatment by objection, patience, US

associational life, which is probably an incidental effect among this particular subgroup. But by filtering out Republican objectors from non-objectors (the remaining 66 percent of Republican respondents), we are left with an important observation: non-objectors still become significantly less likely to value patience (p = 0.01) in response to the foreign interference treatment. That is, patience is *still* less important in response to foreign interference, notably among Republican *non*-objectors. Figure 6.5 presents this finding alongside Democratic impatience, which is statistically significant among objectors only.

Non-objectors are a large and diverse group of respondents who showed that they did pay attention to the foreign interference treatment but did not express disagree with it. They may agree with the premise of interference, they may be unsure about interference, or maybe they were unaware they could express objection. The fact that this finding endures, regardless of whether objectors are included or not in the Republican subset, is cause for concern for American democracy. Losing forbearance can be a logical response to information on electoral interference; recognizing that sometimes your side loses elections can understandably feel futile if the election itself is compromised. By the same logic, one should think voting matters less if the election is not conducted fairly.

But a decline in forbearance among incumbent supporters is a red flag for fortifying a citizenship to fend off backsliding. Among

Republicans (and Democratic objectors), patience is *exceptionally fragile*, susceptible to winning and losing as well as perceived costs and benefits of challenging the status quo. In the polarization scenario, across cases, we saw patience was the luxury of the incumbent; patience for winning and losing is easier if you're already the winner. But evidence of its decline in the face of a threat that challenges status quo benefits is not good for democracy. It is clear evidence that the forbearance required to serve as a soft guardrail in democratic institutions is weak. It raises concerns that we can't count on incumbents to do the right thing if their power is challenged, or if the next election involves losing (as evidenced by Republican claims of fraudulent voting, ballot stuffing, attempts to delegitimize the Electoral College count, and the insurrection of January 6, 2021). In short, declining patience fundamentally weakens the liberal foundation for democratic stability.

To summarize, Americans overall express more patriotism and less patience in response to foreign interference in elections. Looking at results by positional incentives, we observe Republicans as consistently likely to devalue impatience, while Democrats remain largely unaffected. Partisan left challengers did not respond to threat information with more vigilance or being informed. Only by filtering out treatment objectors did support for citizenship norms become visible. Meanwhile, other positional outsiders – those who identify as independents or support third parties – are strongly affected, increasingly valuing friends of other opinions (p = 0.06) and two items of national belonging. Without overinterpreting this finding, these could be general anti-partisan, pro-system views. In the end, heterogenous treatment effects by partisanship helpfully explain what looked like weak initial results in the aggregate. Even these muted responses are sobering after the fact; individuals unevenly define obligations of a good citizen in response to an objective threat to democratic institutional integrity.

6.3.2 United Kingdom

Turning to the UK, where the foreign interference treatment also only had modest effects in aggregate, we see much larger differences when we disaggregate respondents by partisanship. In Figure 6.6, partisan left challengers – in this case, supporters of Labour – not only value "feeling British" and "support government" but strongly activate behavioral dimensions of obligation, including vigilance ("keep watch") and

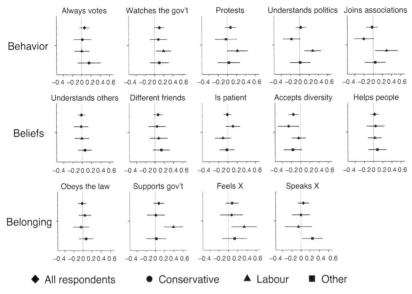

FIGURE 6.6. Foreign interference treatment by partisanship, UK

information-seeking (unlike the US).[38] Moreover, where partisan left challengers are significantly more likely to value understanding politics ("being informed") in response to the treatment, partisan incumbents show the opposite, by significantly devaluing it. A similar pattern is present for joining associations.

While partisan left challengers embrace the hypothesized characteristics of civic obligation – that of vigilance and being informed, partisan right incumbents exhibit predicted demobilization and defensive positions. Specifically, we see that the aggregate result of declining acceptance of diversity in response to foreign interference is driven primarily by Conservative supporters. This is unlike the polarization treatment, where we saw the same result but for Labour supporters as well as Leave voters. Outside of this item, we do not have evidence that partisan right incumbents uniquely repudiate any other liberal democratic values. Yet, alongside this declining support for diversity, greater support for belonging among partisan left challengers suggests a general rise in nationalism during democratic crisis that would only generate more threat to minorities, immigrants, and marginalized groups. Partisan right incumbents do

---

[38] This confirms the finding by MacKuen et al., "Civic Engagements: Resolute Partisanship or Reflective Deliberation."

not exhibit significant change on these items in response to the foreign interference treatment, which is not to say they do not matter in the face of threat, but that responses were statistically indistinguishable from the apolitical control condition.

However, because the election in question was not about choosing parties but positions on Brexit, we need to look at this new issue cleavage to see how citizens assess status quo preserving versus status quo challenging incentives. In the case of the 2016 referendum, these align with Brexit position, not partisanship.[39] Brexit was an issue that ran orthogonal to partisanship – there were prominent "Leave" and "Remain" elites in both parties, and mass opinions were strongly divided. Within David Cameron's Cabinet, prominent members supporting EU membership included Cameron himself but also Chancellor George Osborne, Foreign Secretary Phillip Hammond, and Home Secretary Theresa May. Prominent members supporting Leave included Justice Secretary Michael Gove. Beyond the Cabinet, the Conservative party was split 60:40 in support of EU membership.[40] And Labour Leader Corbyn's endorsement of the Remain campaign was notably belated and lukewarm, recognizing the cross section of supporters within the party (and perhaps his own belief), with one *Guardian* headline declaring "Labour Voters in the Dark about Party's Stance on Brexit."[41] Meanwhile, all regional parties (with the exception of government-supporting Democratic Unionist Party of Northern Ireland) supported Remain.

To explore the effects of this newly salient, cross-partisan political identity, Figure 6.7 presents citizenship norms in response to foreign interference by Brexit vote. Switching the axis of polarization, we observe similar positional incentives at work. Outcome/status quo challengers (Remain voters along with abstainers) became more vigilant ("watch government"), valued information-seeking and patriotism ("feeling British") in response to the foreign interference treatment. Among

---

[39] Hobolt, Leeper, and Tilley. "Divided by the Vote: Affective Polarization in the Wake of Brexit."

[40] UK In a Changing World. "Which Conservative Ministers are Campaign to Leave and Remain in the EU," available at https://ukandeu.ac.uk/fact-figures/which-conservative-ministers-are-campaigning-to-leave-and-remain-in-the-eu/ (accessed April 16, 2019).

[41] Mason, Rowena. "Labour Voters in the Dark about Party's Stance on Brexit, Research Says." *The Guardian,* May 20, 2016. Available at www.theguardian.com/politics/2016/may/30/labour-voters-in-the-dark-about-partys-stance-on-brexit-research-says (accessed April 16, 2019).

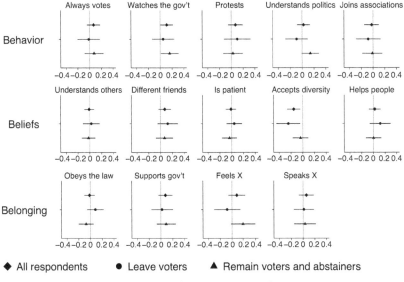

FIGURE 6.7. Foreign interference treatment by Brexit vote, UK

Leavers, information on foreign interference in the Brexit election only makes them value diversity less.

The takeaway is that both partisanship and Brexit vote may be enduring and stable social cleavages, but partisanship is deeper-cutting and produces far more pernicious consequences – particularly when it comes to community-oriented values and liberal democratic norms – in a majoritarian system. Foreign interference logically mobilizes Remainers to value political action but does not yield the same level of engaged citizens that partisanship produced in the same context.

Finally, as with the US, I ran an objection analysis.[42] In total, 16.3 percent of respondents who got the foreign interference treatment objected to it. This is close to the overall US rate (18 percent), but we see a significant difference in how emotional British respondents were (conforming to national stereotypes). Recall that 15 percent of objections among Americans were also emotional; among British respondents, only 7 percent of those who objected were also emotional. Some examples of

---

[42] Each respondent was coded three times, randomized across a team of seven coders. For objection, all three coders agreed in 85.09 percent of the cases (Kappa = 0.610). For emotion, all three coders agreed in 88.8 percent of the cases (Kappa = 0.249). A respondent was ultimately coded as "objecting" or "emotional" if two out of three scores were coded as such.

British objections illustrate the point. One respondent expressed government distrust in their objection: "I do feel that there is danger of influence
from other governments on elections but wonder if it's really as widespread as we are being led to believe or if it's actually our own governments trying to give us a new enemy to focus on." A second echoed this
with negative system affect: "we do not need to look at foreign inter-
ferrance [sic]. There is a lot of interference from both left- and right-wing
extremists."[43] Several respondents noted surprise, that they did not know
about Russian meddling in the Brexit campaign or election. One explanation for this is that motivated reasoning was a messier process, as the
issue at stake was orthogonal to party ID. To wit, Leavers and Remainers
(and including nonvoters) express similar rates of objection – 18 and 15
percent, respectively.[44] This suggests that unlike in the US, among UK
voters, questioning the legitimacy of a result is not seen as tantamount to
defending the outcome. Finally, in contrast to the US, we do not see any
relationship between objecting to the treatment and citizenship norms.[45]

6.3.3 Germany

Like the UK, Germany requires two views: positionality and partisanship.
Positionality lets us run a first-cut test of incentives, grouping coalition
partners (CDU/CSU and SPD) and major parties outside of government in
a residual, challenger category. A partisan lens then lets us interrogate by
party directly (including five parties, and a category for other), observing
left parties in both the challenger and incumbent positions. This allows
for a more careful analysis of left and right parties both in and out of
power, to assess the role of positional incentives versus programmatic
preferences.

Beginning with governing positions, Figure 6.8 organizes responses by
support for parties in government and outside of it. From this different

---

[43] As an illustration of this point, allow me to quote an additional respondent who
expressed agreement: "It is correct that there is foreign influence; however, the belief that
it is election fraud is misplaced. The influence is cultural with Marxism/communism/
transgenderism/hate white people etc. All the madness of the 'progressive' left, they are
the infiltrated ones, and no I'm not a right-winger I'm just not a Corbynite/progressive."
[44] These figures are the likelihood of, say, Leavers to object the out of the total number of
Leavers. Of Leavers that objected out of the total number of treatment recipients (N =
619), objection rate was 7.9 percent. For Remainers, it was slightly higher, at 8.4 percent.
[45] The only exception is for joining associations, where objection leads to a
negative evaluation.

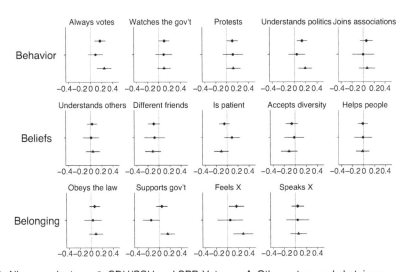

◆ All respondents   ● CDU/CSU and SPD Voters   ▲ Other voters and abstainers

FIGURE 6.8. Foreign interference treatment by coalition participation, Germany

vantage point (and by pooling responses into large categories), the foreign interference vignette makes challengers significantly more active (valuing voting, protesting, understanding politics), impatient (at the 90 percent level), and supportive of democratic institutions (support government and feeling German). Along behavioral items, supporters of parties that are not in government look a lot like Remainers in the UK and Democrats in the US. This affirms a type of mobilizing effect of electoral losers. The vignette had no significant effect on status quo incumbents, with the exception of declining support in government as an attribute of good citizenship. I flag this finding – like in polarization – to investigate whether this is a sign of SPD frustration.

Overall, these findings comport with our general expectations of competitive democracy, where outsiders necessarily feel more mobilized than the status quo insiders in power. Even supporting government *by those who voted for government* is negatively affected by the foreign interference treatment, suggesting a surprisingly robust concern in preserving the integrity of democratic institutions. But these results do not support the theoretical expectation that consensus-based systems minimize asymmetry in citizen responses. In this view, we only observe challenger parties doing the work.

Like the British case, Germany requires a second test for considering how citizenship responds to status quo versus challenger incentives.

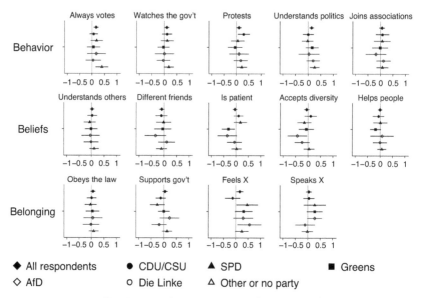

FIGURE 6.9. Foreign interference treatment by partisanship, Germany

Drilling down to the partisan level in Figure 6.9, we see evidence that is consistent with a citizen-centered theory of democratic instability, where the mainstream partisan left and right both value similar attributes of active citizenship, though they are not significant at the individual level (unlike at the aggregate level). Since this is a multiparty system, many of the significant aggregate results are insignificant at the individual party level (due to size and variation within group). Yet we can still discuss trends. The overall picture is consensus, expressed in two ways: (1) citizens are not mobilized by interference to change their understanding of citizenship in accordance with partisanship; and (2) supporters of both left and right parties exhibit similar patterns where they are. That is, in a positive-sum game system, individuals jointly value active citizenship to jointly protect institutions as a public good.

Looking closer at behavior, we see a broad set of significant aggregate results but null results by partisanship. As aggregate results remain stable, this is evidence consistent with the idea that when partisan stakes are lower, citizens interpret obligation by democratic principles not partisan gains. That results are null does not suggest a lack of concern but an already-high level of awareness of the importance of these attributes across groups. The government's priming of vigilance no doubt contributed to this salience. Notably, the only significant result that survives multiparty subsetting is that CDU/CSU supporters are more likely to value protesting in response to the foreign interference treatment (p = 0.02), a trait typically associated with the partisan left rather than with the center-right CDU/CSU.

Moving to liberal democratic beliefs, the foreign interference treatment did not change citizens' understanding of civic obligation when we separate respondents by partisanship. And, as we saw in the results in Chapter 4, these valuations were already high across all parties to begin with, with the unsurprising exception of the illiberal AfD. In response to foreign interference, the AfD become significantly less likely to value patience (p = 0.07) and accept diversity (p = 0.03). Diversity support was already low to begin with (an average 2.9/5), that the AfD could break through a basement effect (p = 0.03) is remarkable. The Greens are also less likely to exhibit patience (p = 0.02) in response to foreign interference, consistent with a general expectation that patience is not a virtue among status-seeking challengers. And, as signposted earlier, SPD posts a significant (p = 0.08) and negative result on "support government," expressing real frustration with coalition partnership.

Finally, the effect of foreign interference on "feeling German" was significant at the aggregate level, and moving to the partisan level we see this effect is significant for all three parties on the left: SPD, Greens, and Die Linke. These echo results from the other two cases, that the partisan left expresses a type of patriotism in response to foreign interference. Again, independent of significant, jingoistic correlates – like "speaking German" or not accepting diversity – "feeling German" in response to an external infiltration on democratic institutions suggests a type of democratic pride and institutional defensiveness. This illustrates the utility in asking a broad range of citizenship items, but also the importance of context. For individuals, national identification may only be activated when confronted by a national out group. That the Greens also appear to approach a significant result for "speaking German" (p = 0.09) alongside patriotism may be a direct concern about Russian influence specifically and a point of contrast to the far left Die Linke, which pulls more heavily from a post-communist, nostalgic demographic.

In checking for objection and emotional responses among German respondents,[46] there are two observations worth noting. First, objection

---

[46] Each respondent was coded three times, randomized across a team of six coders. For objection, all three coders agreed in 95.5 percent of the cases (Kappa = 0.721). For emotion, all three coders agreed in 90.5 percent of the cases (Kappa = 0.447).

among Germans was the lowest across the three cases – only 6 percent of the respondents who received the foreign interference treatment objected to it, reflecting its widespread discussion and unambiguous nature in the run-up to the 2017 federal election. Anecdotally, the open-ended German responses were far more preoccupied with the Russian character of interference than the interference itself, compared to British and American responses. Almost all objections mention Russia (unlike the other cases), and several objectors reported Russian heritage: "I read about Russia's alleged interference in the Western elections, etc. I do not believe a word, that is a clear propaganda of the West against Russia. I myself come from central Russia" and "Everyone is picking at Russia (my country of origin), which I, as a German who was born and raised there, perceive as absolutely asocial. Germans should rather focus on the Americans, because in my eyes these are the biggest warmakers of all."[47] Among those that objected, the only significant effect of the foreign interference treatment is the increased importance on understanding politics (perhaps reflecting an insecurity in not knowing more already or an emotional response to believing the treatment was incorrect).

In sum, Germany is a good example of how positional incentives moderate threat. Unlike foreign interference in the US and UK, both of which were heavily politicized and inevitably refracted through the lens of partisanship, Germany's consensus system engenders a different sense of political efficacy and problem-solving.[48] Germans mobilize across partisan divides not out of altruism but, consistent with the positive-sum incentives of a consensus-based system, out of mutual interest. So while there were no significant effects that really distinguish one party from another in how supporters view citizenship norms, only by framing their political interests by the "win or lose" dichotomy typical to majoritarian systems do we see positional incentives play out.

A respondent was ultimately coded as "objecting" or "emotional" if two out of three scores were coded as such. Across treatments, 33.3 percent of those who objected were also emotional.

[47] Other responses in this vein were more aggressive: "Stimmungsmache gegen Russland!"(Cheap propaganda against Russia) and even "Die Lügenpresse verbreitet Lügen über Russland." (The lying press spreads lies about Russia, Lügenpresse being a loaded term adopted by the Nazis in reference to Jewish, communist, and foreign press and recently repopularized by the far right).

[48] Specifically, PR systems provide more opportunities for representation and therefore increase participation and instill efficacy. Karp, and Banducci. "Political Efficacy and Participation in Twenty-Seven Democracies: How Electoral Systems Shape Political Behaviour."

6.4 CONCLUSION

How do citizens define obligation in response to foreign interference in election? In each case, citizens hold attitudes that reflect positional incentives, where responding as incumbents undermines existing status quo and challenging could yield potential gains. In the US, UK, and Germany, this meant challenger partisans were the most responsive to electoral interference, agreeing that good citizens are vigilant, informed, and exhibit national pride. These effects are strongest in majoritarian systems, where disrupting the status quo yields more direct and immediate payoffs.

There are also some country-specific findings worth revisiting. In the US, we see real division between partisan right winners who exhibit impatience and "objectors" (sore winners), who dismiss the premise of interference altogether. Neither the UK nor Germany exhibited the degree of treatment objection or the significance of objection on good citizenship values. The deep politicization of Russian interference in the US, and the fatigue that accompanies half a decade of nonresponse made this a tough test for the theory. Still, once we account for some respondents' objections to the very premise of foreign interference, we begin to see positional incentives of challengers, especially nonpartisans. By contrast, the UK is a cleaner example of mobilization among the status quo challengers, where Labour supports embrace several items of engaged citizenship as well as patriotism, while Conservatives become less engaged and accepting of diversity.

And Germany is unique to the three cases where we see strong effects of interference as a democratic threat from a positional perspective but not so much from a partisan one. This too is consistent with our expectation of positive-sum systems: either responses are strong across all partisan groups (polarization) or weak and null, as we see here. Strong positional incentives based on coalition position show the experiment worked, so we can rely on this external validity to bring confidence to our theory. In Germany, while challenger dynamics are similar to the US and UK, they only become apparent when sorting individuals by coalition status, and not by individual partisanship.

Lots of social identities – from gender to Brexit to education – shape citizenship norms. But partisanship has revealed itself – time and time again in this chapter – to be the most problematic for national unity in response to democratic crisis because it shapes incentives for responding to democratic problems that may upend democracy itself. These incentives are the clearest in zero-sum systems. Given the significant role of partisanship in setting norms of good citizenship in response to electoral interference, it does not require much creativity to imagine the long-term consequences. First, where only partisan challengers are mobilized, both the problem and the solution become politicized. This only attenuates differences between parties. Second, where partisan incumbents recognize the costs in responding, the likelihood of continued and unchecked electoral violations – along with a slew of other instances of democratic backsliding – are likely to take place. Third, rewarding quiescence and politicizing challenger responses only hollows out the necessary overlaps that hold together inherent differences in national citizenship and substantiates common goals for national unity. Without this foundation, citizen response to threat only makes democratic hard times harder. The next – and last – chapter moves to this very problem.

7

Conclusion

The late Congressman and civil rights icon John Lewis wrote in his last essay that "Democracy is not a state. It is an act."[1] In other words, democracy is a continual process, not a stable outcome. Lewis continued to argue that democracy must be renewed with each generation, through voting and participation, as well as by learning the lessons of the past. At the center of this renewal are not benevolent lawmakers, protecting the rights of the vulnerable and underrepresented, but citizens. He writes about "ordinary people with extraordinary vision."

So what are ordinary people doing to safeguard democracy? When confronted with real threats to democracy in a time of democratic crisis, how do citizens see their role? In this book, I have examined the effect of democratic threat on citizenship norms across two types of crisis (polarization, foreign interference in elections) and in three liberal democratic countries (the US, UK, and Germany). My results show that citizenship norms become divided and partisan in response to democratic threat. To explain these findings, I introduce the concept of positional incentives, where citizens saw their role in responding to democratic hard times according to the party they support. Citizens who support parties that benefit from acknowledging and responding to threats to democracy (i.e., out-of-government challengers) reacted in ways that differ from citizens that support parties that might be undermined by acknowledging and responding to threats (i.e., incumbents). This division between status quo

---

[1] John Lewis. "Together, You Can Redeem the Soul of Our Nation." *The New York Times*, July 30, 2020.

beneficiaries and challengers weakens the overlapping consensus of citizenship norms necessary for national unity and democratic stability.

The details of these asymmetrical responses vary by *institutional context*. In the US and UK, we saw strong responses to threats to democracy among opposition party supporters. When confronted with polarization, Democrats and Labour supporters place a higher value on tolerance, while right party supporters either turned away from citizenship norms of obligation or were unmoved by information about threats to democracy. Institutional incentives in majoritarian systems facilitate these outcomes, pushing citizens to an "us versus them" approach to politics. By contrast, in Germany we find partisans that support both in- and out-of-government parties – on the left and the right – responding to threats to democracy. Unlike the two-party polarization of majoritarian systems, consensus systems offer more opportunities for positive-sum politics, where acknowledging and responding to democratic problems are less costly for everyone. One of the advantages of a cross-national study is being able to identify variation across systems, which pushes us to think about democratic citizenship norms more generally.

My analysis also reveals variation by the *type* of democratic threat. In the US, challengers expressed a strong response to polarization, but a much more muted response to electoral interference. To explain this, I proposed that polarization exists among citizens, whereas electoral interference is distant and institutional in a way that may reduce a citizen's interest and ability to respond. That the threat of foreign electoral interference was real and heavily politicized over a period of three years preceding the survey also weakens citizen agency and interest. This is important. Recent work in political science shows that foreign electoral interference weakens institutional trust, but there are real ways in which the *politics* of a threat can numb citizens to their duty. By contrast, we saw British and German supporters of opposition parties were more activated by foreign interference. In both, we see strong support for an engaged citizen and national allegiance among those who oppose the government. In Germany, supporters of both government and opposition parties value mobilization to preserve election integrity.

Last, we see that citizen responses across all three cases exhibit what I term correspondence: Individuals see the threat of polarization as comprising a decline in tolerance and respond with liberal democratic norms, and see the threat of foreign interference as one that invites behavioral vigilance and patriotism. This is key: The type of threat conditions the type of citizenship response. Citizens understand what's happening to their system, and what citizens are capable of doing in the face of threat.

Overall, this comparison across advanced democracies shows the deep consequences of democratic threat on citizenship norms. Democratic threat fractures consensus over core citizenship values, in which only some citizens recognize and respond to threat. Moreover, the very attributes that both sides need to embrace to support democratic institutions in hard times – the attributes of good citizenship that citizens normally agree upon in day-to-day politics – are the very ones that exhibit asymmetry: tolerance, forbearance, vigilance, and being politically informed.

There are some important differences across the three countries. Backsliding is not a uniquely American phenomenon, but we see some exceptional features in American mass opinion in the face of threats to democracy. First, in the US, we observe impatience among *incumbent supporters* while in Germany we see it among *opposition supporters*. This has important normative implication. We might rightly understand why challengers in democratic systems express impatience, as they are eager to take another swing at gaining power. But what accounts for why we see it among winners? Why do Republicans reject patience? This was a concern at the center of Levitsky and Ziblatt's analysis, that Republican power holders do not exhibit norms of forbearance (or mutual tolerance). Here we see evidence that mass public opinion mirrors this elite impatience. We do not observe the same kind of impatience among Conservative supporters in the UK.

There is a second dimension to the American response to democratic threat that may provide a bit of optimism. Unlike British respondents, American respondents do not become more nationalistic or intolerant to diversity in response to either democratic threat. Among British respondents, threats increase intolerance and nationalism. Facing a threat of polarization, Britons on the left and right express more support for feeling British, while supporters of the left also express more support for speaking English and less support for diversity. These results are similar for Remainers. In Germany, supporters of the left (SPD, Greens, and Die Linke) also respond to foreign interference threat with greater support for patriotism. But, in the case of foreign interference, this result aligns to theoretical expectation, where an external threat – in which a foreign government is named – elicits a rallying-around-the-flag effect. However, that we see this result among British respondents in response to domestic polarization is concerning. Elsewhere, I show that this result is also produced in response to an immigration threat: Labour supporters become more nationalistic and less tolerant.[2]

Many would view these nationalistic values as a feature of British politics, where ethnoculturalism structures a post-Brexit world.[3] But the comparison here raises a second, related possibility: Diversity is less entrenched in national identity. For decades, the UK was upheld as a model of multiculturalism, though its race relations and immigrant politics were certainly no paragon of inclusion.[4] Unlike the US and its two and a half century-long history of immigration, migration scholars characterize countries like the UK and Germany as comparative recent receivers, with immigration largely beginning in the post–World War II era. And while a 2021 report by the UK's Commission on Race and Ethnic Disparities found "no evidence of systemic or institutional racism,"[5] the fierce backlash and criticism to this report suggests otherwise.

The takeaway here is that we observe a strong emphasis on national identity by both the left and right in response to both threats in the UK, and not in the US. And while these attributes of good citizenship are typically reserved to the partisan right in everyday citizenship, the left embraces them as well in response to democratic threat in the European cases. As I said, this might be an encouraging result for the US, that the left does not become more nationalistic in response to democratic that, like they do in more recent immigrant-receiving societies of Western Europe.

A more sober reflection, however, would acknowledge that the diversity that gets scapegoated in the US might not be that related to immigrant-status (e.g., who "feels" American, who speaks English) but race, where systematic discrimination is an enduring feature of American politics. I did not, for example, ask about civic obligation in response to the democratic threat of voter suppression. Writing in 2021, when legislation in states like Georgia and Texas aim to undermine voting rights that disproportionally affect Black Americans, this is arguably the most direct threat to democracy today, but one that has no comparison in

---

[2] Goodman. "Immigration Threat, Partisanship, and Democratic Citizenship: Evidence from the Us, Uk, and Germany."

[3] Sobolewska, and Ford. *Brexitland: Identity, Diversity and the Reshaping of British Politics.*

[4] Erik Bleich. *Race Politics in Britain and France: Ideas and Policymaking since the 1960's.* Cambridge, UK, New York: Cambridge University Press, 2003.

[5] Commission on Race and Ethnic Disparities. "Commission on Race and Ethnic Disparities: The Report." (London: CRED, March 2021), 77.

European democracies. Nor did I ask whether "a good citizen is white" or "shares in national ancestry" (though this is a question that appears in the ISSP National Identity survey). Elsewhere, Wright finds American respondents on average hold achievable definitions of national belonging (versus ascriptive),[6] but these definitions are malleable and subject to change in the context of things like immigration. I highlight this as a critical avenue for additional work and recognize the important research that has already examined racial identity, citizenship norms, and belonging.[7]

This raises some further considerations for thinking about scope conditions in studying divided citizenship norms. First, the timing of the study does not allow me to vary the party in power in each country, meaning that both winner-take-all systems had governments led by parties on the right. One strategy for trying to disentangle incumbency from party preferences was in the inclusion of Germany as a case study, in which a long-serving grand coalition included a left party, the SPD. An additional strategy was in testing different political cleavages other than partisanship. In studying Brexit "winners" versus "losers," we saw that – by and large – positional dynamics explained which citizens responded to democratic threat and which did not. Partisanship is more than a political ideology or policy platform; party government also creates a set of positional incentives.

Second, it was important for threats to resonate with respondents. Attitudes in response to hypothetical events are hypothetical as well, but what we wanted to know here was how citizens react to real experiences, framed as democratic threat. Most studies of democratic backsliding that focus on citizens examine their attitudes toward democracy and democratic values, and these have documented broad declines in support for democracy[8] and increasing tolerance for authoritarianism.[9] In this book, we have looked directly at citizen attitudes about *their role* in democratic hard times. That means that threats had to be real, to allow citizens to

---

[6] Matthew Wright. "Diversity and the Imagined Community: Immigrant Diversity and Conceptions of National Identity." *Political Psychology* 32, no. 5 (2011): 837–62.

[7] Niambi M. Carter, and Efrén O. Pérez. "Race and Nation: How Racial Hierarchy Shapes National Attachments." Ibid. 37, no. 4 (2016): 497–513; Niambi Michele Carter. *American While Black: African Americans, Immigration, and the Limits of Citizenship.* New York: Oxford University Press, 2019.

[8] Mounk. *The People Vs. Democracy: Why Our Freedom Is in Danger and How to Save It.*

[9] Graham, and Svolik. "Democracy in America? Partisanship, Polarization, and the Robustness of Support for Democracy in the United States."; Ariel Malka et al. "Who Is Open to Authoritarian Governance within Western Democracies? ." *Perspectives on Politics* (2020), doi:10.1017/S1537592720002091.

think through expectations for themselves and others. This precluded comparisons to cases like Canada, which had center of left governments in power but no experience with electoral interference. In fact, the Canadian government coordinated detailed plans to preempt interference and misinformation, including encouraging the typically tight-lipped intelligence services to be transparent about threats to the democratic process.[10] Although a limitation of this book, examining how citizens respond to real democratic threats under center-left or left governments is an opportunity for future research.

Third, threat to democracy had to be comparative in scope – that is, experienced across national political systems. Recall the objective was not just to learn about national citizenship norms but about democratic citizenship across systems. This precluded examining threats that may be more consequential and nationally specific, like the rise of far right parties in Germany or voter suppression efforts in the US. Polarization is an example where the substance of the threat type varied cross-nationally – political in the US, issue-based in the UK, social cleavages in Germany – but the general phenomenon of polarization is common enough to enable cross-case comparison.

However, a citizen-centered theory of democratic instability provides explicit guidelines for approaching new cases, new threats, and expanding scope conditions. Beginning with the observation that citizens choose which threats they respond to and how, we expect citizenship norms to adjust in line with partisan incentives. That is, democratic threat creates "us versus them" dynamics in majoritarian systems. When political identities produce different understandings of threat and different citizen commitments in response to threat, this attenuates or severs overlapping norms of consensus. Without this national unity, citizenship cannot prevent democratic erosion. In fact, emerging differences in citizenship norms may actually catalyze democratic erosion.

7.1 HOW DIVIDED CITIZENSHIP MAKES DEMOCRATIC PROBLEMS WORSE

The stakes of divided citizenship cannot be overstated. If a moment of democratic crisis turns members of one party toward liberal democratic

---

[10] For example, Canadian Centre for Cyber Security. "2019 Update: Cyber Threats to Canada's Democratic Process." available at https://cyber.gc.ca/en/guidance/2019-update-cyber-threats-canadas-democratic-process (accessed March 2, 2021).

citizenship norms and members of another against those same norms, this is a threat to democracy itself. Democratic politics under such conditions is not about safeguarding institutions that support meaningful contestation: A partisan rejection of liberal democratic norms means rejecting the soft guardrails that make democracy work. Democratic politics becomes about maintaining positions for status quo winners at any cost, including democracy. In this scenario, individuals respond to threats to democracy not as citizens but as partisans, acting to protect what's best for "their side" even if it means sacrificing democracy in the process.

This phenomenon of divided citizenship seems, at a superficial level, like just another example of polarization. But the true danger is that – unlike polarization – a partisan citizenship is directly incompatible to democratic stability. Democracy is a political system that provides structure for disagreement and partisan rancor, but vigorous disagreement is sustained through mutual commitments to the rule of law, tolerance, forbearance, and other liberal democratic values. The one thing democrats cannot disagree on are the terms of democracy itself. If individuals do not agree on what comprises a democratic threat, or on what democratic citizens should do in response to one, then it is hard to imagine what productive steps might be taken to repair a broken democratic system.

I signposted in the Introduction that I was going to make three arguments in this book. The first two arguments were empirical: Citizenship is a foundational institution for democratic stability (Chapters 2–4) and citizenship becomes divided in hard times when individuals respond to democratic threat as partisans (Chapters 5 and 6). Citizens simultaneously hold partisan interests and democratic values, but the evidence here shows when partisanship can overwhelm citizens' democratic commitments. This, then, is my third argument: Divided citizenship makes democratic problems worse.

There are at least three ways that divided citizenship exacerbates democratic dysfunction. First, with divided citizenship, there is *no objective definition of what constitutes a threat*. We can identify changes to institutions, subversions of rule of law, and deprivation of voting rights for citizens as objective signs of democratic backsliding. But the survey experiments in this book show what is anecdotally apparent in national politics across advanced democracies, which is that how elites and citizens define threats to democracy is subjective and open to interpretation. One person's voter suppression is another person's defense of rule of law. The problem is that when there is no such thing as an objective threat – when partisans decide what is or is not threatening based on their positional interests – there are few incentives for partisans to cooperate in the defense of democracy. Defending democracy cannot just be the preoccupation of power challengers. Those who hold power must also want to preserve the rules of the game. They must want to see the value in future games.

The second reason that divided citizenship makes democratic problems worse is that it exposes *fundamental disagreement over what democracy is*. The problem is not just that elites and citizens interpret democratic problems differently, but that some lack core commitments to democracy to begin with. This did not appear to be the case in everyday citizenship (Chapter 4), but threats to democracy may activate latent antidemocratic attitudes. In other words, heightening the salience of threats to democracy may weaken some of these norms of mutual tolerance, allowing some citizens to admit or reveal that they have loose or superficial commitments to democracy to begin with. And when individuals hold different core values of citizenship, it reflects different meanings of democracy itself. Russ Dalton illustrates the point well: "Democratic and Republican politicians are both strong believers in good citizenship and advocates for more democracy – but they have very different ideas about how the values of Americans should be changed."[11] And, as this quote suggests, citizen-level differences respond to elite cues.

Comparing state responses to electoral interference between the US and Germany is illustrative of this difference. Motivated reasoning not only guided US Republicans to reject Russian electoral interference as a threat, it also increased support for Russia, where the number of Republicans who believed that Russia was friendly to the US rose from 22 percent in 2014 to 40 percent in 2018.[12] In her opening testimony before Trump's Impeachment inquiry, former Russia director for the National Security Council Fiona Hill put this concern succinctly: "When we are consumed by partisan rancor, we cannot combat these external forces as they seek to divide us against each another, degrade our institutions, and destroy the faith of the American people in our

---

[11] Dalton. *The Good Citizen: How a Younger Generation Is Reshaping American Politics*, 47.
[12] Gallup. "Republicans More Positive on U.S. Relations with Russia." July 13, 2018. Available at https://news.gallup.com/poll/237137/republicans-positive-relations-russia.aspx (accessed April 2, 2021).

democracy."[13] Now imagine what would happen if some crises occur *because* the ruling party does not exhibit commitments to liberal democracy.

These problems are more pronounced in winner-take-all systems,[14] and we should worry about status quo institutional deficiencies of these systems as much as active backsliding. This includes polarization. Polarization weakens democratic citizenship not just because it promotes political factions, but also because it elevates and simplifies partisan differences at the expense of other competing interests and values. Polarization also hurts the most vulnerable in society, by encouraging illiberalism, extremism, and violence. We can think of other ways in which institutional deficiencies make solving democratic problem harder, especially if we start to look at counter-majoritarianism. The point is that these systems start at a disadvantage.

Last, partisan citizenship makes solving problems more difficult because *the solutions themselves become politicized*. The problem *and* the solution become subject to partisan division. This exacerbates differences, pushes groups further apart, and makes national unity more unlikely. This makes resolving democratic problems intractable. If only half the country thinks that something is threatening, they will not recognize the proposed solution as necessary or even legitimate. It generates the quintessential negative feedback loop.

7.2 WHAT CAN WE DO ABOUT IT?

Divided citizenship is unlike other democratic challenges. To alleviate negative partisanship, empathy and intergroup contact are often prescribed. To address structural polarization, elites might adopt consensus-building measures, like building broad coalitions beyond traditional allies, or consider large-scale institutional and electoral reforms.[15]

---

[13] NPR. "Fiona Hill, David Holmes Opening Statements for Thursday's Impeachment Hearing." November 21, 2019. Available at www.npr.org/2019/11/21/781415139/read-impeachment-witness-fiona-hills-opening-statement-for-thursday-s-hearing (accessed November 22, 2019).

[14] For more on this, Michael Miller finds "non-winner-take-all institutions, high media accuracy, low partisanship, and citizen support for democracy typically promote democratic survival." Michael K. Miller. "A Republic, If You Can Keep It: Breakdown and Erosion in Modern Democracies." *The Journal of Politics* 83, no. 1 (2021): 198–213.

[15] For example, Lee Drutman. *Breaking the Two-Party Doom Loop: The Case for Multiparty Democracy in America.* New York: Oxford University Press, 2020.

To increase participation, one might, as Hahrie Han describes, do "the hard work of investing in the institutions, processes, and practices of civil society, the economy, and governance."[16] But what do you do when citizens understand the goals and problems of democracy differently? What happens when one side thinks the solution to democratic backsliding is more liberal democracy while the other side thinks the solution is less?

Many suggest the answer lies in more (or better) civic education. Research shows civic education can teach citizens about political life, rights and responsibilities of citizenship,[17] increase engagement[18] and political voice[19] in young people, and ultimately, empower citizens to do the "hard work" of investing in and protecting democracy.[20] Civic education is certainly important wherever we see a decline in political knowledge and interest.[21] In the case of the US, civic education can have a big impact on young people with less exposure to information about the US political system at home.[22] And evidence from Europe shows more education for citizens generally can reduce intolerance by reducing anti-immigrant attitudes.[23]

But I think that the evidence in this book suggests that this "civic deficit" is less a problem of being uninformed and more of a lack of will. We see across both polarization and foreign interference threats that citizens match problems with appropriate solutions. For example, partisan challengers in the US and UK expressed appropriate responses to

---

[16] Hahrie Han. "Problems of Power." *Stanford Social Innovation Review* Winter (2020): 6.

[17] Steven E. Finkel, and Amy Erica Smith. "Civic Education, Political Discussion, and the Social Transmission of Democratic Knowledge and Values in a New Democracy: Kenya 2002." *American Journal of Political Science* 55, no. 2 (2011): 417–35; Steven E. Finkel. "Can Democracy Be Taught?." *Journal of Democracy* 14, no. 4 (2003): 135–51; Steven E. Finkel. "Civic Education and the Mobilization of Political Participation in Developing Democracies." *Journal of Politics* 64, no. 4 (2002): 994–1020.

[18] Matthew D. Nelsen. "Cultivating Youth Engagement: Race & the Behavioral Effects of Critical Pedagogy." *Political Behavior* 43, no. 2 (2021): 751–84.

[19] Matthew D. Nelsen. "Teaching Citizenship: Race and the Behavioral Effects of American Civic Education." *Journal of Race, Ethnicity, and Politics* 6, no. 1 (2021): 157–86.

[20] Levitsky, and Ziblatt. *How Democracies Die.*

[21] M. Kent Jennings. "Political Knowledge over Time and across Generations." *Public Opinion Quarterly* 60, no. 2 (1996): 228–52.

[22] David E. Campbell, and Richard G. Niemi. "Testing Civics: State-Level Civic Education Requirements and Political Knowledge." *American Political Science Review* 110, no. 3 (2016): 495–511.

[23] Charlotte Cavaillé, and John Marshall. "Education and Anti-Immigration Attitudes: Evidence from Compulsory Schooling Reforms across Western Europe." Ibid. 113, no. 1 (2019): 254–63.

polarization – that it requires more tolerance and not, say, protesting or voting. The problem is not, as Lupia and McCubbin's book *The Democratic Dilemma* asks, "can citizens learn what they need to know"?[24] but can they do what they need to do? Do they want to? For democracy to endure, how do you teach, in the words of Larry Diamond, "leaders and citizens [to] internalize the spirit of democracy"[25]? Whatever its many benefits, there is no evidence that civic education can overcome the barrier of motivated reasoning.

This raises a second point: What is the ideal content of civic education? What sort of curriculum could build more agreement between citizens on recognizing democratic problems and solutions? There is significant variation in what countries count as civic education – content ranges from history, politics, and national symbols to financial skills and human rights. For immigrants, the fundamentals of citizenship center on cultural integration, but include understanding the political process, liberal democratic values, and enabling individuals to be autonomous.[26] But I think the German Federal Ministry of the Interior gets the concept exactly right when they describe civic education as "non-partisan but not impartial; it is grounded in the values and interpretation of democracy found in our Constitution. ... Civic education should start precisely where social consensus in a democracy is threatened."[27]

If existing civic curricula cannot assume that consensus exists, and cannot create consensus on core democratic values, this invites a more creative approach. We need to think outside the box of what constitutes "civic education"; perhaps it might include media literacy and debate skills. Or perhaps alongside a civic education curriculum that highlights rule of law and mutual tolerance, citizens – just like naturalizing immigrants – need to take an oath of citizenship. Immigrants in each case explicitly pledge to uphold liberal democratic values, but there is no equivalent for native-born citizens. The goal is to unite citizens behind protecting and preserving liberal democracy. To do so, they need to understand and agree on group goals – what democracy is and that it is

---

[24] Arthur Lupia, and Mathew D. McCubbins. *The Democratic Dilemma: Can Citizens Learn What They Need to Know?* (New York: Cambridge University Press, 1998).

[25] Diamond Larry. *The Spirit of Democracy: The Struggle to Build Free Societies Throughout the World* (New York: Times Books/Henry Holt and Co., 2008), 294.

[26] Goodman. *Immigration and Membership Politics in Western European.*

[27] Bundesministerium des Innern für Bau und Heimat. Available at www.bmi.bund.de/EN/ topics/community-and-integration/civic-education/civic-education-node.html (accessed April 7, 2021).

worth protecting – and the role of citizens in doing so. This may include combating misinformation; it may also include new exercises to rebuild intergroup trust. These are exciting possibilities worth exploring.

Where does that leave us? The most optimistic take is that just as threats to democracy may be temporary, mutual ties of tolerance, engagement, and commitments to rule of law may prove resilient. Political party fortunes rise and fall, and today's incumbent may be tomorrow's challenger. But while these changes may produce a civic reawakening, the partisan citizenship that I have uncovered in this book may be pushing us down another path. And we may only be at the beginning of this path that leads to a dark period for democracy, where democratic obstacles reveal themselves through slow-moving or piecemeal increments in time. Cross-cutting ties may continue to erode, and in time, prove harder to renew or repair.

I regret that this book raises more questions than provides answers. I do not know if there are real world policy solutions to the problem of divided citizenship. Nor could there be any simple resolution to a seemly intractable problem. How do you sell citizens on the values of democracy – and the role they play in preserving it – if they do not experience its bounty or if they reject it? And how do you maintain national unity when there are citizens within it that disagree on the fundamental values of democracy, including their role in preserving it? Given the strong force that elite messaging exerts on citizens, it seems that any path forward in hard times begins with elites coming together to define norms of consensus. This is impossible if there are actors of bad faith, or if the Republican Party – in the case of the US – remains committed to antidemocratic measures to preserve its hold on political power.

The key to democratic stability in diverse societies is not that political differences become homogenized or reduced, but that they are balanced and bound together through cross- cutting ties. These are the values and obligations of citizenship. But we can no longer afford to assume that citizenship demarcates a unified community that shares beliefs, values, and norms about civic duty. There are cleavages *in* citizenship that democratic hard times activate. And it is the work of this generation and generations to come to ensure the overlapping norms and group goals that form the foundation of citizenship – and, through it, democracy – are strong.

Appendix 1 Summary Statistics

United States

Variable	Obs	Mean	SD	Min	Max
Always Vote	2295	4.559	0.882	1	5
Obey Laws	2293	4.381	0.871	1	5
Keep Watch	2295	4.547	0.754	1	5
Associations	2273	3.421	1.153	1	5
Help People	2292	4.236	0.925	1	5
Others Opinions	2294	4.274	0.86	1	5
Friends Different	2281	3.982	1.029	1	5
Patience	2286	4.298	0.858	1	5
Support Govt	2203	3.179	1.13	1	5
Protest	2243	3.785	1.157	1	5
Informed	2303	4.479	0.799	1	5
Accept Diversity	2294	4.397	0.976	1	5
Feel American	2243	4.049	1.224	1	5
Speak English	2295	3.817	1.385	1	5
Female	2334	0.558	0.497	0	1
Age	2334	51.352	16.99	18	94
College Graduate	2334	0.338	0.473	0	1
Race1 (Black)	2334	0.094	0.292	0	1
Race2 (other, non-white)	2334	0.199	0.399	0	1
Reg_Midwest	2334	0.22	0.414	0	1
Reg_Northeast	2334	0.171	0.377	0	1
Reg_South	2334	0.371	0.483	0	1
Reg_West	2334	0.238	0.426	0	1

United Kingdom

Variable	Obs	Mean	SD	Min	Max
Always Vote	2546	4.31	1.027	1	5
Obey Laws	2564	4.351	0.845	1	5
Keep Watch	2520	4.029	0.97	1	5
Associations	2492	2.944	1.184	1	5
Help People	2542	4.069	0.922	1	5
Others' Opinions	2556	4.285	0.778	1	5
Friends Different	2553	4.045	0.937	1	5
Patience	2537	4.263	0.823	1	5
Support Govt	2429	3.057	1.079	1	5
Protest	2454	3.503	1.115	1	5
Informed	2536	3.813	1.004	1	5
Accept Diversity	2544	4.195	1.057	1	5
Feel British	2519	3.698	1.308	1	5
Speak English	2554	4.121	1.131	1	5
Female	2613	0.507	0.5	0	1
Age	2613	48.232	17.082	18	89
College	2613	0.326	0.469	0	1
Race1 (Black)	2613	0.025	0.156	0	1
Race2 (Asian, mixed, other)	2613	0.073	0.261	0	1
Reg_East Midlands	2613	0.069	0.254	0	1
Reg_East of England	2613	0.086	0.28	0	1
Reg_Greater London	2613	0.122	0.327	0	1
Reg_North East England	2613	0.041	0.197	0	1
Reg_North West England	2613	0.107	0.309	0	1
Reg_Northern Ireland	2613	0.031	0.172	0	1
Reg_Scotland	2613	0.085	0.279	0	1
Reg_South East England	2613	0.133	0.339	0	1
Reg_South West England	2613	0.091	0.287	0	1
Reg_Wales	2613	0.047	0.211	0	1
Reg_West Midlands	2613	0.096	0.295	0	1
Reg_Yorkshire and the Humber	2613	0.093	0.29	0	1

Germany

Variable	Obs	Mean	SD	Min	Max
Always Vote	2437	4.425	0.964	1	5
Obey Laws	2442	4.037	0.916	1	5
Keep Watch	2444	4.127	0.937	1	5
Associations	2375	3.092	1.094	1	5
Help People	2440	4.156	0.876	1	5
Others Opinions	2442	4.135	0.88	1	5

Variable	Obs	Mean	SD	Min	Max
Friends Different	2412	3.711	1.025	1	5
Patience	2387	3.919	0.924	1	5
Support Govt	2353	2.811	1.035	1	5
Protest	2407	4.072	0.966	1	5
Informed	2409	4.165	0.889	1	5
Accept Diversity	2434	4.016	1.076	1	5
Feel German	2399	3.273	1.368	1	5
Speak German	2449	4.133	1.079	1	5
Female	2490	0.514	0.5	0	1
Age	2490	48.452	17.048	18	89
College	2490	0.394	0.489	0	1
Race1 (Immigrant-origin, white)	2490	0.084	0.278	0	1
Race2 (Immigrant-origin, non-white)	2490	0.084	0.278	0	1
Reg_Baden Württemberg	2490	0.134	0.34	0	1
Reg_Bayern	2490	0.156	0.363	0	1
Reg_Berlin	2490	0.04	0.196	0	1
Reg_Brandenburg	2490	0.026	0.159	0	1
Reg_Bremen	2490	0.01	0.102	0	1
Reg_Hamburg	2490	0.022	0.147	0	1
Reg_Hessen	2490	0.076	0.265	0	1
Reg_Mecklenburg Vorpommern	2490	0.02	0.14	0	1
Reg_Niedersachsen	2490	0.084	0.278	0	1
Reg_Nordrhein Westfalen	2490	0.221	0.415	0	1
Reg_Rheinland Pfalz	2490	0.053	0.224	0	1
Reg_Saarland	2490	0.01	0.1	0	1
Reg_Sachsen	2490	0.052	0.222	0	1
Reg_SachsenAnhalt	2490	0.032	0.175	0	1
Reg_SchleswigHolstein	2490	0.037	0.188	0	1
Reg_Thüringen	2490	0.026	0.159	0	1

Appendix 2   Balance Tests: Polarization

United States

Variable	(1) Control group	(2) Treatment group	(3) Difference	(4) Standardized Difference
Female	0.579	0.553	−0.027	−0.038
	(0.494)	(0.498)	(0.285)	
Age	51.178	51.758	0.580	0.024
	(17.398)	(16.851)	(0.498)	
Black	0.091	0.083	−0.008	−0.020
	(0.288)	(0.277)	(0.576)	
Other, non-white	0.197	0.212	0.014	0.025
	(0.398)	(0.409)	(0.473)	
College	0.342	0.337	−0.005	−0.007
	(0.475)	(0.473)	(0.844)	
Reg_Midwest	0.217	0.215	−0.001	−0.002
	(0.412)	(0.411)	(0.955)	
Reg_Northeast	0.184	0.165	−0.018	−0.034
	(0.387)	(0.372)	(0.335)	
Reg_South	0.341	0.396	0.056*	0.081
	(0.474)	(0.489)	(0.021)	
Reg_West	0.259	0.223	−0.036	−0.060
	(0.438)	(0.417)	(0.092)	
Observations	822	780	3,111	

United Kingdom

Variable	(1) Control group	(2) Treatment group	(3) Difference	(4) Standardized Difference
Female	0.530	0.529	−0.000	−0.001
	(0.499)	(0.500)	(0.985)	
Age	49.339	49.444	0.106	0.004
	(17.041)	(17.292)	(0.909)	
Black	0.020	0.026	0.006	0.028
	(0.141)	(0.160)	(0.465)	
Asian, mixed, other	0.066	0.059	−0.008	−0.023
	(0.249)	(0.235)	(0.553)	
College	0.335	0.323	−0.012	−0.018
	(0.472)	(0.468)	(0.631)	
Reg_East Midlands	0.070	0.074	0.004	0.010
	(0.256)	(0.262)	(0.795)	
Reg_East of England	0.088	0.083	−0.005	−0.012
	(0.284)	(0.277)	(0.753)	
Reg_Greater London	0.118	0.106	−0.011	−0.026
	(0.323)	(0.309)	(0.503)	
Reg_North East England	0.035	0.037	0.002	0.007
	(0.184)	(0.189)	(0.857)	
Reg_North West England	0.108	0.108	−0.000	−0.001
	(0.311)	(0.311)	(0.982)	
Reg_Northern Ireland	0.033	0.034>	0.001	0.006
	(0.177)	(0.181)	(0.882)	
Reg_Scotland	0.087	0.082	−0.005	−0.013
	(0.282)	(0.274)	(0.742)	
Reg_South East England	0.140	0.133	−0.007	−0.014
	(0.347)	(0.340)	(0.711)	
Reg_South West England	0.095	0.094	−0.001	−0.002
	(0.293)	(0.292)	(0.964)	
Reg_Wales	0.045	0.052	0.008	0.025
	(0.207)	(0.223)	(0.502)	
Reg_West Midlands	0.085	0.096	0.010	0.025
	(0.280)	(0.294)	(0.504)	
Reg_Yorkshire and the Humber	0.096	0.100	0.004	0.010
	(0.295)	(0.301)	(0.798)	
Observations	738	648	3,225	

Germany

Variable	(1) Control group	(2) Treatment group	(3) Difference	(4) Standardized Difference
Female	0.509	0.499	−0.010	−0.014
	(0.500)	(0.500)	(0.700)	
Age	47.655	49.965	2.310**	0.097
	(17.205)	(16.564)	(0.009)	
Immigrant-origin (white)	0.091	0.087	−0.004	−0.009
	(0.287)	(0.282)	(0.812)	
Immigrant-origin (non-white), other	0.091	0.087	−0.004	−0.009
	(0.287)	(0.282)	(0.812)	
College	0.369	0.396	0.027	0.039
	(0.483)	(0.489)	(0.288)	
Reg_Baden Württemberg	0.118	0.157	0.039*	0.079
	(0.323)	(0.364)	(0.031)	
Reg_Bayern	0.159	0.148	−0.011	−0.022
	(0.366)	(0.355)	(0.549)	
Reg_Berlin	0.042	0.040	−0.002	−0.008
	(0.201)	(0.196)	(0.820)	
Reg_Brandenburg	0.022	0.027	0.004	0.019
	(0.148)	(0.161)	(0.599)	
Reg_Bremen	0.011	0.010	−0.001	−0.006
	(0.105)	(0.101)	(0.876)	
Reg_Hamburg	0.016	0.022	0.006	0.031
	(0.126)	(0.147)	(0.398)	
Reg_Hessen	0.073	0.072	−0.001	−0.002
	(0.261)	(0.259)	(0.946)	
Reg_Mecklenburg Vorpommern	0.021	0.015	−0.006	−0.034
	(0.144)	(0.121)	(0.363)	
Reg_Niedersachsen	0.078	0.087	0.009	0.023
	(0.269)	(0.282)	(0.535)	
Reg_Nordrhein Westfalen	0.239	0.233	−0.005	−0.009
	(0.426)	(0.423)	(0.817)	
Reg_Rheinland Pfalz	0.062	0.049	−0.013	−0.041
	(0.242)	(0.215)	(0.265)	
Reg_Saarland	0.007	0.004	−0.003	−0.028
	(0.086)	(0.066)	(0.456)	
Reg_Sachsen	0.063	0.041	−0.022	−0.070
	(0.244)	(0.199)	(0.061)	

(continued)

(continued)

	(1)	(2)	(3)	(4)
Variable	Control group	Treatment group	Difference	Standardized Difference
Reg_Sachsen Anhalt	0.026	0.027	0.001	0.002
	(0.159)	(0.161)	(0.952)	
Reg_Schleswig Holstein	0.032	0.040	0.008	0.029
	(0.177)	(0.196)	(0.434)	
Reg_Thüringen	0.029	0.028	−0.001	−0.002
	(0.167)	(0.165)	(0.953)	
Observations	805	677	3,155	

Appendix 3 Balance Tests: Foreign Interference

		United States		

	(1)	(2)	(3)	(4)
Variable	Control group	Treatment group	Difference	Standardized Difference
Female	0.579	0.541	−0.038	−0.054
	(0.494)	(0.499)	(0.131)	
Age	51.178	51.116	−0.061	−0.003
	(17.398)	(16.686)	(0.943)	
Black	0.091	0.108	0.017	0.039
	(0.288)	(0.310)	(0.272)	
Other, non-white	0.197	0.187	−0.010	−0.018
	(0.398)	(0.390)	(0.621)	
College	0.342	0.333	−0.009	−0.013
	(0.475)	(0.472)	(0.723)	
Reg_Midwest	0.217	0.228	0.012	0.020
	(0.412)	(0.420)	(0.583)	
Reg_Northeast	0.184	0.164	−0.020	−0.037
	(0.387)	(0.370)	(0.306)	
Reg_South	0.341	0.377	0.036	0.054
	(0.474)	(0.485)	(0.135)	
Reg_West	0.259	0.231	−0.028	−0.046
	(0.438)	(0.422)	(0.197)	
Observations	822	732	3,111	

United Kingdom

Variable	(1) Control group	(2) Treatment group	(3) Difference	(4) Standardized Difference
Female	0.530	0.519	−0.011	−0.016
	(0.499)	(0.500)	(0.680)	
Age	49.339	49.517	0.178	0.008
	(17.041)	(16.314)	(0.845)	
Black	0.020	0.023	0.002	0.011
	(0.141)	(0.149)	(0.771)	
Asian, mixed, other	0.066	0.058	−0.008	−0.024
	(0.249)	(0.234)	(0.533)	
College	0.335	0.341	0.006	0.009
	(0.472)	(0.474)	(0.811)	
Reg_East Midlands	0.070	0.076	0.005	0.015
	(0.256)	(0.265)	(0.700)	
Reg_East of England	0.088	0.084	−0.004	−0.010
	(0.284)	(0.278)	(0.790)	
Reg_Greater London	0.118	0.110	−0.008	−0.018
	(0.323)	(0.313)	(0.643)	
Reg_North East England	0.035	0.047	0.012	0.041
	(0.184)	(0.211)	(0.280)	
Reg_North West England	0.108	0.115	0.006	0.014
	(0.311)	(0.319)	(0.713)	
Reg_Northern Ireland	0.033	0.032	−0.000	−0.001
	(0.177)	(0.177)	(0.983)	
Reg_Scotland	0.087	0.084	−0.003	−0.007
	(0.282)	(0.278)	(0.859)	
Reg_South East England	0.140	0.129	−0.010	−0.021
	(0.347)	(0.336)	(0.579)	
Reg_South West England	0.095	0.090	−0.004	−0.011
	(0.293)	(0.287)	(0.782)	
Reg_Wales	0.045	0.044	−0.001	−0.004
	(0.207)	(0.204)	(0.922)	
Reg_West Midlands	0.085	0.105	0.020	0.047
	(0.280)	(0.307)	(0.218)	
reg_Yorkshireandthe Humber	0.096	0.084	−0.012	−0.030
	(0.295)	(0.278)	(0.436)	
Observations	738	619	3,225	

Germany

Variable	(1) Control group	(2) Treatment group	(3) Difference	(4) Standardized Difference
Female	0.509	0.570	0.061*	0.086
	(0.500)	(0.495)	(0.019)	
Age	47.655	48.264	0.610	0.025
	(17.205)	(16.676)	(0.491)	
Immigrant-origin (white)	0.091	0.068	−0.023	−0.060
	(0.287)	(0.252)	(0.109)	
Immigrant-origin (non-white), Other	0.091	0.068	−0.023	−0.060
	(0.287)	(0.252)	(0.109)	
College	0.369	0.464	0.095**	0.137
	(0.483)	(0.499)	(0.000)	
Reg_Baden Württemberg	0.118	0.131	0.013	0.029
	(0.323)	(0.338)	(0.434)	
Reg_Bayern	0.159	0.151	−0.008	−0.016
	(0.366)	(0.358)	(0.659)	
Reg_Berlin	0.042	0.043	0.001	0.002
	(0.201)	(0.203)	(0.955)	
Reg_Brandenburg	0.022	0.030	0.007	0.032
	(0.148)	(0.169)	(0.384)	
Reg_Bremen	0.011	0.010	−0.001	−0.006
	(0.105)	(0.101)	(0.876)	
Reg_Hamburg	0.016	0.024	0.007	0.038
	(0.126)	(0.152)	(0.300)	
Reg_Hessen	0.073	0.080	0.006	0.017
	(0.261)	(0.271)	(0.640)	
Reg_Mecklenburg Vorpommern	0.021	0.022	0.001	0.005
	(0.144)	(0.147)	(0.891)	
Reg_Niedersachsen	0.078	0.084	0.006	0.015
	(0.269)	(0.278)	(0.677)	
Reg_Nordrhein Westfalen	0.239	0.202	−0.036	−0.062
	(0.426)	(0.402)	(0.095)	
Reg_Rheinland Pfalz	0.062	0.056	−0.006	−0.018
	(0.242)	(0.230)	(0.628)	
Reg_Saarland	0.007	0.015	0.007	0.049
	(0.086)	(0.121)	(0.175)	
Reg_Sachsen	0.063	0.055	−0.009	−0.026
	(0.244)	(0.227)	(0.481)	
Reg_Sachsen Anhalt	0.026	0.037	0.011	0.044

(continued)

(*continued*)

Variable	(1) Control group	(2) Treatment group	(3) Difference	(4) Standardized Difference
	(0.159)	(0.189)	(0.231)	
Reg_Schleswig Holstein	0.032	0.038	0.006	0.023
	(0.177)	(0.192)	(0.525)	
Reg_Thüringen	0.029	0.022	−0.006	−0.029
	(0.167)	(0.147)	(0.437)	
Observations	805	677	3,155	

References

Abramowitz, Alan I., and Kyle L. Saunders. "Ideological Realignment in the US Electorate." *The Journal of Politics* 60, no. 3 (1998): 634–52.

Abramowitz, Alan I., and Steven Webster. "The Rise of Negative Partisanship and the Nationalization of US Elections in the 21st Century." *Electoral Studies* 41 (2016): 12–22.

Achen, Christopher H., and Larry M. Bartels. *Democracy for Realists: Why Elections Do Not Produce Responsive Government.* Vol. 4. Princeton, NJ: Princeton University Press, 2017.

Adam, Karla, and William Booth. "Rising Alarm in Britain over Russian Meddling in Brexit Vote." *Washington Post*, November 17, 2017.

Adorno, Theodor W., Else Frenkel-Brunswik, Daniel J. Levinson, and R. Nevitt Sanford. *The Authoritarian Personality.* New York: Norton, 1950.

Ahlquist, John S., Nahomi Ichino, Jason Wittenberg, and Daniel Ziblatt. "How Do Voters Perceive Changes to the Rules of the Game? Evidence from the 2014 Hungarian Elections." *Journal of Comparative Economics* 46, no. 4 (2018): 906–19.

Albertson, Bethany, and Shana Kushner Gadarian. *Anxious Politics: Democratic Citizenship in a Threatening World.* New York: Cambridge University Press, 2015.

Aldama, Abraham, Mateo Vásquez-Cortés, and Lauren Elyssa Young. "Fear and Citizen Coordination against Dictatorship." *Journal of Theoretical Politics* 31, no. 1 (2019): 103–25.

Alex-Assensoh, Yvette M. *Democracy at Risk: How Political Choices Undermine Citizen Participation and What We Can Do about It.* Washington, DC: Brookings Institution Press, 2005.

Almond, Gabriel, and Sidney Verba. *The Civic Culture: Political Attitudes and Democracy in Five Nations.* Princeton, NJ: Princeton University Press, 1963.

Altemeyer, Robert A., and Bob Altemeyer. *The Authoritarian Specter.* Cambridge, MA: Harvard University Press, 1996.

Anderson, Christopher J., Andre Blais, Shaun Bowler, Todd Donovan, and Ola Listhaug. *Losers' Consent: Elections and Democratic Legitimacy.* Oxford: Oxford University Press, 2005.

Anderson, Christopher J., and Christine A. Guillory. "Political Institutions and Satisfaction with Democracy: A Cross-National Analysis of Consensus and Majoritarian Systems." *American Political Science Review* 91, no. 1 (1997): 66–81.

Appleby, Jacob, and Christopher M. Federico. "The Racialization of Electoral Fairness in the 2008 and 2012 United States Presidential Elections." *Group Processes & Intergroup Relations* 21, no. 7 (2018): 979–96.

Bail, Christopher A., Lisa P. Argyle, Taylor W. Brown, et al. "Exposure to Opposing Views on Social Media Can Increase Political Polarization." *Proceedings of the National Academy of Sciences* 115, no. 37 (2018): 9216–21.

Baldassarri, Delia, and Andrew Gelman. "Partisans without Constraint: Political Polarization and Trends in American Public Opinion." *American Journal of Sociology* 114, no. 2 (2008): 408–46.

Barber, Benjamin. *Strong Democracy: Participatory Politics for a New Age.* Berkeley CA: University of California Press, 2003.

Bartels, Larry M. "Uninformed Votes: Information Effects in Presidential Elections." *American Journal of Political Science* 40 (1996): 194–230.

Benedetto, Giacomo, Simon Hix, and Nicola Mastrorocco. "The Rise and Fall of Social Democracy, 1918–2017." *American Political Science Review* 114, no. 3 (2020): 928–39.

Berinsky, Adam J. "Assuming the Costs of War: Events, Elites, and American Public Support for Military Conflict." *The Journal of Politics* 69, no. 4 (2007): 975–97.

Berman, Sheri. *Democracy and Dictatorship in Europe: From the Ancien Régime to the Present Day.* Oxford: Oxford University Press, 2019.

  The Social Democratic Moment. Cambridge, MA: Harvard University Press, 1998.

Berman, Sheri, and Hans Kundnani. "The Cost of Convergence." *Journal of Democracy* 32, no. 1 (2021): 22–36.

Berman, Sheri, and Maria Snegovaya. "Populism and the Decline of Social Democracy." *Journal of Democracy* 30, no. 3 (2019): 5–19.

Bermeo, Nancy. "On Democratic Backsliding." *Journal of Democracy* 27, no. 1 (2016): 5–19.

Bermeo, Nancy Gina. *Ordinary People in Extraordinary Times: The Citizenry and the Breakdown of Democracy.* Princeton, NJ: Princeton University Press, 2003.

Bisgaard, Martin. "How Getting the Facts Right Can Fuel Partisan-Motivated Reasoning." *American Journal of Political Science* 63, no. 4 (2019): 824–39.

Bisgaard, Martin, and Rune Slothuus. "Partisan Elites as Culprits? How Party Cues Shape Partisan Perceptual Gaps." *American Journal of Political Science* 62, no. 2 (2018): 456–69.

Blais, André. *To Vote or Not to Vote: The Merits and Limits of Rational Choice Theory.* Pittsburgh, PA: University of Pittsburgh Press, 2000.

Blais, André, and Christopher H. Achen. "Civic Duty and Voter Turnout." *Political Behavior* 41, no. 2 (2019): 473–97.

Blais, André, Carol Galais, and Danielle Mayer. "Is It a Duty to Vote and to Be Informed?" *Political Studies Review* 17, no. 4 (2019): 328–39.

Bleich, Erik. *Race Politics in Britain and France: Ideas and Policymaking since the 1960s.* Cambridge and New York: Cambridge University Press, 2003.

Blinder, Scott, Robert Ford, and Elisabeth Ivarsflaten. "Discrimination, Antiprejudice Norms, and Public Support for Multicultural Policies in Europe: The Case of Religious Schools." *Comparative Political Studies* 52, no. 8 (2019): 1232–55.

Blumer, Herbert. "Race Prejudice as a Sense of Group Position." *Pacific Sociological Review* 1, no. 1 (1958): 3–7.

Bolzendahl, Catherine, and Hilde Coffé. "Are 'Good' Citizens 'Good' Participants? Testing Citizenship Norms and Political Participation across 25 Nations." *Political Studies* 61 (2013): 45–65.

Bonikowski, Bart. "Nationalism in Settled Times." *Annual Review of Sociology* 42 (2016): 427–49.

Bonikowski, Bart, and Paul DiMaggio. "Varieties of American Popular Nationalism." *American Sociological Review* 81, no. 5 (2016): 949–80.

Bosniak, Linda. *The Citizen and the Alien: Dilemmas of Contemporary Membership.* Princeton, NJ: Princeton University Press, 2006.

Boxell, Levi, Matthew Gentzkow, and Jesse M. Shapiro. "Cross-Country Trends in Affective Polarization." NBER Working Paper No. 26669. Cambridge, MA: National Bureau of Economic Research, 2020.

Brubaker, Rogers. *Citizenship and Nationhood in France and Germany.* Cambridge, MA: Harvard University Press, 1992.

Bush, Sarah Sunn, and Amaney A. Jamal. "Anti-Americanism, Authoritarian Politics, and Attitudes about Women's Representation: Evidence from a Survey Experiment in Jordan." *International Studies Quarterly* 59, no. 1 (2015): 34–45.

Calvo, Ernesto, and Timothy Hellwig. "Centripetal and Centrifugal Incentives under Different Electoral Systems." *American Journal of Political Science* 55, no. 1 (2011): 27–41.

Campbell, Angus, Philip E. Converse, Warren E. Miller, et al. *"The American Voter."* Ann Arbor, MI: University of Michigan Press, 1960.

Campbell, Angus, Philip Converse, Warren E. Miller, et al. *The American Voter.* [in English] Midway Reprints. Chicago, IL: University of Chicago Press, 1960.

Campbell, David E. "Civic Engagement and Education: An Empirical Test of the Sorting Model." *American Journal of Political Science* 53, no. 4 (2009): 771–86.

Campbell, David E., and Richard G. Niemi. "Testing Civics: State-Level Civic Education Requirements and Political Knowledge." *American Political Science Review* 110, no. 3 (2016): 495–511.

Capoccia, Giovanni. *Defending Democracy: Reactions to Extremism in Interwar Europe.* Baltimore: Johns Hopkins University Press, 2005.

Carsey, Thomas M., and Geoffrey C. Layman. "Changing Sides or Changing Minds? Party Identification and Policy Preferences in the American Electorate." *American Journal of Political Science* 50, no. 2 (2006): 464–77.

Carter, Niambi M., and Efrén O. Pérez. "Race and Nation: How Racial Hierarchy Shapes National Attachments." *Political Psychology* 37, no. 4 (2016): 497–513.

Carter, Niambi Michele. *American While Black: African Americans, Immigration, and the Limits of Citizenship*. New York: Oxford University Press, 2019.

Cavaillé, Charlotte, and John Marshall. "Education and Anti-Immigration Attitudes: Evidence from Compulsory Schooling Reforms across Western Europe." *American Political Science Review* 113, no. 1 (2019): 254–63.

Chou, Winston, Rafaela Dancygier, Naoki Egami, et al. "Competing for Loyalists? How Party Positioning Affects Populist Radical Right Voting." *Comparative Political Studies* (2021) Online first, https://doi.org/10.1177/0010414021997166.

Claassen, Christopher. "Does Public Support Help Democracy Survive?". *American Journal of Political Science* 64, no. 1 (2020): 118–34.

Coffé, Hilde, and Catherine Bolzendahl. "Partisan Cleavages in the Importance of Citizenship Rights and Responsibilities." *Social Science Quarterly* 92, no. 3 (2011): 656–74.

Colomer, Josep M. *Political Institutions: Democracy and Social Choice*. Oxford: Oxford University Press, 2001.

Conover, Pamela Johnston, Ivor M. Crewe, and Donald D. Searing. "The Nature of Citizenship in the United States and Great Britain: Empirical Comments on Theoretical Themes." *The Journal of Politics* 53, no. 3 (1991): 800–32.

Converse, Philip E. "The Nature of Belief Systems in Mass Publics." In *Ideology and Discontent*, edited by David E. Apter, 1–74. New York: The Free Press of Glencoe, 1964.

Corstange, Daniel, and Nikolay Marinov. "Taking Sides in Other People's Elections: The Polarizing Effect of Foreign Intervention." *American Journal of Political Science* 56, no. 3 (2012): 655–70.

Crouch, Colin. *Coping with Post-Democracy*. Vol. 598. London: Fabian Society, 2000.

Crozier, Michel, Samuel P. Huntington, and Joji Watanuki. *The Crisis of Democracy*. Vol. 70: New York: University Press New York, 1975.

Dahl, Robert. *Pluralist Democracy in the United States: Conflict and Consent*. Chicago: Rand McNally, 1967.

   Polyarchy: Participation and Opposition. New Haven, CT: Yale University Press, 1973.

Dahl, Robert A. "What Political Institutions Does Large-Scale Democracy Require?". *Political Science Quarterly* 120, no. 2 (2005): 187–97.

Dahl, Robert Alan. *Democracy and Its Critics*. New Haven, CT: Yale University Press, 1989.

Dalton, Russell J. *Citizen Politics: Public Opinion and Political Parties in Advanced Industrial Democracies*. Los Angeles: CQ Press, 2013.

   "Citizenship Norms and the Expansion of Political Participation." *Political Studies* 56, no. 1 (2008): 76–98.

   Democratic Challenges, Democratic Choices. The Erosion of Political Support in Advanced Industrial Democracies (Comparative Politics). UK: Oxford University Press, 2004.

The Good Citizen : How a Younger Generation Is Reshaping American Politics. [in English] Washington, DC: CQ Press, 2008.

The Good Citizen: How a Younger Generation Is Reshaping American Politics. Washington, DC: CQ press, 2021.

Dalton, Russell J., and Martin P. Wattenberg. *Parties without Partisans: Political Change in Advanced Industrial Democracies*. New York: Oxford University Press, 2002.

Dalton, Russell J., and Christian Welzel. *The Civic Culture Transformed: From Allegiant to Assertive Citizens*. New York: Cambridge University Press, 2014.

Dawson, James, and Seán Hanley. "What's Wrong with East-Central Europe?: The Fading Mirage of The" Liberal Consensus"." *Journal of Democracy* 27, no. 1 (2016): 20–34.

Day, Martin V., Susan T. Fiske, Emily L. Downing, et al. "Shifting Liberal and Conservative Attitudes Using Moral Foundations Theory." *Personality and Social Psychology Bulletin* 40, no. 12 (2014): 1559–73.

De Vries, Catherine E., and Sara B. Hobolt. *Political Entrepreneurs: The Rise of Challenger Parties in Europe*. Princeton, NJ: Princeton University Press, 2020.

Diamond, Larry. *Developing Democracy: Toward Consolidation*. Baltimore: Johns Hopkins University Press, 1999.

Doorenspleet, Renske. "Electoral Systems and Good Governance in Divided Countries." *Ethnopolitics* 4, no. 4 (2005): 365–80.

Downs, Anthony. "An Economic Theory of Political Action in a Democracy." *Journal of Political Economy* 65, no. 2 (1957): 135–50.

Druckman, James N., Erik Peterson, and Rune Slothuus. "How Elite Partisan Polarization Affects Public Opinion Formation." *American Political Science Review* (2013): 57–79.

Drutman, Lee. *Breaking the Two-Party Doom Loop: The Case for Multiparty Democracy in America*. New York: Oxford University Press, 2020.

Easton, David. *A Framework for Political Analysis*. Vol. 25: Englewood Cliffs, NJ: Prentice-Hall, 1965.

Evans, Geoffrey, and Anja Neundorf. "Core Political Values and the Long-Term Shaping of Partisanship." *British Journal of Political Science* (2018): 1–19.

Fieldhouse, Edward, David Cutts, and Jack Bailey. "Who Cares If You Vote? Partisan Pressure and Social Norms of Voting." *Political Behavior* (2020): 1–20.

Finkel, Eli J., Christopher A. Bail, Mina Cikara et al. "Political Sectarianism in America." *Science* 370, no. 6516 (2020): 533–36.

Finkel, Steven E. "Can Democracy Be Taught?". *Journal of Democracy* 14, no. 4 (2003): 137–51.

"Civic Education and the Mobilization of Political Participation in Developing Democracies." *Journal of Politics* 64, no. 4 (2002): 994–1020.

Finkel, Steven E., and Amy Erica Smith. "Civic Education, Political Discussion, and the Social Transmission of Democratic Knowledge and Values in a New Democracy: Kenya 2002." *American Journal of Political Science* 55, no. 2 (2011): 417–35.

Fiorina, Morris P., and Samuel J. Abrams. "Political Polarization in the American Public." *Annual Review of Political Science* 11 (2008): 563–88.

Fiorina, Morris P., Samuel J. Abrams, and Jeremy Pope. *Culture War? The Myth of a Polarized America.* Boston MA: Longman Publishing Group, 2006.

Flynn, D. J., Brendan Nyhan, and Jason Reifler. "The Nature and Origins of Misperceptions: Understanding False and Unsupported Beliefs About Politics." *Political Psychology* 38, no. S1 (2017/02/01 2017): 127–50.

Foa, Roberto Stefan, and Yascha Mounk. "The Signs of Deconsolidation." *Journal of Democracy* 28, no. 1 (2017): 5–15.

Ford, Robert, and Will Jennings. "The Changing Cleavage Politics of Western Europe." *Annual Review of Political Science* 23 (2020): 295–314.

Fukuyama, Francis. *Political Order and Political Decay: From the Industrial Revolution to the Globalization of Democracy.* London, UK: Profile Books, 2014.

Gadarian, Shana Kushner, Sara Wallace Goodman, and Thomas B. Pepinsky. "Partisanship, Health Behavior, and Policy Attitudes in the Early Stages of the Covid-19 Pandemic." *PLOS ONE* 16, no. 4 (2021): e0249596.

Galston, William A. *Anti-Pluralism: The Populist Threat to Liberal Democracy.* New Haven, CT: Yale University Press, 2017.

Garrett, R. Kelly, and Natalie Jomini Stroud. "Partisan Paths to Exposure Diversity: Differences in Pro-and Counterattitudinal News Consumption." *Journal of Communication* 64, no. 4 (2014): 680–701.

Gidron, Noam, James Adams, and Will Horne. *American Affective Polarization in Comparative Perspective.* Elements in American Politics. Cambridge, UK: Cambridge University Press, 2020.

"How Ideology, Economics and Institutions Shape Affective Polarization in Democratic Polities." 2018.

Ginsburg, Tom, and Aziz Z. Huq. *How to Save a Constitutional Democracy.* Chicago, IL: University of Chicago Press, 2018.

Goodman, Sara Wallace. "'Good American Citizens': A Text-as-Data Analysis of Citizenship Manuals for Immigrants, 1921–1996." *Journal of Ethnic and Migration Studies* 47, no. 7 (2020): 1474–97.

Immigration and Membership Politics in Western European. New York, NY: Cambridge University Press, 2014.

"Immigration Threat, Partisanship, and Democratic Citizenship: Evidence from the US, UK, and Germany." *Comparative Political Studies* (2021), Online first, https://doi.org/10.1177/0010414021997165

Goodman, Sara Wallace, and Hannah M. Alarian. "National Belonging and Public Support for Multiculturalism." *Journal of Race, Ethnicity and Politics* 6, no. 2 (2021): 305–33.

Goodwin, Matthew, and Caitlin Milazzo. "Taking Back Control? Investigating the Role of Immigration in the 2016 Vote for Brexit." *The British Journal of Politics and International Relations* 19, no. 3 (2017): 450–64.

Goren, Paul. "Party Identification and Core Political Values." *American Journal of Political Science* 49, no. 4 (2005): 881–96.

Graham, Matthew H., and Milan W. Svolik. "Democracy in America? Partisanship, Polarization, and the Robustness of Support for Democracy in the United States." *American Political Science Review* 114, no. 2 (2020): 392–409.

Greene, Steven. "Understanding Party Identification: A Social Identity Approach." *Political Psychology* 20, no. 2 (1999): 393–403.

Groenendyk, Eric W., and Antoine J. Banks. "Emotional Rescue: How Affect Helps Partisans Overcome Collective Action Problems." *Political Psychology* 35, no. 3 (2014/06/01 2014): 359–78.

Haggard, Stephan, and Robert Kaufman. *Backsliding: Democratic Regress in the Contemporary World*. New York, NY: Cambridge University Press, 2021.

Han, Hahrie. "Problems of Power." *Stanford Social Innovation Review* Winter (2020): 6.

Harper, Caroline, Richard Kerbaj, and Tom Wheeler. "Revealed: The Russia Report." *The Sunday Times*, 17 November 2019, www.thetimes.co.uk/art icle/revealed-the-russia-report-kz6c9mwxf.

Hetherington, Marc J. "Resurgent Mass Partisanship: The Role of Elite Polarization." *American Political Science Review* 95, no. 3 (2001): 619–31.
"Putting Polarization in Perspective." *British Journal of Political Science* 39, no. 2 (2009): 413–48.

Hibbing, John R., and Elizabeth Theiss-Morse. *Stealth Democracy: Americans' Beliefs About How Government Should Work*. New York, NY: Cambridge University Press, 2002.

Hirschman, Albert O. *Exit, Voice, and Loyalty: Responses to Decline in Firms, Organizations, and States*. Vol. 25. Cambridge, MA: Harvard University Press, 1970.

Hobolt, Sara B. "The Brexit Vote: A Divided Nation, a Divided Continent." *Journal of European Public Policy* 23, no. 9 (2016/10/20 2016): 1259–77.

Hobolt, Sara B., Thomas J. Leeper, and James Tilley. "Divided by the Vote: Affective Polarization in the Wake of Brexit." *British Journal of Political Science* (2020): 1–18.

Hoerner, Julian, and Sara Hobolt. "Unity in Diversity? Polarization, Issue Diversity and Satisfaction with Democracy." *Journal of European Public Policy* 27, no. 12 (2020): 1838–57.

Hopkins, Daniel J., John Sides, and Jack Citrin. "The Muted Consequences of Correct Information About Immigration." *The Journal of Politics* 81, no. 1 (2019): 315–320.

Horowitz, Donald L. "Democracy in Divided Societies." *Journal of Democracy* 4, no. 4 (1993): 18–38.
Ethnic Groups in Conflict, Updated Edition with a New Preface. Berkeley: University of California Press, 2000.

Horton, John. *Political Obligation*. Basingstoke and New York, NY: Palgrave Macmillan, 2010.

Howard, Marc Morjé. *The Weakness of Civil Society in Post-Communist Europe*. New York, NY: Cambridge University Press, 2003.

Huber, John, and Ronald Inglehart. "Expert Interpretations of Party Space and Party Locations in 42 Societies." *Party Politics* 1, no. 1 (1995): 73–111.

Huddy, Leonie. "From Social to Political Identity: A Critical Examination of Social Identity Theory." *Political Psychology* 22, no. 1 (2001): 127–56.

Huddy, Leonie, Alexa Bankert, and Caitlin Davies. "Expressive Versus Instrumental Partisanship in Multiparty European Systems." *Political Psychology* 39 (2018): 173–99.

Huddy, Leonie, Lilliana Mason, and Lene Aarøe. "Expressive Partisanship: Campaign Involvement, Political Emotion, and Partisan Identity." *American Political Science Review* 109, no. 1 (2015): 1–17.

Huntington, Samuel P. *Political Order in Changing Societies*. New Haven, CT: Yale University Press, 2006.

Hur, Aram. "Is There an Intrinsic Duty to Vote? Comparative Evidence from East and West Germans." *Electoral Studies* 45 (2017): 55–62.

Inglehart, Ronald. *The Silent Revolution: Changing Values and Political Styles among Western Publics*. Princeton, NJ: Princeton University Press, 1977.

Inglehart, Ronald, and Pippa Norris. "Trump and the Populist Authoritarian Parties: The Silent Revolution in Reverse." *Perspectives on Politics* 15, no. 2 (2017): 443–54.

Iversen, Torben, and David Soskice. "Information, Inequality, and Mass Polarization: Ideology in Advanced Democracies." *Comparative Political Studies* 48, no. 13 (2015): 1781–813.

Iyengar, Shanto, Yphtach Lelkes, Matthew Levendusky, Neil Malhotra, and Sean J. Westwood. "The Origins and Consequences of Affective Polarization in the United States." *Annual Review of Political Science* 22 (2019): 129–46.

Iyengar, Shanto, Gaurav Sood, and Yphtach Lelkes. "Affect, Not Ideology: A Social Identity Perspective on Polarization." *Public Opinion Quarterly* 76, no. 3 (2012): 405–31.

Iyengar, Shanto, and Sean J Westwood. "Fear and Loathing across Party Lines: New Evidence on Group Polarization." *American Journal of Political Science* 59, no. 3 (2015): 690–707.

Janoski, Thomas. *Citizenship and Civil Society: A Framework of Rights and Obligations in Liberal, Traditional, and Social Democratic Regimes*. New York, NY: Cambridge University Press, 1998.

Jennings, M. Kent. "Political Knowledge over Time and across Generations." *Public Opinion Quarterly* 60, no. 2 (1996): 228–52.

Johnston, Richard. "Party Identification: Unmoved Mover or Sum of Preferences?". *Annual Review of Political Science* 9 (2006): 329–51.

Karp, Jeffrey A., and Susan A. Banducci. "Political Efficacy and Participation in Twenty-Seven Democracies: How Electoral Systems Shape Political Behaviour." *British Journal of Political Science* 38, no. 2 (2008): 311–34.

Kaufman, Robert R., and Stephan Haggard. "Democratic Decline in the United States: What Can We Learn from Middle-Income Backsliding?". *Perspectives on Politics* 17, no. 2 (2019): 417–32.

Klar, Samara, and Yanna Krupnikov. *Independent Politics*. New York, NY: Cambridge University Press, 2016.

Klar, Samara, Yanna Krupnikov, and John Barry Ryan. "Affective Polarization or Partisan Disdain?: Untangling a Dislike for the Opposing Party from a Dislike of Partisanship." *Public Opinion Quarterly* 82, no. 2 (2018): 379–90.

Klüver, Heike, and Jae-Jae Spoon. "Helping or Hurting? How Governing as a Junior Coalition Partner Influences Electoral Outcomes." *The Journal of Politics* 82, no. 4 (2020): 1231–42.

Kriesi, Hanspeter. "Restructuration of Partisan Politics and the Emergence of a New Cleavage Based on Values." *West European Politics* 33, no. 3 (2010): 673–85.

Kriesi, Hanspeter, Edgar Grande, Romain Lachat, et al. *West European Politics in the Age of Globalization*. New York, NY: Cambridge University Press, 2008.

Kriesi, Hanspeter, Ruud Koopmans, Jan Willem Duyvendak, et al. *New Social Movements in Western Europe: A Comparative Analysis*. London, UK: University College London Press, 1995.

Laakso, Markku, and Rein Taagepera. ""Effective" Number of Parties: A Measure with Application to West Europe." *Comparative Political Studies* 12, no. 1 (1979): 3–27.

Lajevardi, Nazita, and Marisa Abrajano. "How Negative Sentiment toward Muslim Americans Predicts Support for Trump in the 2016 Presidential Election." *The Journal of Politics* 81, no. 1 (2019/01/01 2018): 296–302.

Lane, Robert E. "The Tense Citizen and the Casual Patriot: Role Confusion in American Politics." *The Journal of Politics* 27, no. 4 (1965): 735–60.

Langton, Kenneth P., and M. Kent Jennings. "Political Socialization and the High School Civics Curriculum in the United States." *American Political Science Review* 62, no. 3 (1968): 852–67.

Larry, Diamond. *The Spirit of Democracy: The Struggle to Build Free Societies Throughout the World*. New York, NY: Times Books/Henry Holt and Co, 2008.

Lassen, David Dreyer. "The Effect of Information on Voter Turnout: Evidence from a Natural Experiment." *American Journal of Political Science* 49, no. 1 (2005): 103–18.

Lau, Richard, and David Redlawsk. *How Voters Decide: Information Processing During Election Campaigns*. New York, NY: Cambridge University Press, 2006.

Lavine, Howard G., Christopher D. Johnston, and Marco R. Steenbergen. *The Ambivalent Partisan: How Critical Loyalty Promotes Democracy*. New York, NY: Oxford University Press, 2012.

LeBas, Adrienne. "Can Polarization Be Positive? Conflict and Institutional Development in Africa." *American Behavioral Scientist* 62, no. 1 (2018/01/01 2018): 59–74.

Lee, Frances E. *Beyond Ideology: Politics, Principles, and Partisanship in the US Senate*. Chicago, IL: University of Chicago Press, 2009.

"How Party Polarization Affects Governance." *Annual Review of Political Science* 18 (2015): 261–82.

Insecure Majorities: Congress and the Perpetual Campaign. Chicago, IL: University of Chicago Press, 2016.

Lenz, Gabriel S. *Follow the Leader?: How Voters Respond to Politicians' Policies and Performance*. Chicago, IL: University of Chicago Press, 2013.

Levendusky, Matthew. *How Partisan Media Polarize America*. Chicago, IL: University of Chicago Press, 2013.

The Partisan Sort: How Liberals Became Democrats and Conservatives Became Republicans. Chicago, IL: University of Chicago Press, 2009.

Levendusky, Matthew S. "Americans, Not Partisans: Can Priming American National Identity Reduce Affective Polarization?". *The Journal of Politics* 80, no. 1 (2018): 59–70.

Levin, Dov H. "A Vote for Freedom? The Effects of Partisan Electoral Interventions on Regime Type." *Journal of Conflict Resolution* 63, no. 4 (2019): 839–68.

"When the Great Power Gets a Vote: The Effects of Great Power Electoral Interventions on Election Results." *International Studies Quarterly* 60, no. 2 (2016): 189–202.

Levitsky, Steven, and Daniel Ziblatt. *How Democracies Die*. New York, NY: Crown, 2018.

Lewis, John. "Together, You Can Redeem the Soul of Our Nation." *The New York Times*, July 30, 2020.

Lijphart, Arend. *Democracies: Patterns of Majoritarian and Consensus Government in Twenty-One Countries*. New Haven, CT: Yale University Press, 1984.

Patterns of Democracy. Government Forms and Performance in Thirty-Six Countries. New Haven, CT: Yale University Press, 1999.

The Politics of Accommodation; Pluralism and Democracy in the Netherlands. [in English] Berkeley, CA: University of California Press, 1968.

"Unequal Participation: Democracy's Unresolved Dilemma Presidential Address, American Political Science Association, 1996." *American Political Science Review* 91, no. 1 (1997): 1–14.

Lin, Winston. "Agnostic Notes on Regression Adjustments to Experimental Data: Reexamining Freedman's Critique." *The Annals of Applied Statistics* 7, no. 1 (2013): 295–318.

Linz, Juan J. *Crisis, Breakdown and Reequilibration*. Baltimore, MD: Johns Hopkins University Press, 1978.

"The Perils of Presidentialism." *Journal of Democracy* 1, no. 1 (1990): 51–69.

Linz, Juan J., and Alfred C. Stepan. "Toward Consolidated Democracies." *Journal of Democracy* 7, no. 2 (1996): 14–33.

Linz, Juan José, and Alfred C. Stepan. *The Breakdown of Democratic Regimes*. Baltimore: Johns Hopkins University Press, 1978.

Lipset, Seymour Martin. "*Political Man: The Social Bases of Politics*." Doubleday & Co., 1959.

Lipset, Seymour Martin, and Stein Rokkan, eds. *Party Systems and Voter Alignments: Cross-National Perspectives*. Vol. 7. New York, NY: Free Press, 1967.

Lodge, Milton, and Charles S Taber. *The Rationalizing Voter*. New York, NY: Cambridge University Press, 2013.

Lupia, Arthur, Mathew D. McCubbins, and Lupia Arthur. *The Democratic Dilemma: Can Citizens Learn What They Need to Know?*. New York, NY: Cambridge University Press, 1998.

Lupu, Noam. "Party Polarization and Mass Partisanship: A Comparative Perspective." *Political Behavior* 37, no. 2 (2015/06/01 2015): 331–56.

Macedo, Stephen. *Diversity and Distrust: Civic Education in a Multicultural Democracy*. Cambridge, MA: Harvard University Press, 2009.

MacKuen, Michael, Jennifer Wolak, Luke Keele, et al. "Civic Engagements: Resolute Partisanship or Reflective Deliberation." *American Journal of Political Science* 54, no. 2 (2010): 440–58.

Mainwaring, Scott. *Rethinking Party Systems in the Third Wave of Democratization: The Case of Brazil*. Palo Alto, CA: Stanford University Press, 1999.

Malka, Ariel, Yphtach Lelkes, Bert N. Bakker, et al. "Who Is Open to Authoritarian Governance within Western Democracies?". *Perspectives on Politics* (2020), doi:10.1017/S1537592720002091.

Marcus, George E., Elizabeth Theiss-Morse, John L. Sullivan, et al. *With Malice toward Some: How People Make Civil Liberties Judgments*. New York, NY: Cambridge University Press, 1995.

Marshall, Thomas. *Citizenship and Social Class and Other Essays*. Cambridge, UK: Cambridge University Press, 1950.

Mason, Lilliana. *Uncivil Agreement: How Politics Became Our Identity*. Chicago, IL: University of Chicago Press, 2018.

McCarty, Nolan, Keith T. Poole, and Howard Rosenthal. *Polarized America: The Dance of Ideology and Unequal Riches*. Cambridge, MA: MIT Press, 2016.

McCoy, Jennifer, Tahmina Rahman, and Murat Somer. "Polarization and the Global Crisis of Democracy: Common Patterns, Dynamics, and Pernicious Consequences for Democratic Polities." *American Behavioral Scientist* 62, no. 1 (2018): 16–42.

McCoy, Jennifer, and Murat Somer. "Toward a Theory of Pernicious Polarization and How It Harms Democracies: Comparative Evidence and Possible Remedies." *The ANNALS of the American Academy of Political and Social Science* 681, no. 1 (2019): 234–71.

Mechkova, Valeriya, Anna Lührmann, and Staffan I. Lindberg. "How Much Democratic Backsliding?". *Journal of Democracy* 28, no. 4 (2017): 162–69.

Merolla, Jennifer L., and Elizabeth J. Zechmeister. "Threat and Information Acquisition: Evidence from an Eight Country Study." *Journal of Experimental Political Science* 5, no. 3 (2018): 167–81.

Mill, John Stuart. *Collected Works*. Toronto, CA: University of Toronto Press, 1963.

Miller, David. "Immigrants, Nations, and Citizenship." *Journal of Political Philosophy* 16, no. 4 (2008): 371–90.

Miller, Michael K. "A Republic, If You Can Keep It: Breakdown and Erosion in Modern Democracies." *The Journal of Politics* 83, no. 1 (2021): 198–213.

Miller, Steven V. "Economic Threats or Societal Turmoil? Understanding Preferences for Authoritarian Political Systems." *Political Behavior* 39, no. 2 (2017/06/01 2017): 457–78.

Milner, Henry. *Civic Literacy: How Informed Citizens Make Democracy Work*. Hanover, NH: University Press of New England, 2002.

Mondak, Jeffery J. "Public Opinion and Heuristic Processing of Source Cues." *Political Behavior* 15, no. 2 (1993): 167–92.

Mounk, Yascha. *The People Vs. Democracy: Why Our Freedom Is in Danger and How to Save It*. Cambridge, MA: Harvard University Press, 2018.

Mudde, Cas. *Populist Radical Right Parties in Europe*. Cambridge, UK: University Press Cambridge, 2007.

Mutz, Diana C. "Status Threat, Not Economic Hardship, Explains the 2016 Presidential Vote." *Proceedings of the National Academy of Sciences* 115, no. 19 (2018): E4330–E39.

Nelsen, Matthew D. "Cultivating Youth Engagement: Race & the Behavioral Effects of Critical Pedagogy." *Political Behavior* 43, no.2 (2021): 1–34.
"Teaching Citizenship: Race and the Behavioral Effects of American Civic Education." *Journal of Race, Ethnicity, and Politics* 6, no. 1 (2021): 157–86.
Nelson, Thomas E., Zoe M. Oxley, and Rosalee A. Clawson. "Toward a Psychology of Framing Effects." *Political Behavior* 19, no. 3 (1997): 221–46.
Norris, Pippa. *Critical Citizens: Global Support for Democratic Government.* New York, NY: Oxford University Press, 1999.
"Global Party Survey, 2019." Harvard Dataverse, 2020, www.globalpartysurvey.org/.
"It Happened in America." *Foreign Affairs* (2021).
Why Electoral Integrity Matters. New York, NY: Cambridge University Press, 2014.
Norris, Pippa, Sarah Cameron, and Thomas Wynter. *Electoral Integrity in America: Securing Democracy.* New York: Oxford University Press, 2018.
Norris, Pippa, and Ronald Inglehart. *Cultural Backlash: Trump, Brexit, and Authoritarian Populism.* New York, NY: Cambridge University Press, 2019.
Orenstein, Mitchell *Alexander. Out of the Red: Building Capitalism and Democracy in Postcommunist Europe.* Ann Arbor, MI: University of Michigan Press, 2001.
Pearlman, Wendy. "Narratives of Fear in Syria." *Perspectives on Politics* 14, no. 1 (2016): 21–37.
Pepinsky, Thomas. "Why the Impeachment Fight Is Even Scarier Than You Think." *Politico*, October 31, 2019. https://www.politico.com/magazine/story/2019/10/31/regime-cleavage-229895/.
Pepinsky, Thomas B. *Economic Crises and the Breakdown of Authoritarian Regimes: Indonesia and Malaysia in Comparative Perspective.* New York: Cambridge University Press, 2009.
Persson, Mikael. "Education and Political Participation." *British Journal of Political Science* 45, no. 3 (2015): 689–703.
Petersen, Michael Bang, Martin Skov, Søren Serritzlew, et al. "Motivated Reasoning and Political Parties: Evidence for Increased Processing in the Face of Party Cues." *Political Behavior* 35, no. 4 (2013): 831–54.
Poole, Keith T., and Howard L. Rosenthal. *Ideology and Congress*: New Brunswick, NJ: Transaction Publishers, 2007.
Popper, Karl. *The Open Society and Its Enemies.* London, UK: Routledge, 1945.
Powell, G. Bingham. "American Voter Turnout in Comparative Perspective." *American Political Science Review* 80, no. 1 (1986): 17–43.
Powell, G. Bingham, and G. Bingham Powell Jr. *Elections as Instruments of Democracy: Majoritarian and Proportional Visions.* New Haven, CT: Yale University Press, 2000.
Przeworski, Adam. *Capitalism and Social Democracy.* New York, NY: Cambridge University Press, 1986.
Crises of Democracy. New York, NY: Cambridge University Press, 2019.
Putnam, Robert D. *Bowling Alone: The Collapse and Revival of American Community.* New York, NY: Simon & Schuster, 2000.
Making Democracy Work: Civic Traditions in Modern Italy. Princeton, NJ: Princeton University Press, 1993.

Quillian, Lincoln. "Prejudice as a Response to Perceived Group Threat: Population Composition and Anti-Immigrant and Racial Prejudice in Europe." *American Sociological Review* 60, no. 4 (1995): 586–611.

Rabushka, Alvin, and Kenneth A. Shepsle. *Politics in Plural Societies*. New York, NY: Pearson, 2009.

Rahn, Wendy M. "The Role of Partisan Stereotypes in Information Processing About Political Candidates." *American Journal of Political Science* (1993): 472–96.

Rawls, John. *Political Liberalism*. New York, NY: Columbia University Press, 2005.

Redlawsk, David P. "Hot Cognition or Cool Consideration? Testing the Effects of Motivated Reasoning on Political Decision Making." *The Journal of Politics* 64, no. 4 (2002): 1021–44.

Reiljan, Andres. "'Fear and Loathing across Party Lines' (Also) in Europe: Affective Polarisation in European Party Systems." *European Journal of Political Research* 59, no. 2 (2020): 376–96.

Reny, Tyler T., Loren Collingwood, and Ali A. Valenzuela. "Vote Switching in the 2016 Election: How Racial and Immigration Attitudes, Not Economics, Explain Shifts in White Voting." *Public Opinion Quarterly* 83, no. 1 (2019): 91–113.

Riker, William H., and Peter C. Ordeshook. "A Theory of the Calculus of Voting." *The American Political Science Review* 62, no. 1 (1968): 25–42.

Rokeach, Milton. *The Open and Closed Mind*. New York, NY: Basic Books, 1960.

Rosenblum, Nancy L. *On the Side of the Angels: An Appreciation of Parties and Partisanship*. Princeton, NJ: Princeton University Press, 2010.

Runciman, David. *How Democracy Ends*. London, UK: Profile Books, 2018.

Rustow, Dankwart A. "Transitions to Democracy: Toward a Dynamic Model." *Comparative Politics* 2, no. 3 (1970): 337–63.

Sartori, Giovanni. *Parties and Party Systems: A Framework for Analysis*. Cambridge, UK: Cambridge University Press, 1977.

Satherley, Nicole, Kumar Yogeeswaran, Danny Osborne, and Chris G. Sibley. "If They Say "Yes," We Say "No": Partisan Cues Increase Polarization over National Symbols." *Psychological Science* 29, no. 12 (2018): 1996–2009.

Schattschneider, Elmer Eric. *The Semi-Sovereign People: A Realist's View of Democracy in America*. New York, NY: Holt, Rinehart and Winston, 1960.

Schildkraut, Deborah J. *Press "One" For English: Language Policy, Public Opinion, and American Identity*. Princeton, NJ: Princeton University Press, 2005.

Schumpeter, Joseph A. *Capitalism, Socialism and Democracy*. New York, NY: Harper & Brothers, 1942.

Scott, James C. *Seeing Like a State: How Certain Schemes to Improve the Human Condition Have Failed*. New Haven, CT: Yale University Press, 1998.

Sedelmeier, Ulrich. "Anchoring Democracy from Above? The European Union and Democratic Backsliding in Hungary and Romania after Accession." *JCMS: Journal of Common Market Studies* 52, no. 1 (2014): 105–21.

Shulman, Stephen, and Stephen Bloom. "The Legitimacy of Foreign Intervention in Elections: The Ukrainian Response." *Review of International Studies* 38, no. 2 (2012): 445–71.

Sides, John, Michael Tesler, and Lynn Vavreck. *Identity Crisis: The 2016 Presidential Campaign and the Battle for the Meaning of America*. Princeton, NJ: Princeton University Press, 2018.

Skitka, Linda J., Christopher W. Bauman, and Edward G. Sargis. "Moral Conviction: Another Contributor to Attitude Strength or Something More?". *Journal of Personality and Social Psychology* 88, no. 6 (2005): 895.

Slater, Dan. "Democratic Careening." *World Politics* 65, no. 4 (2013): 729–63.

Slothuus, Rune, and Claes H. De Vreese. "Political Parties, Motivated Reasoning, and Issue Framing Effects." *The Journal of Politics* 72, no. 3 (2010): 630–45.

Smith, Rogers M. *Civic Ideals: Conflicting Visions of Citizenship in US History*. New Haven, CT: Yale University Press, 1999.

Sobolewska, Maria, and Robert Ford. *Brexitland: Identity, Diversity and the Reshaping of British Politics*. Cambridge, UK: Cambridge University Press, 2020.

Sobolewska, Maria, Silvia Galandini, and Laurence Lessard-Phillips. "The Public View of Immigrant Integration: Multidimensional and Consensual. Evidence from Survey Experiments in the UK and the Netherlands." *Journal of Ethnic and Migration Studies* 43, no. 1 (2017): 58–79.

Spiro, Peter J. *Citizenship: What Everyone Needs to Know*. New York: Oxford University Press, 2019.

Spoon, Jae-Jae, and Heike Klüver. "Responding to Far Right Challengers: Does Accommodation Pay Off?". *Journal of European Public Policy* 27, no. 2 (2020): 273–91.

Spoon, Jae-Jae, and Christopher J. Williams. "'It's the Economy, Stupid': When New Politics Parties Take on Old Politics Issues." *West European Politics* 44, no. 4 (2020): 802–24.

Spoon, Jae-Jae, and Heike Klüver. "Party Convergence and Vote Switching: Explaining Mainstream Party Decline across Europe." *European Journal of Political Research* 58, no. 4 (2019): 1021–42.

Stokes, Donald E. "Spatial Models of Party Competition." *The American Political Science Review* 57, no. 2 (1963): 368–77.

Sullivan, John L., James Piereson, and George E. Marcus. *Political Tolerance and American Democracy*. Chicago, IL: University of Chicago Press, 1982.

Svolik, Milan W. "Polarization Versus Democracy." *Journal of Democracy* 30, no. 3 (2019): 20–32.

Tajfel, Henri, Michael G. Billig, Robert P. Bundy, and Claude Flament. "Social Categorization and Intergroup Behaviour." *European Journal of Social Psychology* 1, no. 2 (1971): 149–78.

Tajfel, Henri, and John C. Turner. "An Integrative Theory of Intergroup Conflict." *The Social Psychology of Intergroup Relations* 33, no. 47(1979): 74.

Tesler, Michael. "The Return of Old-Fashioned Racism to White Americans' Partisan Preferences in the Early Obama Era." *The Journal of Politics* 75, no. 1 (2012): 110–23.

Theiss-Morse, Elizabeth. *Who Counts as an American? : The Boundaries of National Identity*. [in English] Cambridge UK, New York NY: Cambridge University Press, 2009.

Tilly, Charles. "Citizenship, Identity and Social History." *International Review of Social History* 40, no. S3 (1995): 1–17.

Tomz, Michael, and Jessica L. P. Weeks. "Public Opinion and Foreign Electoral Intervention." *American Political Science Review* (2020): 1–18.

Tsebelis, George. *Veto Players: How Political Institutions Work*. Princeton, NJ: Princeton University Press, 2002.

Turner, John, and Henri Tajfel. *Social Identity and Intergroup Relations*. New York, NY: Cambridge University Press, 1982.

Vachudova, Milada. "Ethnopopulism and Democratic Backsliding in Central Europe." *East European Politics* 36, no. 3 (2020): 318–40.

Europe Undivided: Democracy, Leverage, and Integration after Communism. New York, NY: Oxford University Press , 2005.

"From Competition to Polarization in Central Europe: How Populists Change Party Systems and the European Union." *Polity* 51, no. 4 (2019): 689–706.

Valentino, Nicholas A., Vincent L. Hutchings, Antoine J. Banks, et al. "Is a Worried Citizen a Good Citizen? Emotions, Political Information Seeking, and Learning Via the Internet." *Political Psychology* 29, no. 2 (2008): 247–73.

Van der Meer, Tom W. G., Jan W. Van Deth, et al. "The Politicized Participant: Ideology and Political Action in 20 Democracies." *Comparative Political Studies* 42, no. 11 (2009): 1426–57.

Vasilopoulos, Pavlos. "Terrorist Events, Emotional Reactions, and Political Participation: The 2015 Paris Attacks." *West European Politics* 41, no. 1 (2018): 102–27.

Waldner, David, and Ellen Lust. "Unwelcome Change: Coming to Terms with Democratic Backsliding." *Annual Review of Political Science* 21 (2018): 93–113.

Walzer, Michael. *Obligations: Essays on Disobedience, War, and Citizenship*. Cambridge, MA: Harvard University Press, 1970.

Wan, Amy J. *Producing Good Citizens: Literacy Training in Anxious Times*. Pittsburgh, PA: University of Pittsburgh Press, 2014.

Wattenberg, Martin P. *Where Have All the Voters Gone?* Cambridge, MA: Harvard University Press, 2002.

Watts, Jake, and Tim Bale. "Populism as an Intra-Party Phenomenon: The British Labour Party under Jeremy Corbyn." *The British Journal of Politics and International Relations* 21, no. 1 (2019): 99–115.

Webster, Steven W., and Alan I. Abramowitz. "The Ideological Foundations of Affective Polarization in the US Electorate." *American Politics Research* 45, no. 4 (2017): 621–47.

Weingast, Barry R. "The Political Foundations of Democracy and the Rule of Law." *American Political Science Review* 91, no. 2 (1997): 245–63.

Wellman, Elizabeth Iams, Susan D. Hyde, and Thad E. Hall. "Does Fraud Trump Partisanship? The Impact of Contentious Elections on Voter Confidence." *Journal of Elections, Public Opinion and Parties* 28, no. 3 (2018): 330–48.

Welzel, Christian. *Freedom Rising*. New York, NY: Cambridge University Press, 2013.

Welzel, Christian, and Ronald Inglehart. "The Role of Ordinary People in Democratization." *Journal of Democracy* 19, no. 1 (2008): 126–40.

Westwood, Sean J., Shanto Iyengar, Stefaan Walgrave, et al. "The Tie That Divides: Cross-National Evidence of the Primacy of Partyism." *European Journal of Political Research* 57, no. 2 (2018): 333–54.

Whiteley, Paul. "Does Citizenship Education Work? Evidence from a Decade of Citizenship Education in Secondary Schools in England." *Parliamentary Affairs* 67, no. 3 (2012): 513–35.

Whiteley, Paul, Monica Poletti, Paul Webb, and Tim Bale. "Oh Jeremy Corbyn! Why Did Labour Party Membership Soar after the 2015 General Election?". *The British Journal of Politics and International Relations* 21, no. 1 (2019): 80–98.

Wilson, David C., and Paul R. Brewer. "The Foundations of Public Opinion on Voter ID Laws: Political Predispositions, Racial Resentment, and Information Effects." *Public Opinion Quarterly* 77, no. 4 (2013): 962–84.

Wright, Matthew. "Diversity and the Imagined Community: Immigrant Diversity and Conceptions of National Identity." *Political Psychology* 32, no. 5 (2011): 837–62.

  "Policy Regimes and Normative Conceptions of Nationalism in Mass Public Opinion." *Comparative Political Studies* 44, no. 5 (2011): 598–624.

Wright, Matthew, Jack Citrin, and Jonathan Wand. "Alternative Measures of American National Identity: Implications for the Civic-Ethnic Distinction." *Political Psychology* 33, no. 4 (2012): 469–82.

Ypi, Lea. "Political Commitment and the Value of Partisanship." *American Political Science Review* 110, no. 3 (2016): 601–13.

Zaller, John. *The Nature and Origin of Public Opinion*. New York, NY: Cambridge University Press, 1992.

  The Nature and Origins of Mass Opinion. New York, NY: Cambridge University Press, 1992.

Ziblatt, Daniel. *Conservative Political Parties and the Birth of Modern Democracy in Europe*. New York, NY: Cambridge University Press, 2017.

Index